Deference and Defiance in
Nineteenth-Century Japan

WILLIAM W. KELLY

Deference and Defiance in Nineteenth-Century Japan

PRINCETON UNIVERSITY PRESS

PRINCETON, NEW JERSEY

Copyright © 1985 by Princeton University Press
Published by Princeton University Press, 41 William Street,
Princeton, New Jersey 08540
In the United Kingdom: Princeton University Press,
Guildford, Surrey

Library of Congress Cataloging in Publication Data will be
found on the last printed page of this book

ISBN 0-691-09417-9

This book has been composed in Linotron Bembo

Clothbound editions of Princeton University Press books
are printed on acid-free paper, and binding materials are
chosen for strength and durability

Printed in the United States of America by
Princeton University Press
Princeton, New Jersey

For my parents

CONTENTS

LIST OF FIGURES   *ix*

LIST OF TABLES   *xi*

LIST OF MAPS   *xii*

PREFACE   *xiii*

1 Class, Community, and Party in 19th-Century
  Collective Protest   *3*

2 Shōnai and Sakai Domain   *26*

3 Honorable Subjects . . . : The Anti-Transfer
  Protests of 1840–41   *66*

4 . . . And Unruly Mobs: The Ōyama Disturbances
  of 1844   *105*

5 Restoration in Shōnai   *121*

6 Initiative and Inertia: The Second Sakata Prefecture   *155*

7 Cash Taxes, Suppressed Reforms, and Falsified
  Expenditures   *173*

8 From the Headmen's Compounds to the Council
  of State   *205*

9 The Government Responds: The Numa Hearings
  and the Kojima Court   *230*

10 Aftermath   *261*

11 Concluding Reflections   *284*

vii

CONTENTS

APPENDIX: Early Spring Rice Prices and Domain
Mean Tax Levels, 1697–1862   *292*

CHARACTER LIST   *297*

REFERENCES   *301*

INDEX   *319*

LIST OF FIGURES

1 A lacquered *wappa* from the Shōnai region.
Courtesy of Chidō hakubutsukan, Tsuruoka.   2
2 Sakata town and harbor with shipping. Anonymous
handscroll attributed to late 17th or early 18th
century.
Courtesy of Honma bijutsukan, Sakata.   36
3 A meeting of Kuromori Village residents at their temple.
Yume no ukihashi, 1841 original, scene 5.
Courtesy of Chidō hakubutsukan, Tsuruoka.   81
4 Petitioning at Edo Castle. *Yume no ukihashi*, 1841
original, scene 14.
Courtesy of Chidō hakubutsukan, Tsuruoka.   85
5 Assembly of Tagawa protestors at Nakagawa Yachi,
April 1841. *Yume no ukihashi*, 1841 original, scene 54.
Courtesy of Chidō hakubutsukan, Tsuruoka.   87
6 Banners displayed at the Nakayama Yachi assembly,
April 1841. *Yume no ukihashi*, 20th-century copy.
Courtesy of Tsuruoka-shi kyōdo shiryōkan,
Tsuruoka.   90
7 An 1841 protest banner featuring melon (*uri*) imagery.
Courtesy of Gyokuryū-ji Temple, Eji Village.   92
8 A *tengu* mask.
Courtesy of Dewa no Yuki shiryōkan, Ōyama.   97
9 Celebrations in Tsurugaoka. *Yume no ukihashi*, 1841
original, scene 82.
Courtesy of Chidō hakubutsukan, Tsuruoka.   100
10 A sketch map and listing of Ōyama town *sake* brewers.
Tōkō shōnin kan.
Courtesy of Tsuruoka-shi kyōdo shiryōkan,
Tsuruoka.   108
11 Conveying the arrested Ōyama protestors to the Shiono
hearings. *Hojōki*.
Courtesy of Tsuruoka-shi kyōdo shiryōkan,
Tsuruoka.   115
12 Scenes from the Matsugaoka Project. Scenes a, b, and c
from the *Ryōsōchō* scroll. Scene d: squad photograph
(late 1870s).
Courtesy of Matsugaoka kaikon kinenkan, Haguro-
chō.   158

ix

13 Some of the principals in the Wappa Disturbances.
   Courtesy of Tsuruoka-shi kyōdo shiryōkan,
   Tsuruoka.   162
14 The head of Ōshio Heihachirō. Hanging scroll, 1850s.
   Courtesy of Kōkyō bunko, Sakata.   210
15 Mori Tōemon featured on the cover of Ueki Emori's
   1879 pamphlet, *Jiyū minken ron.*
   Courtesy of Yamagata-ken shi hensan iinkai,
   Yamagata.   258
16 After the Meiji Agricultural Methods.
   Courtesy of Mr. Kasuga Norio, Tsuruoka.   279

LIST OF TABLES

1 Levels of Rural Administration, Shōnai Domain, 1861   *31*
2 Rotation of Village Group Headmen Assignments: The Example of Tentō Hayanosuke   *32*
3 Contributions and Uncollected Loans to Sakai Domain from Main Honma House, 1843-1874   *39*
4 Registered and Cultivated Holdings of Sakurabayashi Village Residents, 1768-1868   *50*
5 Changes in the Landholdings of Yogorō (#5), 1768-1868   *54*
6 Tenants of Yogorō's Holdings, 1868   *55*
7 General Budget Estimates, Shōnai Domain, 1811   *61*
8 Registered Holdings of Shōnai Petitioners to Other Domains, Spring 1841   *95*
9 Grievances of the Tengu League in Its Eighteen-Clause Petition to Sakata Prefecture, December 1869   *140*
10 Itemizations of Taxes and Levies, Ōyodokawa Village, 1872   *168*
11 Itemizations of Taxes and Levies, Ōyodokawa Village, 1873   *170*
12 Distribution of Registered Landholdings in Twelve Villages Involved in the Kojima Suit   *265*
13 Distribution of Landholdings in Takazaka Village, 1879   *265*
14 Acreage and Tenancy Rents before and after Land Adjustment Projects, Sakai-shinden Village, Akumi County   *280*

LIST OF MAPS

1 The Shōnai region   27
2 Akumi   28
3 Tagawa   29

PREFACE

Osorenagara Shōnai nigun no hyakushō tomo ittō onageki moshiagesōrō kakitsuke no koto . . .

With all deference, the humble cultivators of the two counties of Shōnai unite in bringing this written appeal of distress . . .

So began the distress petitions that cultivators' representatives carried to the shogun's capital of Edo from the northern rice plain of Shōnai in early 1841. On their knees, they pressed them before the palanquins of the shogun's chief councilors at the entrance to Edo Castle. Thirty-four years later, in the spring of 1875, representatives of the next generation of Shōnai cultivators again took to the road for Edo, now Tokyo, the seat of the new Meiji government. This group, however, deposited a legal suit in the petition box that stood before the Superior Court of the new Ministry of Justice. Its title was more sharply inflected:

Kenshi kyokuhi assei no so

A suit against the extreme persecutions of prefectural officials

The 1841 distress petition and the 1875 court suit were two moments in popular protest movements that spread across Shōnai four times in the 19th century. Each in its own manner combined a compliant deference to certain conventions and an implacable defiance of elite expectations. The changing character of these protests, their relationship to one another, and their role in the broader societal transformation of this small rice plain are my concerns in this study.

In the past two decades there has been an impressive outpouring of new research on 19th-century Japan by Japanese and Western scholars. The collapse of the Tokugawa agrar-

xiii

ian state and the 1868 Meiji Restoration of the emperor and reconstitution of central authority remains the analytical pivot, but this recent work has recast our appreciation of how the Tokugawa 19th century and the Meiji 19th century fit together. The intersection of collective protest, political consciousness, and societal change is now a matter of vigorous debate, and I have written this study as a contribution to that reevaluation of how moments of intense, focused action related to the deeper currents of 19th-century social life.

However, I am not by specialty a 19th-century historian, and there is another motivation behind this book as well. It is a stage in my own long-term project as an anthropologist to understand the transformations to modernity of a small Japanese region. It follows an earlier study (Kelly 1982a) of the ecological, economic, and political forces that gave specific form in the 17th and 18th centuries to the plain's agrarian society. In a future work I want to treat certain dimensions of 20th-century Shōnai life as the region has been rewoven into the social patterns and cultural fabric of the contemporary industrial state. Each of these three studies is intended to stand on its own, although I hope that their eventual juxtaposition will illuminate in what ways and under what constraints the people of Shōnai have chosen and created their present lives from their past legacies.

This project has involved me in both ethnographic field work and archival and documentary research. I first came to Shōnai in 1976 for dissertation research and spent eighteen months shuttling between paddy fields and local libraries, between casual socializing in the village where I lived and formal meetings and interviews at the several levels of government offices, agricultural cooperatives, and land improvement districts. I have subsequently returned for four shorter stays of three to six weeks. I continue to enjoy the hospitality and assistance of many Shōnai friends, including Professor Higashiyama Isamu, Professor Watanabe Shunzō, and the Narisawas of Watamae.

This particular study was largely researched and written

during 1982-83, through the generosity of a junior faculty fellowship from Yale University. The Yale Center for International and Area Studies and the Council on East Asian Studies provided supplemental grants for travel to Japan and for expenses of manuscript preparation. It is a pleasure to record my gratitude for this support.

What understanding I have gained of Shōnai's past owes much to lively and dedicated groups of local historians in Tsuruoka, Sakata, and smaller towns across the plain. It is their energy and enthusiasm that has built up two fine local archives, now attached to the city libraries of Tsuruoka and Sakata. Over the last thirty years, they have published extensive, invaluable collections of documents and have written useful contributions to town, regional, and prefectural history series. In my own research for this study, I could find few materials that were not already published in these document collections, and I have relied upon them heavily. On the particular topics of this study, I am especially indebted to the scholarship of Satō Shigerō, now of Niigata University, and Igawa Kazuyoshi of Sakata. Although I depart considerably from their interpretations, I have the utmost respect for their scholarly skills and for their commitment to make Shōnai's past of more than antiquarian interest.

Since my first period in Shōnai, Maeta Mitsuhiko has been a forgiving and patient guide to the intricacies of reading local documents. Akiho Ryo and Hori Shirō at the Tsuruoka-shi kyōdo shiryōkan, Sakai Chūji at the Chidō hakubutsukan, and Tamura Kanzō at the Sakata city history editorial committee office have all been most accommodating in answering questions and providing access to materials. I am indebted to the following institutions and individuals for permission to photograph and use objects and materials as illustrations: Kōkyō bunko (Sakata), Tsuruoka-shi kyōdo shiryōkan, Chidō hakubutsukan (Tsuruoka), Honma bijutsukan (Sakata), Gyokuryū-ji Temple (Eji Village), Dewa no Yuki shiryōkan (Ōyama), Matsugaoka kaikon kinenkan (Ha-

guro), Mr. Kasuga Norio (Tsuruoka), and Yamagata-ken shi
hensan iinkai (Yamagata).

Harold Bolitho, John W. Hall, Marius Jansen, James Scott,
Richard Smethurst, Robert J. Smith, and George Wilson
were all kind enough to offer comments on their readings of
this manuscript. If I have not deferred to all of their suggestions, it is not from willful defiance, but from a recognition
of my limitations.

A CHARACTER list of local and unusual terms and phrases is
included for specialists, but I have tried to avoid frequent
Japanese terms in the text. I have converted all dates to the
Western Gregorian calendar, officially adopted in Japan on
January 1, 1873. Most weights and measures have been rendered in metric equivalents. The only exceptions are the
common volumetric standard of rice, the *koku*, which is
equal to roughly 5 bushels, and the monetary units, the gold
ryō and the post-1871 *yen*. All Japanese names are written
with the family name preceding the given name. I have used
the following abbreviations for references cited frequently in
the text:

MCS: *Mikawa-chō shi*   [The History of Mikawa Town]
OCS: *Ōyama-chō shi*   [The History of Ōyama Town]
SSS: *Sakata-shi shi*   [The History of Sakata City]
TSS: *Tsuruoka-shi shi* [The History of Tsuruoka City]
W: *Wappa sōdō shiryō* [Documents of the Wappa
                         Disturbances]
YKS: *Yamagata-ken shi* [The History of Yamagata
                         Prefecture]

Deference and Defiance in
Nineteenth-Century Japan

1. A lacquered *wappa* from the Shōnai region.

ONE

Class, Community, and Party in 19th-Century Collective Protest

IN THE summer of 1874, a small group of ex-samurai, town merchants, large landholders, smallholding cultivators, and tenants gathered at a house in Tsurugaoka, the former castle town of Sakai Domain. Six years earlier, for much of 1868, Sakai and his retainers had remained loyal to the last Tokugawa shogun and resisted the new Restoration forces, before finally capitulating in October of that year. Initial attempts at direct administration of parts of the former domain proved too difficult for the new Meiji authorities. In late 1871, the Sakai territories—Shōnai Plain and its surrounding mountains—were reconsolidated as a single prefecture, and the old domain elite was installed as the prefectural staff. It was from considerable disaffection with this restored local elite and its policies that such a disparate group secretly met in the midsummer heat. Their discussions gave rise to a radical proposal—a cultivators' shareholding company that would cooperatively market members' rice, pay their taxes, and sell them necessary supplies.

During late July and August these activitists fanned out across Shōnai, explaining the plan and soliciting members at mass village assemblies. Then, after violent confrontations with prefectural troops in early September, they precipitously dropped the plan in favor of vigorous and ultimately successful popular agitations to lodge an eleven-count legal suit against the prefecture with the central authorities in Tokyo. A major demand was the reimbursement of 200,000 *yen*

3

by the prefecture for illegal and excess tax levies. It was widely explained that each person would receive a share of the reimbursement monies that would fill a *wappa*, the local Shōnai term for the shallow, round wooden container that individual cultivators used to carry their mid-day meal to the fields. This was later to give the movement its name—the Wappa Disturbances. The court hearings in 1876 coincided with the comprehensive Land Tax Reform surveys in Shōnai. The court decision was at least a qualified success for the plaintiffs, and the survey produced broad reductions in the land tax burden. With this resolution, the movement dissolved.

. These actions, stretching over three years, were the last of four sustained moments of popular, collective protest on this small rice plain during the 19th century. In 1840-41, an organized protest by cultivators, merchants, and domain elite had scored a rare success in reversing a direct shogunal order that would have transferred the Sakai domain lord to another fief and assigned Shōnai to a notoriously harsh and impoverished family. Then in 1844, town *sake* brewers and residents of seventy-two villages joined in a second "anti-transfer" movement to protest the assignment to Lord Sakai of administrative responsibility for three small shogunate territories within Shōnai. This time they were unsuccessful and harshly punished. The third collective protest came in 1869-71, just after the formation of the new Meiji state; the administrators it sent to the northern half of Shōnai faced a series of coordinated demands for reform of taxation and local governance. Both townspeople and rural cultivators mobilized against village officers, designated merchants, and the administrators themselves. It was in the aftermath of these actions, known as the Tengu Disturbances, that the Wappa Disturbances began.

What follows is a study of these four extended moments during which large numbers of Shōnai residents were moved to express their grievances and indignation. It traces in some detail the course of each movement and sifts the surviving

4

evidence for the social composition of participants and leaders, the claims and the demands advanced, and the language and the standards by which they were justified. Moreover, these four 19th-century cases (a "complete record," as it were, from this region) are juxtaposed to permit comparison. In what ways did they share similar developmental sequences? To what degree did the Tengu and Wappa agitations of the 1870s represent a new and more intense form of protest than those thirty years earlier in the 1840s? And finally, I am seeking here to relate these periods of challenge and crisis to the broader forces transforming Shōnai in the 19th century: the capitalist reorganization of the regional economy and the consolidation of the plain into a resurgent national political authority. In what manner did capitalism and nation-state formation give rise to, and give shape to, these protests? Conversely, how significant were these moments of collective action in giving direction to the particular forms of capitalist economy and state polity in Shōnai by the end of the century? It is toward such questions that the study is directed.

From Wealth to Capital, from Subject to Citizen

There was at one time a history of Tokugawa Japan whose line of narrative might be glibly summarized as follows: expanding markets and commercial transactions underwrote the rise of a merchant class; in turn, this spelled the decline of the political elite, while the peasantry and the rural economy stagnated as one exploitative master replaced another. Our understanding now is quite different. We realize that a burgeoning economy did not debilitate a brittle polity. Seventeenth-century Tokugawa political theory to the contrary, there were no necessary contradictions, but rather an essential mutualism between the tributary relations of overlord and subject and the commercial activities of the merchants, with their circuits of trade in the surpluses of the tribute-takers and the producing subjects. By the mid-17th century,

5

symbiotic ties were fashioned between large urban merchants and shogunal and certain domain authorities, and it was this nexus of the sword and the abacus that was threatened by upstarts—who turned out to be other samurai and other merchants. In the late 18th and early 19th centuries, urban merchant domination of commercial activity was challenged by rural processors and traders, resulting in a competition for market control and, eventually, a "rural-centered growth" (Smith 1973). At the same time, as Bolitho (1974) has demonstrated, the balance of political power was shifting from Edo to the domains, as the domain lords came to behave less as vassals of the shogun and more as rulers of domains. Aggregate per capita output in the rural economy expanded as population stabilized, agricultural production rose, and by-employments increased. Thus, the 17th- and 18th-century collusions of the great merchant houses like the Kōnoike and the shogunal magistrates in Osaka and Edo yielded in the mid-19th century to the mutual dependency of such prospering rural merchants as Shibusawa Ichirō and his local Okabe Domain elders (Chambliss 1965:22-25).

Still, these were at best tendencies of the late Tokugawa. The changing personnel and the shifting political-economic center of gravity were neither uniform nor completed processes. The shogunate endured as the polity's carapace, and large urban centers continued to be the principal markets. Tokugawa society from the mid-1600s through the mid-1800s remained an interlocking mercantile economy and tributary polity.

However, this political and economic decentralization did foster some radically new arrangements, such as protoindustrial manufacturing in some countrysides, and it catalyzed severe ideological debates about the legitimacy of rule and the bases of authority. Just how serious a rupture was precipitated or how smooth a transition was accomplished in the mid- and late 19th century is a matter, we will see shortly, that fundamentally divides historians. But few will deny that by the turn of the 20th century, Japan was an in-

6

terlocking capitalist economy and constitutional state, and the movement from wealth to capital and from subject to citizen were central developments of the 19th century.

I should add that my particular characterization of these developments rests on notions of "capitalism" and "nation-state" that are partisan, though neither polemical nor idiosyncratic. With Eric Wolf (1983) and others, I hold it useful to distinguish between mercantile activity, seeking profits in trade, and capitalist investment, seeking a return in production by deploying purchased labor to produce other commodities:

> Wealth in the hands of holders of wealth is not capital until it controls means of production, buys labor power, and puts it to work, continuously expanding surpluses by intensifying productivity through an ever-rising curve of technological inputs. . . . As long as wealth remains external to the process of production, merely skimming off the products of the primary producers and making profits by selling them, that wealth is *not* capital. (Wolf 1983:78–79; emphasis in original)

Merchants may, as they did for much of Japanese history, draw goods into spheres of trade without directly intervening in the production process itself. Profits become capital only when they seek to direct the means of production and reorder the relations of production. The differences are of profound social consequence, and the distinction should be crucial for non-Marxists and Marxists alike. For only this distinction can deflate that great, putative prime mover of 19th-century social change, commercialization. The tributary polity and mercantile economy was already extensively commercialized at the outset of the century. Shibusawa Ichirō, a rural sericulture promoter who appeared in Chambliss's study of Chiaraijima Village, was a rural merchant of a type common in the late Tokugawa countryside. But his son, Shibusawa Eiichi, was a capitalist, Meiji Japan's preeminent industrialist and banker (Chambliss 1965). It was a capitalist transformation of the economy, not commercial acceleration, that divided father and son. There was money before merchants, merchants before manufacture—and manufacture before capitalist manufacture.

Similarly, there were states and nations before nation-states. The formative processes of nation-states are various and complex, but I am persuaded by Reinhard Bendix that all center on a reconstitution of authority, "as the rule of kings [is] replaced by governments of the people" (1978:4). The nationalization of the state and the politicization of the nation in the last two centuries has involved a redefinition of the legitimacy of authority, from the religious sanctions of kingly rule to the exercise of authority in the name of the people. However, Bendix has cautioned, this modern shift from subject to citizen has not always brought greater popular participation in government; dictatorships and monarchies, too, have ruled "in the name of the people." Indeed, I would suggest that how far the popular mandate has entailed popular participation has depended in each instance on the particular meanings that have been attached to "accountability." In this sense, the two decades between the announcement of a nation-state in the Charter Oath of 1868 and its ratification in the Constitution of 1889 were but the intense midpoint of longer, rancorous debates on just this issue of accountability.

The 19th century in Japan marked the transition from a mercantile economy and tributary polity to a capitalist economy and constitutional polity. These are the broad terms from which I begin to look for the particular formations and mutual connections of polity and economy on the small, coastal rice plain of Shōnai. They are the larger movements along which I seek to plot the actions of its inhabitants. Much social theory proposes that collective protest catalyzes novel economic and political solidarities even as it arises from new economic and political forces (Thompson 1978). What were the patterns of social solidarities and modes of action by which the people of Shōnai resisted or promoted (and in either case gave shape to) the new order?

HISTORIOGRAPHIC PARADIGMS OF 19TH-CENTURY JAPAN

Even if it were possible to secure agreement on the general features of Japan at 1800 and Japan at 1900, students of that century would continue to divide sharply between those who emphasize the lines of continuity between the old Tokugawa order and the new Meiji order and those who highlight the disjunctures of the century. These are fault lines of both the Japanese and Western literatures. It is not relevant here to review these debates exhaustively. However, among these competing formulations, I see several recurring models of class, community, and party as the significant vehicles and products of 19th-century change. To appreciate the forms of collective protest in Shōnai, we must distill these models from the literatures.

Among Japanese scholars, these competing historiographies of continuity or crisis have generally manifested themselves as fractious, internecine debates in a Marxist idiom of class struggle, ignited by the celebrated intellectual and political schism of the 1920s and 1930s between the so-called "Lectures Faction" and the "Labor-Farmer Faction" (Kelly 1982b:7-9). A central issue in these multifaceted debates has been the nature of the Meiji Restoration. Was it a true bourgeois revolution, heralding the replacement of a feudal regime by a monopoly capitalist mode of production? Or, as the majority "Lectures Faction" thinkers insisted, were the gains of the lower samurai and petty bourgeoisie in the towns and countryside usurped by the "parasitic absentee landlords," who supplanted the feudal overlords and established a semi-feudal (han hōken) mode of production, supported by an absolutist state?

Despite the bitter polemics that have divided them, both factions have tended to write unilinear histories of the 19th-century countryside, based on the "internal differentiation of

9

the peasantry" (nōmin kaisō bunkai). Commercialization of production, the success of largeholders in marketing surpluses, the ability of village officers to advance their personal positions, and the land investments of town merchants challenged feudal arrangements with a nascent capitalist mode of production and stratified the peasantry. A common grid stratifies the 19th-century countryside into large, absentee, "parasitic landlords" (kisei jinushi); "village-resident, small landlords" (nōson kojinushi); "wealthy, self-cultivating largeholders" (gōnō); "smallholders" (shōnō) with varying combinations of registered and tenanted parcels; and the "semi-proletariat" (han puro) of marginal tenants, day laborers, and miscellaneous wage workers. The relative contributions of improvements in cultivation methods, structural crises of feudalism, and harvest disasters to this stratification are hotly debated, as is its late 19th-century fate (a retreat to "semi-feudalism" or advance to agrarian capitalism?). But the most typical reading of rural protest in this century has been as a class struggle within this polarizing peasantry, increasingly between the "semi-proletariat" and the resident and non-resident landlords. Class stratification and class struggle, in Shōnai (Satō 1965, Igawa 1972) as elsewhere, have largely delimited the boundaries of interpretation and debate.

This analytical framework, for example, lies behind the work of Aoki Kōji, which requires mention because he is widely cited to support many propositions about the changing patterns of 18th- and 19th-century protest. Building on earlier compilations of Kokushō Iwao, Aoki has made an ambitious attempt to catalogue popular protest incidents in the Tokugawa centuries (Aoki 1966) and the Meiji decades (Aoki 1967). He has revised and folded these into a single, comprehensive chronology that names, locates, estimates numbers, and categorizes 6,889 "rebellions" and "disturbances" between 1590 and 1877 (Aoki 1971). Aoki subscribes to the common tripartite division of collective action into hyakushō ikki, murakata sōdō, and toshi sōdō. The first is frequently translated as "peasant uprising" (e.g., Borton 1938,

Scheiner 1973:590, Bowen 1980), and refers to conflicts between peasants and their feudal overlords. These are distinguished from *murakata sōdō* ("rural disturbances"), which were agitations within the stratified peasantry. Third, there were *toshi sōdō* ("urban disturbances"), agitations of proletarian townspeople against rich merchants, town authorities, or feudal overlords. Very roughly, Aoki and others (e.g., Hayashi 1971:3-40) have argued that the 17th and early 18th centuries were characterized by solidary "all-peasant" risings against the feudal elite, but by the 19th century, stratification was pitting dispossessed cultivators (tenants and laborers) against the privileged elite of the towns and villages. *Hyakushō ikki* gave way to a preponderance of *murakata sōdō* and *toshi sōdō*.

There are several difficulties with Aoki's categorization and typologies that limit the value of his catalogues,[1] but perhaps most pernicious is the implication that class antagonism may be read from distributional stratification (see Brow

---

[1] *Hyakushō ikki*, for example, is a cover term of such proportions as to homogenize a vast range of non-violent petitions and violent confrontations, isolated incidents and organized resistance. For example, the 45 *ikki* listed for Shōnai in Aoki's 1971 volume include: an incident in 1635 in which 7 households absconded from a village (1971:28); the jailing of 27 persons from a mountain village in the spring of 1707 for protesting timbering by another village (ibid.:62); the overnight jailing of 4 cultivators and the house confinement of 3 others, who petitioned in 1764 for increased rice loans (ibid.:127); and the two sustained "anti-transfer" movements of the 1840s discussed in this study (ibid.:255-56, 263). This conceptual ambiguity is compounded, not mitigated, by his classification of *ikki* by predominant mode of protest. That is, he categorizes the 1635 incident as a *chōsan* (absconding), the 1707 timber incident as a *sanron* (a mountain dispute), the 1764 incident as a *gōso* (an illegal direct petition made with some intimidating threat), the first anti-transfer movement of 1840-41 as a *shūso* (a joint, legal petition), and the second movement of 1844 as an *uchikowashi* (a smashing). Not only does a check with source documents in many of the Shōnai examples raise doubts about the appropriateness of his judgments, but the very act of pigeonholing what are usually incidents of multiple motivations and composite strategies has trivialized the variegated expressions of popular discontent.

11

1981). This analytical strategy is widely shared among Marxist historians of 19th-century Japan, but it requires two dubious assumptions. The first has been to identify the class strata of the countryside by the distribution of landholdings (either land registered to the household or cultivated by the household, often only in their village of residence). We will see some of the difficulties of this in the next chapter. The second has been to breathe life in these distributional strata— to assume a consciousness of shared class interests and to presume an antagonism among the thus reified agrarian classes. Too often we are presented with a quick, inevitable sequence of inequality, class, and class struggle. There were certainly tensions unleashed by changing relations of production in the 19th-century countryside, but, as E. P. Thompson has argued eloquently in another context, analyses too often reverse the actual historical sequence:

> To put it bluntly: classes do not exist as separate entities, look around, find an enemy class, and then start to struggle. On the contrary, people find themselves in a society structured in determined ways (crucially, but not exclusively, in productive relations), they experience exploitation (or the need to maintain power over those whom they exploit), they identify points of antagonistic interest, they commence to struggle around these issues and in the process of struggling they discover themselves as classes, they come to know this discovery as class-consciousness. Class and class-consciousness are always the last, not the first, stage in the real historical process. (Thompson 1978:147)

There are several other recent contributions to this Japanese literature on 19th-century rural protest that merit reference in prefacing the Shōnai movements. There has been strenuous argument among Japanese scholars about the reactionary nature or revolutionary potential of rural class struggles. Did the rebellions and disturbances represent conservative resistance to the appropriation by tribute-takers of

12

peasant surpluses, or were they radical challenges to the existing order? In many books and articles, Sasaki Junnosuke has vigorously restated the latter position by emphasizing the millenarian programs of the protesters and rioters in the 1850s and 1860s, "semi-proletarians" who were pushed to extreme visions of social justice and liminal actions by deteriorating rural conditions. Sasaki's narrow interpretation of disturbances in these decades has been challenged by Fukaya (1981:152-60) and Satō Shigerō (1980:13-104). They have argued that these rather special intra-peasantry *yonaoshi* actions gave way to a resurgence of "all-peasant uprisings" (*sōbyakusō ikki*) in the late 1860s and 1870s as rural people realized sufficient solidarity and collective interests to press their advantage against a national elite in disarray.

Yet another interpretation has been advanced by Irokawa Daikichi, doyen of the new "populist" historians, who uphold a historiographic mission akin to the History Workshop in England and the *Annales* school in France, albeit with less institutional coherence. As Gluck (1978) has perceptively observed in an overview of this Japanese "people's history," relations among Marxists, modernists, and populists in Japanese historical circles are complex and often ambiguous. Important differences, though, turn on their respective treatments of the concept of "community" (*kyōdōtai*). For most Marxists, the cohesive (exploitative) solidarity of the Tokugawa village community inhered primarily in the vertical relations of patronage and personal dependency on landlords, main families, and headmen. "Harmony" as a communal value was an ideological weapon of repression. Modernists, too, have a largely negative evaluation of the "community," suspecting that the village smothered self-expression and stifled individual freedom and rationalization. Irokawa and other populists, though, have found a vibrant egalitarianism in the natural, horizontal associations that comprised, for them, the real village collectivity: the pilgrimage groups, labor exchanges, age-grade organizations, rotating credit societies, and so on. These were the meaningful social bonds

13

of the countryside, preserving healthy communal values and quite capable of rising up in common, spirited defense when threatened. Submerged, overwhelmed by the Meiji state, they nonetheless survived to fight new battles a hundred years later in the local citizen protests of the 1960s and 1970s. Irokawa's history is, in that special way, one that highlights, celebrates these continuities, "the survival struggle of the Japanese community" (Irokawa 1975).

A CENTURY CONTINUOUS OR A CENTURY RUPTURED?

In a very different sense, the burden of Western scholarship on 19th-century Japan in the last thirty years has been to demonstrate the essential continuities between the premodern, preindustrial decades of the Tokugawa 19th century and the early modern, industrializing decades of the Meiji 19th century. In part, this was a response to what was considered a mechanistic Marxism in Japan, a Marxism with a rigid model of the disjunctures of feudalism in crisis and an embryonic capitalism struggling to break free. In part, too, the flush of modernization theory and the development problems of newly independent Third World countries prompted Japan specialists to reevaluate Japan's precocious rise to industrial nationhood. The writings of Thomas Smith on "the agrarian origins of modern Japan" (1959) in the later Tokugawa period and its "pre-modern economic growth" (1973) have been seminal. His work and the demographic research of Hayami Akira have laid the basis for a new orthodoxy, a descriptive model of stable population levels and an expanding rural economy for much of the 19th century (Smith 1977; Hanley and Yamamura 1977). Dore (1965) demonstrated the high levels of literacy and the spread of basic education through Tokugawa society. Bellah (1957; cf. 1978) characterized a transformation of religious values in Ishida Baigan's Shingaku movement as fostering a predisposition to industrial work effort and nation-state allegiance. Crawcour (1965) and Hauser (1974) have detailed the sophisticated fi-

14

nancial structures and commercial organizations of the Tokugawa economy, while Robert J. Smith (1960, 1972), Hibbett (1959), and others have described the ward structures
and the lively urban ethos of the Tokugawa cities. All demonstrate in effect the ideological predispositions, the institutional matrices, and the material bases for Japan's rapid and
successful industrialization and urbanization of the late 19th
and early 20th centuries.

Such a perspective is not blind to conflict, but many of the
major, synthetic works have chosen to emphasize these cultural, institutional, and material continuities. They do not
find popular protest to have radically challenged or seriously
deflected the main currents of the century. Evaluation of the
Meiji Restoration, as many have observed, is diagnostic: by
the paradigm of continuity it was a "palace coup d'état," a
circulation of elites. Craig's masterful study of Chōshū con-
cludes:

> The Meiji Restoration was not a revolution, not a
> change in the name of new values—such as *liberté, ega-
> lité*, and *fraternité* in the French Revolution. Rather, it
> was what is far more common in history, a change car-
> ried out in the name of old values. (1961:360)

The most well-developed economic model of growth and
prosperity in the 19th-century countrysides has been that of
Hanley and Yamamura. Their 1977 volume, which documented a position Thomas Smith had sketched more tentatively twenty years before, addressed the question of
whether there was a rising or falling standard of living in the
late 18th and 19th centuries. Was the countryside tumbling
on a downward spiral of poverty and exploitation or was it
ascending an upward curve of surplus production and accumulation? Their answer was most emphatically the latter: on
an aggregate level, in most regions, and among most households, due to expanding output, stable population levels, and
a competitive labor market. I will return later in this study
to the implications for Shōnai of their convincing demon-

15

stration of expanding rural output. It must suffice here to draw attention to their rather narrow characterization of motivations behind this economic and demographic behavior and to their uncertain treatment of the consequences of this behavior. Neither provides ready guidelines for understanding collective protest in the 19th century.

In anthropology, the battles waged across the journal pages between the so-called "formalists," insisting on the universal salience of classical and neoclassical economics, and the "substantivists," equally adamant that production and exchange operates in precapitalist societies by entirely different principles, collapsed in exhaustion some time ago (for a eulogy, see Cancian 1974). The arguments were most useful as a reminder that people everywhere are moved to manipulate what they see as possibilities to what they believe to be their advantage. But acknowledging this general rationality has only heightened our appreciation for the limitations of that special model that is "economic rationality": "the application of scarce means to differentially graded ends to maximize the position of the actor vis-à-vis others" (Rappaport 1979:236). Yet it is the *homo economicus* who populates the Tokugawa countrysides of Hanley and Yamamura. They have insisted, for example, that the controls on family size were deliberate, selective calculations to maximize household position and income:

> As the economy grew, farming became increasingly commercially oriented, and the rural villages were gradually woven into a highly monetized and consumption-oriented society, people began to choose to "trade off" additional children for goods and services or the accumulation of wealth needed to improve or maintain their standard of living and their status within village society. This is equivalent to saying that if a graph were drawn the line connecting the tangencies between the indifference curves representing various levels of income and the slope indicating the rate of wealth-children substi-

16

tution would be curved backwards to the Y-axis that measures the quantity of goods (X-axis measures children). (Hanley and Yamamura 1977:36)

I would argue that one can accept their general proposition that there was widespread, voluntary planning and control of family size without endorsing the stringent logic of their particular explanation. We know enough now about "satisficing" to be suspicious of "maximizing." Both of the desired "ends" of decision making, household status and standard of living, remain vague, unspecified, and disconcertingly asocial. And the formal economic assumption that they can be quantified and arrayed along a single hierarchy of desirability can be dangerously self-fulfilling when only statistical evidence is considered.

Hanley and Yamamura appear ambivalent about whether general prosperity bred contentment or dissatisfaction. In their joint volume, they did not ignore the many "peasant uprisings" in Nambu Domain in the late 18th and 19th centuries, for which they offered a "political economy" (Popkin 1979) explanation. That is, they were to be understood as the largely successful efforts of commercially oriented peasants and merchants to limit domain exactions and official obstacles to free market access. And in a separate article, Yamamura included a disclaimer that "I do not argue that the Tokugawa peasant became happier or more satisfied with life" (Yamamura 1979:319, footnote 84).

Yet the burden of their work suggests that this is just what they do argue. Hanley, in recently proposing there was a "leveling of incomes" in addition to a rising standard of living in mid-century, cited as appropriate Townsend Harris's observation in 1857 that "they are all fat, well clad, and happy looking, but there is an equal absence of any appearance of wealth or of poverty." Hanley concluded that:

In short, income disparities were narrowing and this mitigated the social disruption that could have been ex-

17

pected with the change in government in 1868 and the loss of the samurai's sinecures. (Hanley 1983:191)

In sum, they have made a significant and persuasive demonstration of aggregate economic growth through the 19th century. Shōnai will illustrate, though, that the distribution of output in particular regions, the several cultural calculuses of the "producers," and the social consequences of that aggregate growth are not reducible to their particular model of behavior.

However forceful their advocacy, scholars of the prosperity and continuity perspective are fighting a cross-current of Western historiography, which is perhaps running stronger and deeper these days. It marks a return, with an idealist emphasis quite different from that of most Japanese Marxists, to the disjunctures and moments of radical choice in 19th-century Japan. Two intellectual historians, Harootunian and Najita, have been particularly influential in this reorientation toward what Harootunian (1974:662) has described as those events of "transformative significance" that "reveal a discontinuity in purpose and the field of possibles out of which new purpose is forged." Intellectual history for Harootunian is not the history of ideas or the sociology of knowledge; it is the engagement with and interpretation of "mental structures" as revealed in the discourse among texts. It is this epistemological premise that has sensitized him to the "breakdown" of established discursive fields and "the eruption of new discourse," metaphors he has borrowed from Foucault. The drama of the 19th century was the antagonism of two discursive fields, the challenge of "the new realism" of National Learning (kokugaku) to the older forms of orthodox Neo-Confucianism:

[M]y task is to note the discontinuity in consciousness which kokugakusha disclosed in a new discourse, and to examine its disjunctures and capacity for transformation. Discontinuity, here, represents an attempt to or-

18

ganize a new epistemological field. (Harootunian 1978:69-70)

Najita's metaphors of thought are less volcanic and more botanical; he has written of a Levensonesque "exfoliation of ideas" (1975). Elsewhere, he has juxtaposed bureaucratic loyalty with idealist protest as two opposing "modes of action" associated, respectively, with official shogunate ethical codes and with the radical currents of 19th-century "Restorationism" (1974).

Inspired by this new intellectual history as well as by recent populist history in Japan, other Western scholars are paying increasing attention to 19th-century popular thought: to the complexities of folk morality, peasant culture, and local religious symbolism. Behind many such studies is the shared proposition that it was the moments of crisis in the 19th century that provoked heightened consciousness, the formulation of new standards of behavior, and the articulation of alternative social orders.[2] A central thrust of the recent conference volume, *Conflict in Modern Japanese History* (Najita and Koschmann 1982), is to argue for a radical shift in popular consciousness around the time of—and indeed forming a part of the *core experience* of—the Meiji Restoration. Adopting Najita's and Harootunian's epistemological assumptions, several contributors argued for underlying "textual" connections between the millenarian rioters, the *kōbu gattai* plotters, the *shishi* fanatics, the "smashings" mobs, and other radical actions against the Tokugawa and early Meiji establishments. The following passage from Najita's introduction to the volume stands in stark and instructive contrast to Craig's conclusion cited above:

[2] There are certainly other lessons to be drawn from conflict: "a riot throws light upon the norms of tranquil years, and a sudden breach of deference enables us to better understand the deferential habits which have been broken" (Thompson 1977:251). But these scholars examine periods of crisis to diagnose alternative values and initiatives emergent in them, rather than to reveal the otherwise silent norms of the hegemonic social order.

19

Drastic acts of dissent, risk taking, and spiritual seces-
sion thus reverberated beyond narrow social compart-
ments and social spheres. Common to these varying experiences was an awareness of a breakdown in the
received social, political, and moral universes. An ideological language legitimating dissent evolved and became generally accessible. In varying dimensions, there
was fear and excitement, a sense of disbelief over the
general state of confusion, and an awareness that previous methods could not correct the disarray. All this
was accompanied by a sense of expectation of new possibilities, a flowering of large and small visions based on
an anticipation that unusual things were about to happen
to bring about a renewal, and that, through action de-
fined in a wide variety of ways, new achievements were
indeed possible. (Najita 1982:19; see also Wilson 1983)

Still, those who plumb the depths of mid-century crisis
disagree sharply on how and when significant solidarities coalesced and contested the existing order. For an appreciation
of the Shōnai protests, two of the more important formulations of critical breaks in 19th-century popular consciousness
are those of Irwin Scheiner (1973, 1978) and Roger Bowen
(1980). Scheiner and Bowen differ on two fundamental
points: on *when* a radical shift in popular consciousness occurred and on the *terms* themselves of protest, on the *language*
of indignation. Scheiner emphasizes the utopian, chiliastic visions of popular millenarian movements of the 1850s and
1860s (the *yonaoshi* and *ee ja nai ka* frenzies). Bowen emphasizes the liberal language of constitutional government and
human rights that was catalytic in the "violent incidents"
(*gekka jiken*) of the early and mid-1800s. These imply very
different interpretations of the Shōnai movements.

In his 1978 essay, Scheiner proposed several transformations in the moral language of popular protest in the Tokugawa centuries. The initial Tokugawa moral order, he argued, had implied a "covenant" of mutual obligations

20

between the paternalistic "benevolent lords" and the subordinate "honorable peasants," which offered the deferential peasant a guaranteed subsistence. Lords unmindful of the legitimate limits of exactions risked protest from their subjects seeking to restore moral reciprocity. But growing fiscal troubles brought a "crisis of the covenant." By the late 18th century, pleas for paternal benevolence and images of just rulers were no longer effective prods to lords who refused or were unable to accept moral limits. Peasants turned increasingly to enshrined rebel heroes as the "righteous men" (*gimin*) who would rally support against unjust claims and legitimate movements to restore righteous rule.

By the mid-19th century, there was a second transformation as increasingly distressed and disenchanted peasants began to carry forward "the reform of society" by themselves. The very justifications of the lords' rule were questioned; the *gimin* were no longer extolled merely as "virtuous men" but as *saviors*, who would lead peasants into a new social order. Thus, for example, the fertility and harvest cults of the Maitreya Buddha were reworked as more radical "cargo cults," which awaited the "ships of Maitreya" that would bring retribution to the powerful as well as wealth to the poor. They became justifications for attacking the rich and redistributing their wealth, a vision of leveling society (*yonaoshi*) more radical than earlier agitations for a return to benevolent rule. The peasants' "crisis of the covenant" was, as it were, the vulgate of the intellectuals' crisis of Neo-Confucianism; it was the rural manifestation of the Restorationist critique of the shogunate polity. One link between the rural actions and the dissident elite Restorationists was Hirata Atsutane and his followers, who proselytized a radical communitarianism (Harootunian 1978). Another was the promotion of *gimin* figures like Ōshio Heihachirō, who were glorified by commoners and elite alike as templates of "pure action."

Roger Bowen (1980) does not deny these levelers of the 1850s and 1860s, but he mutes their significance. He dismisses them as limited, prepolitical agitations; they were the rearguard actions of peasants who had yet to see themselves as *political actors*, who had yet to learn to speak in a political language. He has focused instead on several dramatic "violent incidents" (*gekka jiken*) of the early and mid-1880s: those in Fukushima (1882), Kabasan (1884), and Chichibu (1884-85). In each case, he argues for organizational and ideological links between the protestors and activitists in the Movement for Freedom and Popular Rights (*jiyū minken undō*), the popular rights movement of the period that based its demands for representative government and civil liberties on Western liberal principles of natural rights. That is, it was not the millenarian language of moral revival and renewal but the secular political language of universal human rights and democratic representation that transformed the farmer from a passive, prepolitical being, responding to obligations but unaware of rights, into a political actor, demanding democratic reforms in the increasingly bureaucratic, centralized Meiji state and calling on it to make good its initial vision. It was a demand that was violently suppressed by the Meiji authorities, but which nonetheless stands as a true experience of and authentic experiment in democracy.

To Bowen, the shift in political consciousness from feudal subject to active citizen was prompted by the economic transformation of subsistence peasants into commercial farmers. By the late 19th century, he argues, the subsistence-oriented peasant economy had become a liberal market economy of commercialized farmers, and the significant acts of 19th-century protest and rebellion were the progressive actions of such farmers, who "transferred the new economic principles of the market to the political realm" (1980:124).[3] It was not moral "covenant" but political "contract" that they demanded.

Both Scheiner (1982) and Bowen (1980:89, 124, 178) have

[3] Although Bowen does not refer to Hanley and Yamamura's model, one might see them as complementary; Bowen's argument that radical political action resulted from commercialization and prosperity was an outcome not foreseen, and perhaps not acceptable, to Hanley and Yamamura.

been quite critical of the other's work,[4] but beyond these mutual recriminations is some important common ground shared by many who focus on the crises and discontinuities of 19th-century Japan. Both believe that popular consciousness was shaping into a radical and dynamic worldview and was articulating an alternative social vision that forced its way to the surface, either in utopian communal terms or in liberal democratic demands. These were visions that *might* have become the foundations for a different and preferable modernity, had not the increasingly powerful Meiji state intervened and overwhelmed them. Thus the Restoration was a "failed revolution," arrested, incomplete.

Scheiner and Bowen also share a concern with the disruptions of the market on agriculture and the rural economy, and on this point, their models are weakest. Once again, 19th-century economic change is played along an axis of commercialization: the subsistence peasant eagerly embraces the opportunities of the market to become the entreprenurial farmer (Bowen) or else resists the market's immiserating outcomes of tenancy and wage labor and social disintegration (Scheiner). The difficulties with such a view have been

---

[4] Their dispute has clear parallels to debates about the nature of agrarian regimes in other parts of the world. Oakes (1982), for example, has seen capitalist entrepreneurs on the plantations of the antebellum South where Genovese (1969) had found agrarian paternalists. Another debate that has reverberated through peasant studies has been Popkin's (1979) juxtaposition of a "political economy" explanation with Scott's (1976) "moral economy" model of Burmese and Vietnamese peasant behavior in the 1920s and 1930s. Both Scott and Popkin had proposed broad applications of their models. Scott had stressed the ways in which state-building and capitalism undermine "age-old subsistence guarantees." Peasants thus rebel to restore precapitalist securities—if not through appeal to the benevolence of the ruler then through appeal to a more utopian village community order. Popkin characterized most traditional subsistence arrangements as more exploitative than protective of peasant interests. To him, the spread of market relations offers opportunities for the enterprising peasant cultivator; peasant rebellion more often arises when such entreprenurial drives for profit are thwarted. A 1983 symposium in the *Journal of Asian Studies* (42:753-868) has examined both of these positions.

23

sketched above: the rural economy was already commercialized at the outset of the century, and cultivators were drawn
into market relations for a variety of motives that cannot be
reduced to a single model of individual profit-maximizing.
It was not the commercializing of exchange, but the capitalist
reorganization of production that was the thrust of change
in the 19th-century rural economy.

It is not surprising that the experience of Japan's 19th-cen-
tury transition to modernity should generate such different
calculations of its benefits and dislocations. Other literatures
are similarly divided.[5] Nor is it surprising that here, too,
albeit in different cultural idioms, analysts should find community, class, and party as the foci of collective action; they
are the recurring solidarities of modern social theory. They
were certainly the intellectual force field within which I began this study of Shōnai's four protest movements.

And yet, it will become clear in the subsequent chapters
that my initial expectations were frustrated. Neither class interest nor community ideology nor citizen rights goes far in
explaining these enduring, collective actions that were at
once broad in social composition and specific in demands.
Participants were strategically shrewd and ideologically im-
pure, capable of fusing disparate motivations into focused

[5] Compare, for example, the paradigms of 19th-century Japan offered by
Sasaki, Hanley/Yamamura, and Najita/Harootunian and three equally contested formulations of English industrialization. Early analysts such as Marx
and the Hammonds emphasized the misery and desperation in the towns
and countryside—the "classical catastrophic orthodoxy" as Thompson
(1968:214) dubbed it. This was challenged by "a new anti-catastrophic orthodoxy," illustrated by economic historians like Ashton and sociologists
like Smelser, who tracked the continuities of industrial development and
celebrated the prosperity gained from modern economic growth (this "prosperity and continuity" view has been most recently defended by Lindert and
Williamson [1983]). The work of Thompson himself, with others, com-
prises a third perspective, which returns with greater sophistication to the
crises and discontinuities of the English experience, the "blind alleys" and
"the lost causes of the people of the Industrial Revolution" (1968:13, see
also pp. 207-32).

24

action. They could be cautiously deferential and resolutely defiant. It would be patently false to claim that the character of these movements disproves the saliency of class, community, or party in giving voice to aspirations and indignation elsewhere in Japan. But it would be equally mistaken to dismiss the Shōnai protests as marginal, inchoate, and immature or to read them as evidence that, after all, life was good and getting better for the vast majority of rural residents—that they had nothing to protest about. Profound indignation propelled these movements across the plain, and they were to have very considerable consquences both for those who acted and for the region. It is likely that they represented a mode of action that was more common in the 19th-century countryside than either quiescence and acquiescence or radical "pure action." But I must now begin to talk of them and not about them.

TWO

Shōnai and Sakai Domain

SHŌNAI PLAIN is a small, low-lying coastal plain along the Japan Sea in northeastern Honshū (see Map 1). Hemmed in by mountains on three sides, it is protected from the sea by a narrow band of sand dunes. The plain stretches about 50 kilometers north to south, and is bisected mid-way by the broad Mogami River, which crosses the plain to the Japan Sea from its long course in the interior. To the river's north, the plain is only about 6 kilometers wide and is known as Akumi (Map 2). South of the Mogami, in Tagawa, the plain widens to about 15 kilometers (Map 3). In the centuries before 1600, Shōnai was a marshy expanse; only a few rough settlements hugged the plain's perimeter and perched on the higher banks of the small rivers that ran across Akumi and Tagawa. In the medieval centuries it was a frontier zone, attracting only hardy pilgrims to the famous, remote *shugendō* temple complexes on Mts. Haguro, Yudono, and Gassan, "the three mountains of Dewa" (*Dewa sanzan*) that bordered the plain on the southeast. In the 16th century, Shōnai as a buffer and occasional scuffle ground between more settled inland basins and the Echigo plains to the south. Its fortunes changed rapidly after 1600. As in many areas of central and northeastern Japan, irrigation and drainage improvements enabled extensive conversion of the swampy plain to productive paddy lands throughout the 17th and early 18th centuries. It was with optimistic prospects that Sakai Tadakatsu, a close Tokugawa vassal, come to Shōnai in 1622, when he was enfeoffed the plain and its surrounding mountains by the shogun Iemitsu. Weathering several challenges, eleven

26

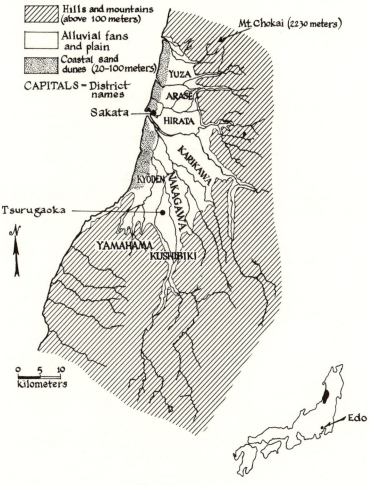

The Shōnei region

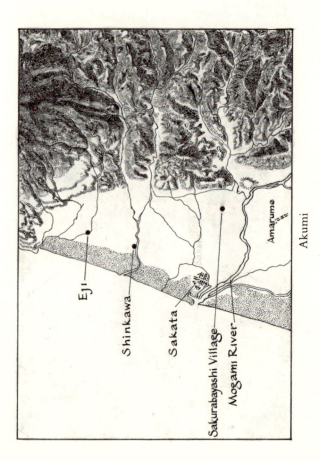

Eji

Shinkawa

Sakata

Sakurabayashi Village

Mogami River

Amarume

Akumi

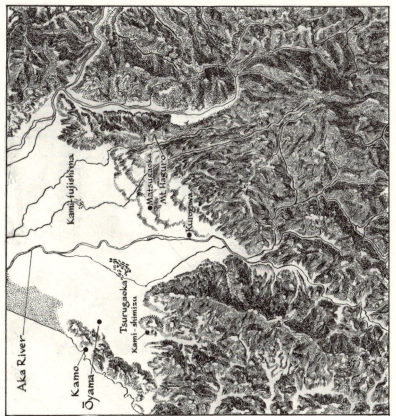

Tagawa

lineal descendants of Tadakatsu followed him as lords of Shōnai.

Sakai Tadakatsu's initial fief grant in 1622 was 140,000 *koku*. This remained the shogunate's official evaluation of Shōnai's productive potential, but Tadakatsu quickly added 50,000 *koku* to the domain's internal assessment (*uchidaka*) with a comprehensive cadastre in the next year. Later additions to the domain registers raised its *uchidaka* to about 225,000 *koku*—its tribute base, as it were—but even this, we will see, considerably understated the actual productivity of the rice monocropped plain. By the early 19th century, the plain was capable of producing about 580,000 *koku* of rice in a very good harvest year.

Like the first Tokugawa shoguns of the larger state system, the early Sakai lords sought to establish a politically secure and economically stable regime by creating a countryside of demilitarized, landholding, and tax-paying peasant households, organized into self-regulating residential settlement units and administered by a hierarchy of officials recruited from among the warrior-retainers of the domain lord. Implicit in this order, then, was a tension between hierarchical control and self-regulating autonomy.

Outside of the castle town of Tsurugaoka and the port of Sakata, there were four levels of rural administrative units. The domain included the two "counties" (*gun*) of Akumi and Tagawa. Akumi was divided into three "districts" (*gō*), while the larger Tagawa was partitioned into five districts (a different term, *tōri*, was used for obscure reasons). Districts were subdivided into three to seven "village groups" (*kumi*), each of which was composed of two to forty-nine roughly contiguous "administrative villages" (*mura*). On the plain, these administrative villages were nearly always congruent with nucleated settlements and their surrounding fields. An 1861 map of Shōnai Domain plotted 747 administrative villages organized into thirty-five village groups, which in turn composed the eight districts of the two counties (see Table 1).

TABLE 1
Levels of Rural Administration, Shōnai Domain, 1861

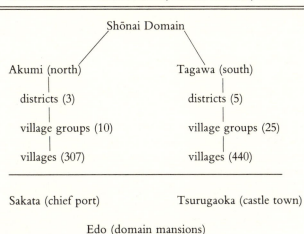

Shōnai Domain

Akumi (north)   Tagawa (south)

districts (3)   districts (5)

village groups (10)   village groups (25)

villages (307)   villages (440)

Sakata (chief port)   Tsurugaoka (castle town)

Edo (domain mansions)

SOURCE: *Dewa Shōnai nigun ezu* (facsimile of 1861 map).

By the mid-1600s, Sakai's retainer band reached a stable level of about 2,500 persons at two levels. The 500 upper-rank retainers were enfeoffed warriors used to fill the administrative hierarchy. Below them were another 2,000 stipendiary retainers: foot soldiers, guards, service personnel of the castle, falconers, and so on. Most retainers were resident in the castle town. Some manned Kamegaseki, the domain's fortification in Sakata, and others were stationed permanently or temporarily at the three domain mansions in Edo.

The countryside was administered through a hierarchy headed by the domain rural affairs officer. Under him were several officials assigned to a district or pair of districts and drawn from among upper-rank retainers. They lived in Tsurugaoka and worked at the main administrative offices with small staffs of subordinates. For most matters, including tax rate adjustments and year-end tax collection, they dispatched these subordinates to their districts. Treating these visiting officials with proper "hospitality" was of course a necessary,

31

delicate, and noisome task for villagers. A private memo from the 1780s advised fellow village officials on the provision of *sake*, food, gifts, and female companionship for tax collection officers and on appropriate behavior when going to town on domain business (SSS 1977:877-78).

Below the district officials were the village group headmen (*ōjoya*), who had general administrative responsibility for a single village group. Theirs was an intermediate and anomalous position. In formal status they were of the cultivator stratum, but for stipend purposes they were treated as lower-rank warrior retainers; they were also accorded the privileges of surname and sword. They lived in large house compounds within the village group, and there was a well-appointed house in the castle town where they lodged while on domain business. Village group residents were assessed the upkeep of this town house, and this was to prove a contentious issue. All village group headmen served at the convenience of district officials, although in fact the post was usually hereditary. Even so, they were frequently shifted around to discourage permanent private interests in particular areas. The Tentō household is a representative illustration (Table 2).

TABLE 2
Rotation of Village Group Headman Assignments:
The Example of Tentō Hayanosuke

	Period of Appointment	Headmanship
1st Generation — 4th Generation	1630?- 1734	Kiyokawa Village Group
5th Generation	1734 - 1790	Karikawa Village Group
6th Generation	1790 - 1794	Miyanouchi Village Group
7th Generation	1794 - 1813	Soegawa Village Group
8th Generation	1813 - 1825	Miyanouchi Village Group
9th Generation	1825 - 1860	Echi Village Group
10th Generation	1860 - 1867	Sanse Village Group
11th Generation	1867 - 1875	Kiyokawa Village Group

SOURCE: Igawa and Satō 1969:12 n. 8.

Thus, the village group headmen were an interface between the warrior stratum officials above and the peasant-stratum village officers below, attracting the suspicions of the domain elite and serving as a focus for the anger of the village group population. They were central figures in all four instances of 19th-century protest. So, too, were the village headmen, whose posts were either hereditary or filled by rotation among some or all of the registered cultivator households.

Complicating the domain's administrative boundaries were three small direct shogunate territories (*tenryō*) within Tagawa (see Map 3). These were contiguous villages around Ōyama, around Amarume, and around Maruoka. Their official assessments totaled 25,000 *koku*, about one-tenth the tribute base of Sakai's domain. These originated as minor fief grants by one of the 17th-century Sakai lords to individuals who died without heirs. By shogunal law, such lands reverted to the shogunate. For some periods it administered these lands directly from a small office in Ōyama, but often it delegated its jurisdiction to the domain. It was just such a transfer of administration in 1844 that provoked strong local opposition—the Ōyama Disturbances described in Chapter Four.

Demographic trends in Shōnai have yet to be rigorously researched, but domain reports to the shogunate suggest that by 1800 the total population in Shōnai Domain and its shogunal pockets was on the order of 185,000 (estimated from YKS 1980:409-31; see TSS 1974:555-57 for local historians' estimates). At the time, the castle town of Tsurugaoka had a population of about 18,000, while the chief port, Sakata, held about 10,000. There were perhaps 7,000 others in the several small towns on the plain—in Tagawa, the small port of Kamo and the *sake* brewing town of Ōyama; in Akumi, the market town of Ichijō and the branch domain town of Matsuyama. The population of the Tagawa countryside was about 83,000, and that of Akumi, about 55,000. On a plain about 530 square kilometers in size, Shōnai's density was about 350 persons per square kilometer. By status stratum, there were on the order of 152,000 cultivators, 20,000 towns-people (artisans and merchants), 2,500 warrior-retainers, and 10,500 warrior-retainer dependents.

The domain's tributary exactions from the rural cultivators consisted of the principal land tax (*honmononari*) and an increasing number of surcharges and ancillary levies (Kelly 1982a:28-37). Except for a "miscellaneous commodities levy" (*komononari*), all of these were nominally due in rice. The 1623 cadastre aimed to survey all arable parcels, assign tax-paying obligation to actual cultivators, and (through inter-village exchanges of parcels) to register all land surrounding a settlement to residents of that settlement. The administrative village was then assigned collective responsibility for gathering the annual tax from each resident household and for meeting the full tax amount. Thus, the thrust of the first domain lords was to establish an isomorphism between land cultivation, tax-paying obligation, and village residency within village "cells" linked hierarchically through an official rural administration to the domain lord.

PROFITABILITY AND VULNERABILITY: THE DYNAMICS OF WEALTH AND INSOLVENCY

In fact, as I have demonstrated in an earlier study (1982a), both the particular patterns by which the plain was gradually converted to paddy land and the expansion of rice trading worked against the realization of this ideal. In the 17th and 18th centuries, the domain offered generous tax concessions to promote paddy land development. Much of the marshy center of the plain was reclaimed for rice cultivation, but these concessions also created tempting tax differentials within and among villages across the plain. Paddy land in cultivation before the 1623 cadastre usually carried principal land tax rates of 45% to 55% of registered yield, while newly developed parcels often carried much lower rates: 20% to 40%. The newer parcels were also given lower quality ratings and were surveyed with a special pole that deliberately undermeasured by up to 20% (see Kelly 1982a:38-40 for details). By the mid- to late-18th century, some town merchants and well-positioned village cultivators had accumulated large holdings of more lightly taxed parcels.

The other spur to paddy land accumulation was the highly commercialized rice trade, with its lucrative potential for mercantile profits. Rice trading was facilitated by the rice voucher system that Tadakatsu instituted in the 1630s; warrior-retainers were given voucher chits equal to their stipendiary rice, which were redeemable at the domain granaries but also negotiable with town merchants for other goods and services. Within two decades, rice dealers in Tsurugaoka and Sakata were organized into monopsonist guilds, and rice exchanges were chartered by the domain (TSS 1974:590-95). Finally, in the late 17th century, the opening of a direct western sea route between the Japan Sea and Osaka was a tremendous boon for Sakata (Figure 2). At the mouth of the long Mogami River, Sakata not only was Shōnai's chief port but also became the transshipment port for the domains in the interior Mogami basins throughout present-day Yamagata Prefecture. By the late 1600s, there were five hundred ships a month coming downriver or in from the sea to Sakata. Saikaku's 1668 portrait of the largest of these early Sakata trading houses, Abumi-ya, illustrates the mercantile prosperity of the rice trade:

> The name of Abumiya Sōzaemon was known to everyone. His grounds, sixty yards broad and a hundred and thirty deep, were packed close with reception buildings and storehouses. The catering departments were an astounding sight. There was a receiver and distributor of rice and bean-curd, a director of firewood, an overseer for fish, a chef, a supervisor of the crockery cupboards, a controller of cakes, a tobacco officer, a tea-room officer, and a bathroom officer. Again, there was even a special runner of errands. Amongst the accountants,

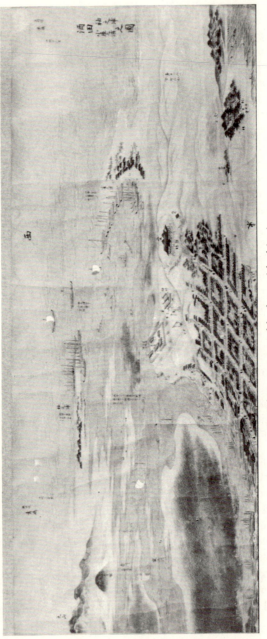

2. Sakata town and harbor with shipping.

there was one for public business, one for private; one for issuing money, one for noting it in the books. With one function, no matter how trifling, apportioned to one man, everything was made to run smoothly. (Sargent 1959:53)

Abumi-ya's preeminence was short-lived, however. Saikaku saw below the scale and opulent hospitality of such large establishments to the precarious and often capricious nature of mercantile fortunes:

The transactions of the Abumiya were as extensive as the plain of Musashi, and it was difficult to keep them under strict control. Brokers' establishments look like the homes of millionaires, but wherever they are, they are built on shaky foundations. The income from the regulation commissions amounts to little, and the temptation is strong for a broker to speculate privately with the goods in his care. If the gamble fails, he calculates that he may easily saddle his client with the losses. When a broker concentrates on brokerage, of course, and takes proper care of his purchases and sales, he has little cause to worry. But the outsider's impression of a broker's finances is far from the truth. There are an amazing number of unsuspected sources of expenses, and running the household on a more economical budget leads inevitably to diminished custom and the rapid decline of the firm. It is only once a year—in the first hour after dawn on New Year's morning—that the balance of a year's losses and gains becomes clear. At any other time it is impossible to check the position. (Sargent 1959:55)

Indeed, Abumi-ya could not sustain its preeminence through the 18th century. It was the subsequent rise of another Sakata house, the Honmas, that was to prove much more important to the shape of 19th-century Shōnai.[1] By

[1] See the valuable dissertation on the Honmas by Johnson (1983). She

1800, the main house was the largest landholder and most powerful financier in the domain—and a central figure in two of the four protest movements. It had been in the late 17th and early 18th centuries that the Honmas gained admittance to the guild of licensed domain rice agents and thus secured a stake in the mutually reinforcing enterprises of rice warehousing, shipping, and domain moneylending. The main house was able to establish several branch houses which it directed in these operations. The main house's most prominent head in the 18th century, Mitsuoka (1732-1801), offered substantial loans and made sizable contributions to the Sakai lords. He was awarded a samurai-equivalency position and then a full samurai rank in the 1760s. He was thereafter solicited in important matters of domain fiscal policy.

An analysis of the main house's account books (in particular, the *daichō*) by Saitō Kiyoshi revealed the enormous scale of Honma contributions and loans to Sakai. In the 117 years from 1756 to 1873, these totaled almost 1,000,000 *ryō* in gold, over 50,000 *kan* in copper, and almost 60,000 *koku* of rice (see Table 3). Honma's private financing to individual households was equally staggering. For the period 1719-1870, Kudō Tadao (1971:33) has collated records of 5,330 private loans to warrior-retainers, townspeople, and cultivators totaling just over 800,000 *ryō*.[2] Thus, Mitsuoka and those who followed him in the headship combined the social statuses of commoner and samurai, political roles of domain subject and domain official, and economic roles of merchant and financier.

describes well the relations forged between Sakai domain and the large Sakata rice dealers and shippers and details the subsequent generations of Honma heads. Unfortunately, she does not distinguish carefully enough between a commercialized economy and a regional capitalism. Honma wealth and influence spanned both.

[2] That is, this excludes official loans to domains. Kudō used a formula of 1 *ryō* = 30,000 present-day *yen* to estimate the present-day value of these loans at nearly 25 billion *yen* (or approximately US $100 million). By the same conversion, Honma's loans and contributions to Sakai Domain would have a present-day value of nearly 30 billion *yen*, or almost $120 million.

38

TABLE 3
Contributions and Uncollected Loans to Shōnai Domain from
Main Honma House 1843-1874

Date	Contributions (sunshikin)	Loans Left Uncollected (saikakukin)
1841-1849		48,772 ryō
1850.12	1,000 ryō	
1851.12		10,000
1842.12		20,000
1855.11	1,800	
1856.3		10,000
1859.7		8,000
1861.3 (intercalary)	2,200	10,000
1863.1	660	6,000
1863.10	10,000	
1864.1	10,000	20,000
1865.9		9,000
1866.4		15,000
1867.9		900
1867.11		18,000
1868.2		12,500
1868.2		15,000
1868.4	61,400	
1868.4	32,000	
1869.3	5,000	
1869.8	50,000	
1871.8	10,000	
1872.4	15,000	
1873.10	16,500	
1874.6	10,000	
Totals, 1843-74	225,560 ryō	203,172 ryō

NOTE: These are totals of cash contributions and uncollected cash loans.
They do not include other gifts and contributions (e.g. 5 cannon in
1853.12 and rice vouchers for 16,000 bags of rice in 1868.4). Dates prior
to 1871 are given in old calendar reckoning.

SOURCE: 1841-1868: TSS 1975a:51 (note that table totals in TSS are incor-
rect; figures have been verified from SSS 1971).
1869-1874: TSS 1975a:202.

The Honmas also became the largest landholders in the domain. Mitsuoka had been the first to divert some of his mercantile wealth to paddy lands, accumulating several hundred hectares of parcels in newly developed, lightly taxed areas of the central plain. Honma paddy holdings in 1800 totaled 588 hectares; by 1830, these had almost doubled. As the main house had used its sixteen branch houses to manage its commercial and financial dealings, so it gradually created a three-tiered hierarchy of land agents to oversee the roughly 2,000 tenants of its paddy land parcels.[3]

Yet the Honma's scale of financial operations and landholding so dwarfed others that it would be highly misleading to see the house as representative. The second largest landholder was the Kamo port merchant Akino Moemon, who accumulated about 140 hectares in the last half of the 18th century and then more than doubled that figure in the next thirty years. Perhaps imitating Honma, Akino, too, designated local cultivator households as agents to initiate and manage agreements with cultivators of holdings, widely scattered over sixty-three villages (see Kelly 1982a:55-57). Even Akino was unusual, however; the several other town merchants with holdings of 50-200 hectares exercised much more limited oversight. In addition to these merchant largeholders, there were a number of village cultivators who became tenanting largeholders in their own right, with holdings of 10-100 hectares by the 19th century (ibid.:55-61 for profiles of Abe Tokusaburō of Sanbongi and Satō Tōzō of Futakuchi). And finally, there were even smaller self-cultivating largeholders with perhaps 5-10 hectares of paddy land. It is hazardous to estimate their numbers in the 19th century, but there must have been over a hundred of them.

Thus, Shōnai *jinushi* ("landlords," but more correctly, tenanting largeholders) included both townspeople and villagers

[3] See Johnson 1983 and Kamagata 1956:214-22 for descriptions of this land administration. In contrast to these and most other writers, I will argue that even the Honma holdings did not extend beyond mercantile investment to a capitalist reorganization of agrarian relations until the 1890s, well into the Meiji period.

and varied widely in the scale and oversight of their hold-ings. They also differed in how they accumulated their hold-ings. There were several methods of land transfer. Outright purchase through the private exchange of a sales document was frequent; because this was illegal, the transaction was generally unregistered or noted only cryptically in the village land books. Also common was the liening of land parcels for a fixed term, often thirty years, in return for a cash loan. The registered holder usually remained as the "tenant" of the lien holder. Honma and Akino tended to prefer the former. But what all of the largeholders shared was an eye for the lightly taxed paddy parcel. And almost all preferred to leave cultivation to tenanting households that relied on family la-bor and tools and kept a share of the crop. Landholding con-centrations did not themselves imply agrarian capitalism.

The underside of such commercial prosperity was the re-curring financial difficulties of the domain and many small-holders. The domain, simply put, was caught between rising expenditures and fixed tributary revenues. Its staff in Edo increased as the domain lord came to spend more and more time at his mansion in Kanda.[4] Lavish living, but also price inflation, ceremonial demands at the shogun's castle, and the occasional, unpredictable, and often quite onerous special levies for shogunate projects—each took its toll. Yet much of this might have been manageable had the domain been able to raise its call on the expanding rice production across the plain. That it could not, and why it could not, were of cardinal significance in casting the shape of 19th-century pol-itics and economy.[5]

---

[4] Like most domain lords, Sakai maintained three mansions in Edo, an "upper," a "middle," and a "lower" compound. The lord himself resided in the upper mansion, which after 1715 was near Kanda Bridge on the north side of the shogun's castle. His middle mansion was in Yanagihara and the lower mansion in Shitaya.

[5] This section recapitulates the argument underlying my previous Shōnai study, which detailed this dynamic of administration, landholding, and pro-duction in order to interpret a particular social arena, irrigation in the plain's major river basin. Here I am trying to call out its more general significance.

By 1820, about 36,000 hectares of the plain's 53,000 hectares were in cultivation—28,000 hectares in rice and 8,000 hectares in non-irrigated crops. We will see that paddy lands were probably then yielding means of 2.1 *koku* per 0.1 hectares. In a good year total production would have been on the order of 580,000 *koku*.[6] In contrast, the registered lands of the domain amounted to only 17,000 hectares of paddy land and 3,000 hectares of non-irrigated crop parcels. Moreover, the mean *assessed* yield per parcel remained unchanged: only about 1.1 *koku* per 0.1 hectares of paddy land and about 0.7 *koku* per 0.1 hectares of other crop parcels. Thus, the domain's total tribute base of about 225,000 *koku* was only slightly more than one-third of the plain's total potential and only just above one-half of Sakai land yields in the early 19th century. It was to this relatively meager tribute base that it applied its schedule of principal and ancillary land taxes.

An obvious solution would have been an upward adjustment of yield standards and/or a new cadastral survey. Such suggestions were occasionally raised (e.g., Igawa 1966:8-9), but there was no comprehensive land resurvey in the 250 years from 1623 until 1874. Instead, the domain found itself dependent for its fiscal survival on periodic transfusions of loans (many of which were later canceled) and contributions from those with commercial wealth. This was both the cause and salvation of its agrarian predicament. Many of the commercially wealthy who were bailing out the domain also had at least modest holdings of lightly taxed lands, and resisted any reforms in the land tax. Their contributions might be seen as "pay-offs" or simply as an alternative form of tribute to the domain. In either view, the relative benefits of land tax reform and merchant loans were never openly debated as courses of action. Crisis by crisis, decade by decade through

---

[6] This is an estimate I reached in my earlier study. I have subsequently discovered a set of calculations by Oyokawa et al. (1953:22-23), who use other domain documents in estimating the plain's productive capacity at 1,333,600 bales by 1800. At the official rate of 1 bale = 0.4 *koku*, this would be 533,440 *koku*. Subtracting direct shogunal and temple territories, the domain territory's capacity would have been about 400,000 *koku*.

the 18th century, the domain fell into supplementing agricultural tribute with such contributions, which brought commercial benefits to those who offered them and, as their paddy holdings increased, protection from higher land taxes. It was a pattern of tribute-taking which neither was devised whole cloth nor emerged spontaneously. Rather, it took shape fitfully and incrementally, with only partial appreciation for its ultimate implications.

It is equally critical to recognize that the surplus which the domain was unable to appropriate was not evenly spread across the countryside. The process of paddy land development and the vagaries of rice cultivation at its northern climatic limits worked hardships on cultivators as well the domain. Agricultural productivity is a contentious issue in Tokugawa studies. Hanley and Yamamura (1977) have argued that rice yields generally rose through the entire period; while this may have been true on a national aggregate level, Shōnai data are equivocal. Our best evidence at the moment is Satō Shigerō's collation of annual harvest samplings from the internal books (*bugari chō*) of three adjacent villages in Kyōden District, together with private records of the Futakuchi Village headman and largeholder, Satō Tōzō. These villages included both older and newly developed paddy parcels, and his data run from 1780 to 1870. He has computed the following twenty-year means:

1780-1800	1.3-1.5 *koku* per actual 0.1 hectares
1800-1830	2.1-2.2 *koku* per actual 0.1 hectares
1830-1850	1.6-1.7 *koku* per actual 0.1 hectares
1850-1870	1.7 *koku* per actual 0.1 hectares

These means suggest rising yields from the late 18th century through the first three decades of the 19th century, with lower mean yields in the next fifty years.[7]

Hanley and Yamamura (1977) attribute the rising yields to

---

[7] Satō 1965. Unfortunately, at present I cannot provide either the deviations around these means or finer breakdowns. Satō has told me that he no longer has the raw tables of annual means from which he derived the twenty-year means, and I have not yet had access to the original records.

new cultivation techniques and tools, better varieties, labor intensification, and increased use of purchased fertilizers of fish meal and oil pressings. Certainly these propelled higher yields in some regions, but the evidence from Shōnai again suggests an important local variant. Igawa (1967) has argued that there were few changes in cultivation techniques on the plain in the latter Tokugawa period, that purchased fertilizers were not used in significant quantities (see also the 1841 memorandum in OCS 1957:200), and that the rice hybridization and variety improvements for which Shōnai farmers became famous did not begin until the Meiji period. Most Tokugawa varieties in Shōnai were of the "thin leaf" (*hosoba*) group (see the Komatsu family records for 1768-1850 in Igawa 1967:274-75). In 1885, a prefectural agricultural agent described the Shōnai thin leaf varieties as strong-stemmed but prone to pests; he estimated that the group yielded below-average harvests in three of five years and above-average harvests in one of five years (ibid.:275). Igawa concluded, and I concur, that Shōnai did not experience a general rise in paddy land productivity. Rather, there was a relative increase in the "profitability" of certain parcels. As the soil quality and water retention of the newer parcels improved, their differential of yield and tribute obligation widened relative to the differentials for the older, higher taxed parcels. It was a pattern of improvement that favored those able to accumulate such parcels—in particular, the largeholders.

Smallholders, then, continued to face sharp harvest fluctuations in their efforts to satisfy tributary tax demands. When unable to meet assessments, they might cover the shortfall in several ways. Relatives, friends, and rotating credit groups (*mujinkō*) could usually provide only limited funds.[8] More drastic measures were usually necessary. Lightly taxed parcels could be pawned or sold to largehold-

[8] This is suggested by the listing of rotating credit groups in the 1790 Sakurabayashi Village *sashibiki chō* (YKS 1980:437-42).

ers. Private lending by village headmen, village group head-men, and district domain officials was proscribed but common. And the domain regularly extended loans at interest to cover taxes and to insure seed and food supplies before the following harvest.[9] Thus in 1793 for example, Fujishima villagers found themselves with 5,700 *koku* of taxes in arrears. Most of this (4,370 *koku*) was from a disasterous harvest thirty-eight years before, in 1755.[10] The annual interest on these back taxes alone amounted to 285 *koku* and 17 *ryō*. It is hardly surprising that by 1793, over half (1,100 *koku*) of the village's registered yield of 2,165 *koku* had been abandoned by the original registered holders (YKS 1980:212-21, especially pp. 217-19).

Smallholders could thus be forced into a downward spiral of selling and pawning their lightly taxed parcels, borrowing from officials, and abandoning heavily taxed parcels. The administrative consequence was that the domain norm of isomorphic residency, cultivation, and tax obligation by village unit proved wholly elusive in Fujishima and elsewhere on the plain. Patterns of registered holdings, cultivation, and settlement were wildly incongruent by the late 18th century. The solidary village was but an administrative fiction. Scheiner's proposition—"Most peasants in the Tokugawa period

---

[9] The latter was known as *tanebujikimai*. In 1749, the domain had instituted advances of rice to villages in the spring to cover shortfalls so that cultivators would have seed rice for planting and food until harvest. The formula was 7.2 *koku* per 100 *koku* of registered village yield. These advances were repayable in rice after harvest at 30% interest, which was to be stockpiled as a reserve fund. The advances were soon made mandatory, but eventually the actual distribution of rice in the spring was discontinued. Only the 30% interest charge was collected in the autumn, payable before all other levies (YKS 1980:1097). This mandatory levy, we will see, was frequently singled out by protestors in the 1870s.

[10] More precisely, the total in arrears was 10,950 bales; while the *koku* was the unit of land valuation, the bale was the unit of tax collection. An official bale in Sakai Domain was 0.4 *koku* (i.e., *shi to iri*), but cultivators were typically required to add 0.12 *koku* to each bale for inspection and in-transit losses. (This contentious surcharge was known as *nobimai*.) Thus the taxpayers needed 5,694 *koku* of rice to tender 10,950 bales.

lived in stable, homogenous hamlets of fifty to one hundred households" (1978:44)—is an unlikely one for Shōnai.

What does this mean for the prospects of collective action? That whatever the force of a communitarian ideology in appeals to a radical reordering of society, it had little basis in the social experience of the 19th-century Shōnai villager. This is not to deny the efficacy of "community" in motivating behavior. Nor is it to ignore the cooperative relations that must have been central to the daily lives of villagers. But the incongruencies of landholding, cultivation, and residency do caution us against assuming the potency of an appeal to the village community in challenging the existing order. Indeed, in Shōnai, the village was often as convenient an organizing unit to protestors as it was for the political elite, but it was rarely an ideological rallying cry.

Still, having delineated domain fiscal insolvency and the perils of smallholder rice cultivation, I want to avoid any suggestion of unrelieved desperation in the countryside. There were several mitigating factors at work. These included the common measures of what some would call the paternalism of tribute-taking elites—or what others have more aptly recognized as the negotiated "moral order" of the tributary relationship (e.g., Scott 1974, Thompson 1971). There were, for example, well-known and frequently activated procedures to secure tax reductions in years of poor harvest. Records of the domain's mean tax rate survive for 219 years (1636-1867; see anon. 1867). They show that this mean exceeded 47% of registered yield in 43 years, was between 45% and 47% in 82 years, and fell between 40% and 45% in 68 years. In 26 years, the domain mean dropped below 40%, after especially poor harvests. In rarer bursts of domain reform initiatives, sweeping debt cancellations benefited smallholders. Other factors were less the procedures of paternalism than the permeability of domain administration. The flood of restrictions against private sales, borrowing, and rice marketing attested primarily to their ineffectiveness. Land abandonment and migration remained options

46

both to those in distress and to those in desire of better opportunities. And smallholders enjoyed insulation from major land tax increases because of the tributelike contributions and uncollected loans offered the domain by large landholding merchants.

One might wonder here about tenancy conditions accompanying the land concentration of the late 18th and early 19th centuries. This has been conventionally interpreted as the differentiation of "peasant proprietorship," with its non-economic calculation of family labor, into a narrow elite of entreprenurial farmers, increasingly oriented toward rational allocation of inputs (and seeking more secure grounding for ownership of land as private property) and a lower stratum of tenants and landless laborers, with little or no security. In fact, for much of the 19th century in Shōnai, tenancy was no more burdensome and indeed not much different from "registered cultivator" status. There are few examples of largeholders' exercising their right to move or remove tenants; the one case in YKS 1980:930-34 occasioned much resistance. While I have yet to discover explicit evidence, it appears that for much of the century there was a "customary" upper limit of "three bags per one hundred sheaves" on the landholder's share of a tenanted parcel.[11] Tenants demanded and expected reductions from the landholder for below-average harvests; the terms for such reductions—*teate* or *teatebiki*—were also used for domain tax concessions. Rarer, more general acts of charity were also expected—for example, Akino Moemon's contribution in 1831 of 300 *ryō* for "the distressed cultivators

[11] *hyakukari sanbyō*. A person buying a parcel or accepting it as a lien never trusted its registered yield and dimensions. Moreover, the pre-Tokugawa unit of sheaves (*soku* or *sokukari*) was used to measure yields and crop shares, rather than the official unit of threshed grain volume (*koku*). One hundred sheaves was approximately 0.1 hectare of medium-grade paddy land; thus, three bales was 1.56 *koku* per 0.1 hectare. In a tenancy agreement (*hyōtazukuri*), the amount rendered by the cultivator was known as *watarikuchimai*. From this, all taxes were subtracted (payment of which remained the cultivator's responsibility), and the balance, the *sakutokumai*, was the landholder's share.

47

of Kyōden District" (*Kyōden tōri nankyū hyakushō sukui no tame sunshikin*; text in YKS 1980:158-60). And finally, we must remember that tenanted holdings usually carried light tax obligations; the shrewd largeholder Abe Tokusaburō amassed 100 hectares that averaged a mere 15% in principal land tax rates. The share that a tenant turned over in taxes and "rent" was seldom more, and often less, than the taxes due on more heavily taxed parcels of a registered cultivator (see, for example, Satō's calculations of Tōzō's tenant arrangements). Indeed, *kosakuryō* and its common English equivalent, "rent," are perhaps inaccurate translations of the early 19th-century term, *watarikuchimai*, which to many cultivators must have seemed nearly identical to their tribute relationship with the domain.

Shōnai, then, saw neither uniform rising prosperity nor widespread dearth and stagnation. Perhaps the most common shared experience was vulnerability—not to absolute deprivation, but to rising and falling household fortunes. What we must keep uppermost in mind was the differential prosperity and poverty across the rural population at any one moment and the fluctuating fortunes for any one household over time.

This tension between stratification and mobility is clearly illustrated in figures which Igawa has gathered for residents of Sakurabayashi Village (Akumi) in the century, 1768-1868 (Table 4).[12] Sakurabayashi was a village in an older area of Hirata District that was developed in the late 16th and early 17th centuries. The village had registered holdings of 256.1501 *koku*; its principal land tax rate, 65%, was high

---

[12] Igawa 1973. Such tables of holdings, of course, abound in the secondary literature on the 19th-century countryside. However, Igawa's work here is unusual and valuable because he has been able to combine a number of records to produce data on *total* registered holdings and cultivation. That is, most similar listings report only holdings and cultivation within the village of residency; thus, they distort actual stratification and are virtually useless in an area such as Shōnai.

even for older villages.[13] By 1768, there was considerable stratification, both in registered holdings and in the self-cultivated acreage of households. Over the next one hundred years, this proved to be a persistent but fluid stratification. There was some movement in and out of the village, but even more, there were continual fluctuations in the holdings of most Sakurabayashi households over the decades: in the size of their holdings, in the balance between registered and tenanted holdings, and in the proportion of holdings which were self-cultivated. (Igawa's data on Yogorō's tenants illustrate a further important feature: tenants did not rely on a single landlord patron: see Tables 5 and 6.) A similar pattern of land stratification and household mobility is suggested by the few other Shōnai cases that have been worked out in detail—for example, Futakuchi Village in the Kyōden District of Tagawa (Satō 1965).

PROTESTS, CRISES, AND REFORMS, 1630-1830

It should be clear, then, that where Hanley and Yamamura highlight aggregate rising fortunes and where Scheiner and Sasaki emphasize the deteriorating condition of a structural class, I prefer to stress the vulnerability of the domain, commercial houses, and cultivator households to both rising and falling fortunes. Such swings intersected at several times in the Tokugawa period to ignite moments of social protest, political crisis, and economic reform. As something of a "pre-history" of 19th-century conflicts, it is instructive to highlight three of the most important of such moments: in the 1630s, the 1670s, and the 1790s.

After the harvest in late 1632, and nine years after Sakai Tadakatsu's cadastre, about 280 cultivators from the northernmost district of the plain abandoned their fields and homes and fled over Mt. Chokai to Akita in protest of the

[13] YKS 1980:446-47. This 1851 document suggests ancillary taxes and loan repayments amounted to an additional 45%!

TABLE 4
Registered and Cultivated Holdings of Sakurabayashi
Village Residents, 1768-1868

	Sakurabayashi Village Residents, 1768			
Household	Total Registered Holdings (koku)	Total Tenanted Lands Cultivated (koku)	Total Lands Let out to Others (koku)	Total Lands Cultivated (koku)
8 Shinnokyoku	29.9		0.2	29.7
16 Kieimon	21.4	7.5	0.2	29.7
Kansaburō	25.6	2.4		28.1
22 Sōbei	19.6	1.9		21.5
12 Shinsuke	8.4	12.5		20.9
Ichijūrō	20.9		0.3	20.7
5 Yogorō	18.0	2.1		20.1
6 Rokubei	17.8			17.8
4 Kanjūrō	11.9	5.2		17.1
2 Kusaburō	15.9			15.9
19 Yobei	5.4	5.6		11.0
21 Chōbei	11.7	0.9	1.6	10.9
15 Ninbei	0.6	6.8		7.5
Kibei	8.5		1.3	7.1
Ichibei	0.1	6.6		6.7
Gonbei	1.5	4.6		6.2
13 Jūsaburō	12.9		9.8	3.1
Kyūshirō	0.1			0.1
Sanjūrō	0.1			0.1
23 Rinshū-ji	3.9	0.8	4.7	0
Totals	234.2	56.9	18.1	273.2
Non-Resident Landholders (6)	57.4		2.5	54.8

50

TABLE 4 (continued)

Sakurabayashi Village Residents, 1790

Household	Total Registered Holdings (koku)	Total Tenanted Lands Cultivated (koku)	Total Lands Let out to Others (koku)	Total Lands Cultivated (koku)
5 Yogorō	37.1	7.4	11.7	32.8
22 Sōbei	27.0			27.0
8 Shinnokyoku	23.1	0.2	0.4	23.0
1 Shinjūrō	18.8	3.8		22.6
2 Kyūsaburō	16.0	6.3		22.3
11 Kanjirō	18.0	4.7	0.5	22.3
10 Tōshirō	21.7	0.6	0.2	22.1
21 Chōbei	13.2	4.8	0.7	17.3
4 Kanjūrō	11.1	4.8	0.7	15.2
14 Rokurobei	13.3	0.1		13.4
6 Rokubei	14.3		1.1	13.3
13 Jūsaburō	13.4		0.3	13.1
15 Ninbei	5.5	6.6		12.2
12 Shinsuke	6.4	4.1		10.5
16 Kiemon	3.7	5.1		8.8
Washichi	8.8	5.5		14.3
Ichibei	0.1	5.4		5.5
17 Kibei	10.7		4.4	6.3
23 Rinshū-ji	3.5			3.5
9 Chōsaku	0.2			0.2
7 Yasuemon	0.2			0.2
19 Yobei	0.2			0.2
Kusaemon	0.2			0.2
Kisaburō	0.1			0.1
Sanjūrō	0.1			0.1
20 Heijirō	0.1			0.1
Totals	266.6	59.4	20.0	306.0
Non-Resident Landholders (8)	61.5		61.5	

TABLE 4 (*continued*)

Household	Sakurabayashi Village Residents, 1838			
	Total Registered Holdings (*koku*)	Total Tenanted Lands Cultivated (*koku*)	Total Lands Let out to Others (*koku*)	Total Lands Cultivated (*koku*)
5 Yogorō	67.1	15.4	10.9	71.6
10 Tōshirō	19.0	11.1	0.3	29.7
1 Shinjūrō	19.4	1.8		21.2
19 Yobei	5.3	11.8		17.1
4 Kanjūrō	9.3	6.8		16.1
2 Heizaemon	15.7	1.7	1.6	15.8
12 Shinsuke	5.2	9.5	0.3	14.3
6 Rokubei	4.3	8.9		13.3
8 Shinnokyoku	18.5	2.9	9.2	12.2
7 Yasuemon	4.3	6.6		11.0
16 Kiemon	3.4	4.9		8.3
11 Kanjirō	18.0	0.6	12.3	6.3
9 Chōsaku	0.2	5.4		5.7
13 Jūsaburō	8.8	3.9	7.2	5.6
15 Ninbei	0.1	5.2	0.1	5.2
18 Kaemon	0.1	4.5		4.6
14 Rokurobei	3.6	0.3		3.8
17 Kibei	5.5	0.2	4.5	1.3
3 Yohachi	9.6		7.8	1.8
22 Sōbei	2.1	0.1	1.5	0.6
20 Heijirō	0.1			0.1
21 Chōbei	0.3			0.3
23 Rinshū-ji	3.0		3.0	
Totals	222.9	101.6	58.7	265.9
Non-Resident Landholders (11)	34.1		34.1	

TABLE 4 (*continued*)

Sakurabayashi Village Residents, 1868

Household	Total Registered Holdings (*koku*)	Total Tenanted Lands Cultivated (*koku*)	Total Lands Let out to Others (*koku*)	Total Lands Cultivated (*koku*)	No. in House- hold*
1 Shinjūrō	26.9			26.9	6 (4)
2 Kyūsaburō	23.7	1.3	0.1	24.9	5 (2)
3 Yohachi	21.7	2.8	1.1	23.4	5 (3)
4 Kanjūrō	11.1	11.8		22.9	7 (4)
5 Yogorō	59.8		37.9	21.9	10 (4)
6 Rokubei	16.7	4.9	4.4	17.2	5 (3)
7 Yasuemon	2.2	17.1			7 (5)
8 Shinnokyoku	20.4	4.3	6.1	18.6	5 (5)
9 Chōsaku	5.0	12.3		17.2	4 (3)
10 Tōshirō	21.3	3.9	8.3	16.9	5 (4)
11 Kanjirō	12.8	0.7		13.6	6 (4)
12 Shinsuke	6.7	3.9		10.6	4 (4)
13 Jūsaburō	4.0	4.1		8.2	5 (4)
14 Rokurobei	5.2	2.7	0.9	7.0	6 (6)
15 Ninbei	0.1	5.9		6.0	4 (1)
16 Kiemon	3.6		2.5	1.1	1 (1)
17 Kibei	0.8	0.3	0.2	0.9	7 (4)
18 Kaemon	0.1			0.1	6 (4)
19 Yobei	0.2			0.2	5 (4)
20 Heijirō	0.1			0.1	6 (3)
21 Chōbei	0.3		0.3		1 (0)
22 Sōbei	4.4	1.1	3.3		2 (2)
23 Rinshū-ji	3.0		3.0		
Totals	250.1	76.0	63.2	260.3	
Non-Resident Landholders (5)	14.0		14.0		

* Parenthesis indicates those between 15 and 55 years old.

SOURCE: Igawa 1973:302-305.

53

TABLE 5
Changes in the Landholdings of Yogorō (#5), 1768-1868

	1768	1790	1825	1838	1850	1868
Registered holdings within village	17.3	22.9	63.8	63.5	57.1	53.5
Registered holdings in other villages	0.7	14.1 (6)	3.8 (7)	3.6 (6)	4.4	6.3
Total tenanted lands cultivated	2.1	7.4	0.4	15.4	10.4	——
Holdings let out to others	——	11.7	9.9	10.9	43.2	37.9
Total lands Cultivated	20.1	32.8	58.3	71.6	28.8	21.9

NOTE: All holdings are expressed in *koku*.
SOURCE: Igawa 1973:313.

increased tax levies.[14] Domain officials held the two village group headmen of the area responsible for the abscondings and arrested them. These headmen had been powerful area leaders before Sakai entered Shōnai, and like other such local chiefs had been melded into the new administrative hierarchy with much mutual suspicion. In early spring of 1633, the cultivators were caught and returned to Shōnai by two individuals who were rewarded with the vacant headman posts. Coincidentally, 1633 was the year when the shogunate began sending inspectors about the country to investigate domain administration; when the first inspector arrived in Shōnai that summer, domain elders kept the two former headmen in prison and tried to suppress news of the incident. When they were released at the end of 1633, one of them, Takahashi Tarozaemon, set off for Edo with his brother. There they presented shogunal officials with a detailed plead-

[14] Documents pertaining to this case appear in YKS 1980:907-13; most may also be found in Nagai 1973:2-17. The incident is discussed in TSS 1974:265-69 and mentioned in Burton 1976:149-50.

TABLE 6
Tenants of Yogorō's Holdings, 1868

Tenant	Household's Registered Holdings (koku)	Household's Total Cultivation (koku)	Total Tenanted Lands (koku)	No. of Households Tenanted From	Amount of Land Let from Yogorō (koku)
#2 Kyūsaburō	23.7	24.9	1.3	4	0.1
#3 Yohachi	21.7	23.4	2.8	2	2.7
#4 Kanjūrō	11.1	22.9	11.8	6	8.1
#6 Rokubei	16.7	21.3	4.9	4	2.2
#7 Yasuemon	2.2	19.3	17.1	7	4.1
#9 Chōsaku	5.0	17.2	12.3	3	2.0
#11 Kanjirō	12.8	13.6	0.7	3	0.1
#12 Shinsuke	6.7	10.6	3.9	4	1.5
#15 Ninbei	0.1	6.0	5.9	3	5.0
#18 Kaemon	3.6	1.5	0.4	1	0.4
Total let to fellow residents					26.2
Yogorō's total tenanted holdings					37.9

SOURCE: Igawa 1973:317.

ing (meyasu) of accusations against the "harsh and oppressive" policies of Sakai. They claimed that Sakai's cadastre had nearly doubled cultivators' tax burden and forced thousands to sell household members into servitude. The domain perversely required those who bought these indentures to return the people, so that there were no longer even those willing to pay advance sums for servants. Their petition was accepted by the senior councilor Matsudaira Nobutsuna, who not only spared Tarozaemon punishment for his act of direct petitioning but awarded him and his brother sizable fief grants. There is no evidence that cultivators received any tax reductions. TSS (1974:267) interprets this in light of Matsudaira's close relationship to Sakai Tadakatsu. Matsudaira's daughter, it seems, married Sakai's son and heir-designate the year before. If Matsudaira were to have punished Tarozaemon, the argument goes, this would have only under-

55

scored Sakai's administrative failings with rival shogunal officials and incited further protests. Rewarding Tarozaemon drew him back into the administration and coopted the threatening local leaders.

The nominal acknowledgment of Tarozaemon's charges must also be evaluated in light of another incident in 1633. This took place in an inland Mogami basin in a domain held by Sakai Tadakatsu's younger brother. There, cultivators presented the visiting shogunal inspector with a petition alleging a decade of suffering and over a thousand deaths from starvation. When this was rejected, thirty-eight persons brought a similar written plea directly to Edo, while hundreds of others stormed the domain castle and beheaded several senior officials. The shogun acted to punish the cultivator leaders and remove the younger Sakai lord from his domain, which reverted to the shogunate. Perhaps fearing a similar escalation of protest, Matsudaira lobbied for, and Sakai Tadakatsu accepted, a quiet resolution.[15]

A second series of incidents forty years later also illustrates the political complexities in which protests took shape and found resolution. By the late 1660s, shogunal levies and domain expenditures were exceeding domain revenues; at the same time, conversion of the plain to paddy land was proceeding apace. In 1671, a promising young retainer, Kōriki Tadabei, was elevated to domain rural affairs officer in an effort to tighten control over production and producers. Kōriki instituted a spring survey, strict tax collection procedures (for example, a tag with the names of the cultivator and the tax collector was to be inserted in each bale submitted), and a 30% interest charge on all unpaid taxes. He encouraged the direct westerly sea route to Ōsaka, where he opened a domain warehouse. In 1677, a visiting shogunal inspector was presented with a petition (*meyasu*) from "all

---

[15] Tadakatsu's younger brother, the now displaced Tadashige, returned to Shōnai, where his plottings to replace Tadakatsu's son and heir with his own son stirred a factional dispute among retainers that continued for much of the 1640s (TSS 1974:273-75).

cultivators of the eight districts" (hachikumi sōbyakushō) that complained bitterly of the high interest charges and the spring survey (which ignored subsequent adverse growing season conditions). Such policies were driving thousands of cultivators from the registered rolls (tsuburebyakushō) into destitution and migration. It alleged that Kōriki violated his own proscriptions on private lending; he, other retainers, and town merchants loaned extensively and were accumulating lucrative new paddy land. These and other charges were repeated in similar petitions over the next few years (brought to Edo, handed to domain elders, fastened to staves in front of village group headmen's compounds, and so on) until Kōriki was finally replaced in 1681.[16]

A third moment of fiscal crisis and policy reform coincided with shogunate's "Kansei Reforms" at the end of the 18th century, but we must also see the domain's initiatives in light of several decades of fiscal pressures and policies that stirred factional controversy. In the mid-1760s, domain elders asked Honma Mitsuoka to execute a financial recovery plan to deal with escalating debts from the profligate spending by the seventh lord and steep ceremonial levies by the shogunate. At the time, both the domain and individual retainers were borrowing heavily from Kansai-area creditors, especially Ōtsu moneylenders and rice dealers, who advanced money on the following year's rice crop (known popularly as Ōtsu kari, "Ōtsu loans"). Honma refinanced these debts with local money, largely his own. The lower interest was appreciated by the retainers, and Honma was able to insure that a much greater proportion of domain rice revenues would now be handled through local Sakata rice dealers. He also attempted to resurrect the moribund reserve granary system by which a special ancillary levy of rice was

---

[16] Most of these petitions were anonymous. When Sōma Hanbei was bold enough to attach his name as "representative" of three Nakagawa District villages, he was executed. He was memorialized as a "righteous person" (gimin) by fellow villagers and the spot where he thrust the document upon officials was consecrated with an Amida statue (Naganuma 1983:66-68).

stockpiled in each village group granary to be loaned in years of harvest shortfalls. It had proven grossly inadequate in the disasterous harvests of 1755 and 1765. Mitsuoka realized that local reserves, properly stockpiled, could stabilize domain revenues and insulate it from calls on its central stocks. Yet these and other measures brought only temporary relief. Within ten years, domain debts mounted to 80-90,000 *ryō*; the annual interest alone was 15,000 *ryō*. The Sakai family history relates that on Tadaari's first visit to Tsurugaoka in 1772 after succeeding to lordship, domain funds in Edo were only sufficient to get the procession halfway home, to Fukushima; cash was hastily sent from Shōnai to allow him to reach Tsurugaoka.[17]

The domain staggered along through the 1780s with more merchant contributions and loans and forced reductions in retainers' annual fief allotments. In Edo in the late 1780s, the new chief councilor, Matsudaira Sadanobu, tried to rebuild shogunate finances with a program based on his grandfather's initiatives fifty years earlier: efficiencies in administration, austerity in samurai spending, further controls on commoner consumption, and other measures to reduce expenditures and increase revenue (Ooms 1975:77-104; Soranaka 1978). In the early 1790s, Matsudaira called upon the Sakai lord, Tadanori, to bring his own domain's sorry finances into order through a similar reform. Heightening the sense of crisis, Tadanori was passed another petition from the countryside, this a long and graphic description of conditions in the Fujishima area of Nakagawa District by a local temple priest, who had access to village books (YKS 1980:212-21; see above, p. 45).

Tadanori turned to his elders and merchant creditors for advice, and shortly received two proposals that reflected very different orientations toward the commercialization of the

[17] TSS 1974:344-45. Earlier that year, the Sakai mansions at Kanda and Shitagaya both burned in one of Edo's larger blazes. Two months later, a fire in Sakata destroyed over 2,000 houses.

rural economy. They also represented serious factional divisions among the domain elite. The first, from Honma Mitsuoka, advised a rationalization of commercial links—another renegotiation of domain debts with its Kansai creditors, a reduction in the proliferating levies on commoners, and a consolidation of their outstanding taxes and loans. He offered to loan the domain 20,000 *ryō* at 5% annual interest and argued that if the domain would then circulate this to the villages at 7%, it would realize a profit that it could apply to its own obligations. Villages in turn could use this low 7% financing to pay off their higher-interest debts and be in a better position to repay this consolidated sum (YKS 1980:222-24).

A far more sanguine picture of commercial dealings was drawn by Mitsuoka's rival for attention, Shirai Yadayū. Shirai was a middle-level retainer and avid proponent of Ogyū Sorai's Neo-Confucianist teachings in the domain. Shirai agreed that the chief difficulty in the countryside was the proliferating number of levies on registered holders. However, he attributed this chiefly to the private lending of public monies by the village, village group, and district officials. Any plan, he warned, that promised solution with yet more loans would fall afoul of such official corruption. Instead he counseled debt cancellation, simplification of taxation, prohibitions against farmers leaving their villages and on merchants acquiring paddy land, more honest administration, and other measures (YKS 1980:200-204).

Only after a two-year struggle between the two factions did Shirai win appointment and approval to attempt his reforms. The centerpiece of his program was a massive cancellation of cultivators' debts. These included outstanding borrowings from the domain of 83,311 bales and 13,892 *ryō* and from domain and local officials of 533,000 bales and 10,100 *ryō*, and all loans from merchants and temples (totals unknown). Among his other reforms were reductions of ancillary levies, assignment of all abandoned parcels to individual cultivators, establishment of a borrowing fund for distressed villages financed by a surcharge on absentee holdings (*konkyū yonaimai*), and reorganization of rural administrative posts (TSS 1974:358-62).

Shirai's program was of only minimal benefit to domain finances if one compares, for example, its 1774 deficit of 27,100 *ryō* (see the budget sheet in Kelly 1982a:47-48) with the projected 1811 deficit of 17,000 *ryō* (Table 7). And in at least some parts of the countryside, lienholders were able to circumvent the debt cancellation by entering their own names on the land registers, dispossessing the cultivator (Naganuma 1983:80-81). Shirai himself was discredited by continued political in-fighting and was replaced in 1811 by a rival faction, allied with Honma, who was once again brought in for counsel and financing.

It was also about this time that Sakai was assigned a section of the Hokkaidō coast to guard. The associated expenses were a further drag on domain coffers, but to the Sakata merchants, and especially to Honma, this initial colonization of "Ezoland" was the opening of another rice market. Honma, now well positioned with the controlling faction, set up a Hokkaidō shipping line. Coinciding with the rising rice demands of an expanding Edo population and Osaka area *sake* brewers and cotton growers, paddy land investment proved lucrative in these first three decades of the 19th century. We have already seen that both Honma and Akino doubled their holdings in this period of prosperity, which came to end about 1830 with a series of poor harvests that threatened political stability and economic solvency.

THE TRIBUTARY/MERCANTILE NEXUS

Shōnai by the early 19th century was a monocropped rice bowl enfeoffed to a single domain lord. Domain revenues, mercantile investment, and the fortunes of 145,000 cultivators were focused on the fluctuating yields and prices of the annual rice crop. Mean rice yields were rising, but much of this escaped the domain because of its particular concessions in promoting paddy land reclamation and its subsequent pat-

TABLE 7

General Budget Estimates, Shōnai Domain, 1811

Tax base	191,218.6 *koku*	
Average principal land tax rate	44%	

Principal land tax revenues	218,754 bales	
Ancillary levies: in rice	46,882	
in gold		7,922 *ryō*
Total revenues	265,636 bales	7,922 *ryō*
Rice expenditures:		
Domain land	15,350 bales	
Upper-rank retainers	112,225	
Lower-rank retainers	50,700	
Village-group headmen, etc.	12,060	
Total expenditures	190,335 bales	
Rice surplus	75,301 bales	
Converted to gold at 35 bales per 10 *ryō* =		21.514 *ryō* 2 *bu*
	Gold balance	29,436 *ryō* 2 *bu*
	Gold expenditures:	
	in Edo	29,105 *ryō*
	in Shōnai	8,968 *ryō* 1 *bu*
	yobikin	2,000 *ryō*
	total	40,073 *ryō* 1 *bu*
	deficit	10,636 *ryō* 1 *bu*

NOTE: These estimates do not include loan repayments; an attached note suggests extraordinary shogunate levies on Sakai were going to add 6,385 *ryō* 2 *bu* to the domain deficit. Compare this to the 1774 balance sheet in Kelly 1982a:47.

SOURCE: TSS 1974:375.

tern of tribute-taking. Yet if production was not "efficiently" extracted by the political elite, neither was its surplus uniformly distributed across the commoner population. Cultivators still faced wide annual yield fluctuations from insect damage, blights, and the vagaries of the northern climate. They were equally vulnerable to market price fluctuations in a highly commercialized rice trade that extended to Edo and Osaka (see Appendix). And they produced rice in hundreds of thousands of paddy parcels that varied widely in their soil and water conditions and in registered tax burdens. Such conditions favored and attracted largeholders with direct and protected market access, most notably the Honmas, although we must remember that even in 1830 the main house's holdings totaled only 4% of the plain's rice acreage. As the Tokugawa period was drawing to a close, then, how and where did Shōnai fit into the paradigm of the protoindustrializing agrarian state with which we concluded the previous chapter?

Farm by-employment and rural cottage industry were significant features of a number of regions. Was there a protoindustrialization of the Shōnai countryside like the cotton processing in the Osaka hinterlands (Hauser 1974), sericulture in the Suwa Basin (Saitō 1982), and paper manufacture and salt extraction in areas of Chōshū (Nishikawa 1981)? I think not. There were extensive networks of part-time and itinerant merchants (*kokake*) and sales agents who bulked small purchases of rice from village households for rice dealers in the towns. A register of petty traders and shopkeepers in Atsumi Village Group drawn up in 1842 listed 118 persons in eleven of its twenty-one villages (YKS 1980:752-57). Two years before, there were 73 licensed merchants and traders in five villages of Oshikiri Village Group, including 10 grain bulkers, 17 peddlars (*bōte*), 18 itinerant greengrocers, 9 greengrocer shops, 5 "second-hand dealers" (*furudōgu uri* and *furute uri*), 7 fishmongers, 3 cotton dealers, 2 vinegar and soy sauce sellers, a haberdasher, and a bean curd maker. A separate listing of craftsmen included carpenters, sawyers, blacksmiths, thatchers, dyers, oil pressers, and malsters.[18]

[18] MCS 1974:177-78. Licensing was the responsibility (and surely also the privilege) of the village group headman; registered cultivators who sought trading or craft licenses needed the additional approval of the rural magistrate.

Yet in spite of such commercial activity, there were few signs of rural industry, of an incipient redeployment of capital and labor that investigators have come to recognize as protoindustrialization (Kriedte et al. 1981; Tilly 1983).

Nor would I characterize the pattern of concentrated, tenanted largeholdings as agrarian capitalism. For most of the 19th century, these largeholders did not turn rice cultivation into a "business enterprise," intensifying cultivation with new methods and rationalizing their employment and deployment of labor. They were quite unlike the "improving landlords" of the early modern English countryside, who rationalized their holdings toward a capital-intensive—and capitalist—agriculture. It is true that Honma and Akino, the two largest landholders, both instituted procedures and a hierarchy of agents for buying and assigning parcels and collecting their crop shares. Essentially, though, they created structures of land administration and surplus extraction parallel to and patterned on the domain's tribute exactions. It is equally significant that until the late 1880s, their investments in technological improvements (especially to the irrigation-drainage networks of the plain; Kelly 1982a), seed varieties, and fertilizers remained minimal. If we hold to the importance of distinguishing "money-begetting-money" and "money-as-capital," we must conclude that there were few signs of an emergent capitalist reorganization of craft or agricultural production in 19th-century Shōnai until its final decade and after the four periods of collective protest.

Rather, domain administration, commercial transactions, and rice cultivation were a mesh of mutually reinforcing and mutually constraining tributary relationships and mercantile activity. It is possible to envision this as a neat triangle of social categories:

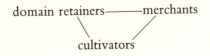

Thus, one might posit a homeostatic force field in which the merchants grew wealthy from domain grain sales and other licensed monopolies while the domain remained solvent through loans, contributions, pay-offs, and give-backs from the merchants. Both exacted tribute from rice cultivators, who in turn tempered these exactions through borrowing, reductions, occasional debt cancellations, and customary limits.

This is a tempting model, but even this is not the most fruitful formulation of 19th-century Shōnai because it tends to reify these categories into monolithic blocs. Nineteenth-century conflict will underscore what the three protest and reform cases of the 1600s and 1700s hinted at: lines of contention were scored along antagonisms among as well as between domain retainers, town merchants, and rural cultivators. Among domain retainers, we have already seen vertical factional struggles for policy and office and horizontal cleavages between higher advisors and local-level officials. Merchants were divided between licensed and unlicensed houses, between those allied to Honma and those antagonistic to his commercial hegemony, and among territorial rivalries of Tsurugaoka, Sakata, and Ōyama.

Rural commercialization, too, could not be reduced to a simple dichotomy of subsistence and profit. All rural cultivators had been drawn into a web of mortgaged lands, cash loans, tenancy, and petty trading. Sometimes it was in desperation, sometimes for accumulation. A paradigmatic shift from peasant farming for subsistence to commercial farming for profit is too crude to capture the multiple orientations to commercial agrarian relations. The rural population of Shōnai by the early 19th century was not a homogenous peasantry. Ownership, cultivation, and residency; household labor and the use of outside labor in transplanting and harvesting; production for consumption, for tribute and rent, for market sales; deployment of labor in farming and non-farming activities; input purchases and output sales—these features of household economy could vary independently of one another to give a structural diversity to the rural population and to permit composite strategies to individual households. "Cultivator" (*hyakushō*) was a term that masked a wide range of production circumstances and market orientations, diverse vulnerabilities and possibilities. Shōnai in 1830 was not a triangle of antagonistic categories but a more dense texture of tributary and mercantile relationships in a commercial rice monoculture.

THREE

Honorable Subjects . . . : The Anti-Transfer Protests of 1840–41

THE INCIDENTS of the 1630s, the 1670s, and the 1790s sketched in the previous chapter stand as the most prominent moments of commoner criticism, elite factional dispute, and domain policy crisis in the Sakai's first two centuries in Shōnai. Yet none involved enduring and collective protest movements. There were joint actions, such as the tens of households absconding over the mountains to Akita in 1632. But not until the 1840s can we identify moments of sustained mass protest: in 1840–41 and again in 1844. The first successfully challenged the shogunate's attempt to replace Sakai with another domain lord; the second was an unsuccessful effort to block Sakai from assuming jurisdiction over the shogunate territories in Shōnai. That these actions followed immediately upon a decade of harvest failures and attendant economic crises raises obvious questions about whether this decade of dearth may have precipitated the subsequent conflicts. Thus it is important to preface our reconstruction of these movements with an outline of the difficulties of the 1830s.

DEARTH AND THE DOMAIN ORDER

For both the shogunate and the domains, the fiscal crises of the late 1700s returned with even greater intensity in the 1830s, a decade of disastrous harvests in much of the country and mounting political tensions in the capital. By the late 1830s, the shogunate was running annual deficits in excess of half a million *ryō* (Beasley 1972:51). A direct challenge to its prerogatives and preeminence was articulated by the young Mito lord Tokugawa Nariaki and several intellectuals in his domain, who pressed to open shogunal policy making to outside "men of talent." Most dramatic of the riots and "smashings" of the decade was the call to popular revolt by the minor shogunal official in Osaka, Ōshio Heihachirō (Morris 1975:180-216, Najita 1970). The uprising was quickly quashed, but Ōshio's defiant gesture and suicide charged the Tenpō imagination as the revenge of the forty-seven samurai of Lord Asano had electrified the Genroku world. In hindsight, historians have dubbed these years (that is, the Tenpō era, 1830-43) the beginning of the end for the shogunate. To Najita, for example, it was the time in which "Restorationism" coalesced as a radical political critique centered in idealistic action.

With much of northeastern Japan, Shonai suffered severe harvest shortfalls and attendant hardships on domain and cultivators alike. These are reflected in the substantial reductions which the domain was forced to take in its principal land tax rate. From a mean of 45.5% in the fifteen-year period, 1812-26, the mean for the next fifteen years fell to 41.1% (see Appendix). The bad weather, unusual pest infestations, and drops in yields began in 1828; the land tax mean that year was 43.3%. In 1830, it was only 40.2% and in 1832, another very poor harvest, it was 41.4%. The rice harvests were even more disastrous in 1833, and the litany of climatic ravages during the growing season suggests the proportions of the crop damage. There were water shortages and abnormally low temperatures during the spring transplanting. This was followed perversely by heavy rains, widespread flooding, and strong winds in July, August, and September. A heavy snowstorm hit on November 7, while the cut sheaves were still drying in the fields, and a month later there was a major earthquake. The rice price mounted

67

steadily with each setback. By October, the local market price was 130% of July prices; after the December earthquake, when harvests in normal years would depress the market, rice prices were 190% of those in July (see Saitō 1982:50, which summarizes private and domain accounts, and TSS 1974:389-93).

The domain reacted quickly. A mid-summer directive prohibited exports from the domain of all grains and legumes. In late October, officials ordered the distribution of 12,000 bales of "charity rice" (osonaemai): 1,000 bales to each of the eight rural districts, to Tsurugaoka and Sakata, to the branch domain of Matsuyama, and to the Ōyama shogunate lands. (The rice was actually distributed after harvest with new rice, implying that the domain had had little or no stocks on hand.) The domain also ordered a halt to all "futures" trading (nobe toribiki) on the rice exchanges in Tsurugaoka and Sakata and a complete moratorium on sake brewing for the year, the first since 1783. Like its ban on exports, this directive was ignored by at least some brewers but probably did limit the volume of rice diverted to brewing. Nor were its warrior-retainers spared; the elders suspended all fief stipends that year, replacing them with smaller "allowances" (onmakai).

The harvest shortfalls forced even deeper land tax concessions than the year before; the 1833 domain mean fell to 37.0%. District officials went around to talk to village officers and tried to draw up a registry of all "indigent people" (konkyūmono), including invalids and sick without relatives. Additional rice was to be distributed to them from domain stocks. In Yamahama District alone, 2,398 indigents were identified and were provided in late December with a month of rations; these were calculated variously at 1.5 to 2.5 go per day (about one-half to three-quarters of a pint). A month later, 3,439 individuals were on the district roles, a 43% increase and representing perhaps 15-20% of the district population. The daily ration formulas, however, were now reduced to 1-1.5 go (Saitō 1982:51-52).

A post-harvest accounting revealed a domain income of

95,425 *koku* for the year, on a total tribute base of about 195,000 *koku* (this includes the basic land tax and all miscellaneous levies). District officials surveying all rice stocks in the domain after the new year estimated a shortfall of 120,000 *koku* below the amounts needed to feed the population through the following harvest. This seems to have been a gross exaggeration, but it inspired enough fear in other officials to purchase rice from Kaga and other domains and to institute a rationing system during 1834 (ibid.:52-55).

Clearly, the dimensions of the harvest shortfall gravely worried domain officials and village group headmen, although I suspect that their bans on exports and *sake* and various rationing systems were largely ineffectual in alleviating hardship. The bans were widely ignored and the rationing was insufficient in scale. Records of the distribution of charity rice for the first eight months of 1834 in twelve villages (ibid.:54-55) are impressive in their detail, but the actual amounts were miniscule. More effective in cushioning the shortages were the suspension of fief stipends and the reductions in land tax rates. The domain also provided amounts of domain rice for sale in each village group; in fact, these sales were often made on loan, and the domain was then to have difficulty securing repayment.

The next fall, 1834, produced a bumper harvest, and the domain tried to insure that reserves were stockpiled in the district granaries. However, low temperatures, flooding, and early winter storms brought very poor harvests for the next three years (1835-37). The concessions that the domain was forced to make in the 1835 land tax reduced that year's tax mean to 32.6%, indicating that the 1834 harvest had not generated much of a surplus. Cultivators continued to borrow from domain stocks; by 1837 in Yamahama District, for example, taxes in arrears and outstanding loans totaled 32,938 bales and 3,242 *ryō*.[1]

[1] An itemization for village group headmen (TSS 1974:401) listed eleven categories of loans and advances from domain officials, one from "landlords," and three from village group and district accounts.

Growing-season weather the following year was equally ominous, and in mid-summer, senior advisors circulated to all village group headmen a proposal to write off all unpaid taxes and loans. Shortly before harvest in 1838 they announced a reform package. They canceled all main and ancillary taxes in arrears and "reorganized" other cultivator debts such that "distressed cultivators" (*nankyū hyakushō*) were relieved of all outstanding obligations. They also reduced ancillary levies ("to bolster the position of indigent cultivators," *konkyū hyakushō*), and added another surcharge (*yonaimai*) of 2.5% on absentee landholders, which was to be added to local reserve stocks. At the same time, they ordered a "complete investigation" of all ancillary and local levies and issued guidelines for distributing local reserves. Half was to go to the general population in times of distress, and half was for the particularly indigent. They emphasized that distribution was to be controlled by the village group headmen and that all shortages were a village group, not domain, responsibility. Thus, the thrust of the reform, like others before, was to try to start over—to eliminate old debts, but to set up a local reserve system so that there would be no need in the future to borrow from the domain's central stocks. This plan was accompanied by other edicts to tighten rural administration. District officials were enjoined to curb their official travel expenses.[2] Each rural magistrate was given three soldiers to accompany him on his rounds to discourage any dissent. The elders intoned against unregistered mortgaging and cash taxes.

Yet Saitō's analysis of village group headmen's books in Yamahama District suggests how district officials themselves subverted these fiscal reforms. Much of the outstanding taxes and loans of the district were in fact advances made by individual district officials to cultivators at interest, for ex-

---

[2] They were to keep their meals simple: *ichijiru issai mushū*, "one soup, one green vegetable, no *sake*" accompanying their rice. This was a stock phrase—see the identical admonition in a 1793 document (YKS 1980:207).

ample when a household could not meet its full tax obligations at the end of the year. The household was cleared on
the village books and began to repay the official privately. I
suspect, though, that in many cases these officials did not
actually tender rice (or rice vouchers) in the household's
name. Rather, the sum was carried on district records as due
from the village group in arrears. Thus, in contrast to merchants' loans on land collateral, these were not mercantile
ventures but private manipulations of administrative records.
This may explain why the district deputies and rural magistrates were willing to carry out the higher officials' order to
cancel old debts, while insisting that the interest due on these
be payable (to themselves). The village group headmen were
then forced to draw down their meager reserve stocks to
repay this interest. Thus, the canceling of old debts did not
allow the building up of granary reserves, as the reforms
intended.[3]

Plagued as the plain was with natural disasters, harvest
shortfalls, and some dubious official maneuvers for over ten
years, it is remarkable that there is virtually no evidence of
violent acts by cultivators or townspeople protesting official
action or inaction and bringing corrupt officials, hoarders, or
price gougers to some rough justice. There were many petitions seeking assistance and dispensation, but my search of
the period's documents has yielded only one record of direct
crowd action. This occurred in mid-October of 1833, when
several hundred residents of five Yamahama District villages
attacked the homes of two local rice miller-dealers, accusing
them of hoarding and price manipulations. It was not until
July of 1834 that final sentences were issued, and they were
harsh: permanent imprisonment (two persons), banishment
from the domain (three), banishment to Akumi (one), lesser
punishments to eleven others, and "reprimands" (*shikari*) to

---

[3] I have drawn here on figures in Saitō 1982:62, but have given them a
rather different interpretation.

all registered cultivators of the villages (YKS 1980:934; cf. Saitō 1982:50).

What are we to make of this apparent quiescence during the same years that saw days of rage in the streets of Edo, Osaka, and several provincial towns? Did the reports of the time and later historians grossly overstate the dimensions of distress and/or ignore the conscientiousness and effectiveness of official relief measures? I think neither. There was real suffering and widespread setbacks, which domain measures did not well cushion. The drop in mean tax rates, the ballooning local debt, the spate of testimonials of hardship,[4] and the extraordinary injunctions of domain officials all bespeak crop shortfalls and rural dislocations on an unprecedented scale. All the same, "famine" remained but a vivid rhetorical image in petitions and memoranda. There was, fortunately, no documented starvation, although weakened resistance was probably responsible for a brief typhoid epidemic in and around Sakata (Saitō 1982:58).

One has to wonder, though, if fine calibrations of hungry stomachs and angry voices—impossible anyway—do not misdirect our efforts to appreciate the forces that impel or tranquilize discontent. In their probing essay on "dearth and the social order in early modern England," Walter and Wrightson (1976) questioned our tendency to assume that dearth always breeds disorder:

> It is difficult to exaggerate the extent to which people in the late sixteenth and early seventeenth century were conscious of the threat of dearth. Periodic harvest disaster and food shortage were the spectre which haunted

[4] See examples in Saitō 1982. Some of these memorials were fervidly sensationalist. Others offered practical advice on "famine foods" to ward off hunger and malnurishment; one list included burdock leaves, yarrow leaves, snake gourd stems, wisteria leaves, beech tree leaves, mare's tail, and other items normally composted even by a rural population that assiduously exploited wild vegetation for their diet (Naganuma 1983:86). Such advice was widespread; see, for example, the facsimile of an 1837 listing of "famine foods" from central Japan in Akiyama et al. 1979:18.

early modern Europe, one of the principal factors contributing to the profound insecurity of the age. Traditionally historians have tended to emphasize the threat which dearth posed to the social order. We wish to qualify such assumptions by suggesting that the consequences of dearth were of a more complex nature. For, while it could undoubtedly contribute to social disorder, there is evidence that the awareness of dearth, the memory of its past, and fear of its future occurrence, could serve as an active element in the maintenance of social stability. A consciousness of dearth, we believe, could strengthen the values and relationships upon which the social order rested, at least in the context of early modern England. (1976:22; see Greenough 1983 for a similar discussion of the cultural meanings of subsistence and their more tragic implications for behavior during 20th-century Bengali famines.)

In 19th-century Japan, too, the sharply fluctuating yields (albeit around a gradually rising mean) and the chronic precariousness of domain finances gave a highly charged and often effective rhetorical edge to mention of "harvest shortfalls," "famine," and "indigent cultivators." Yet the cultural phrasing of state-cultivator relations was rather different in 19th-century Japan from early modern England or the recent Bengali past.

A distinctive feature of Tokugawa Japan was the prevalence of written petitioning as a longstanding, well-defined pathway to express discontent; in the reverse direction, of course, there was an even greater proliferation of written directives to enjoin or proscribe. By the 19th century, the "right" of commoners to petition had been sharply circumscribed by shognate officials; nonetheless, it remained the channel of first resort, the most common way to seek redress for wrong and relaxation from excess. The conventions of petitioning were widely known: the etiquette and procedures for submission, the typical appeal to the subordinates' "distress" and the superiors' "grace," the deferential phrases, the syntatic constructions were all highly standardized, as we will often see in this study.[5]

The frequency of petitioning can be understood as part of a more general persistence of commoner litigation in spite of official discouragement. This included the endemic "incidents" (*ikken*) at the local level, whose charges, countercharges, and testimony filled the voluminous notebooks of the village group headmen's document chests: complaints and disputes between households or villages over land, water, money, and other daily contentions (see Henderson's 1975 compendium of village "contracts" and the numerous cases in Kelly 1982a). There was also a steady stream of commoners before the shogunate courts seeking judgments in civil litigation. Henderson has given us a vivid account of such litigation in the dogged efforts of Nuinosuke, a rural entrepreneur from the outskirts of Edo, to gain satisfaction at the Edo Finance Commission in 1808 (Henderson l965:131-62). For five months he sought judgment against a teahouse operator who had defaulted on a property transaction totaling 50 *ryō*. He was guided throughout by the innkeeper of the special "suit inn" (*kujiyado*) were he lodged.[6] He remained undeterred through seven hearings, twelve

[5] Even calligraphic style was conventionalized. The Shōren-in school of calligraphy had become widely popular in the early Tokugawa period and had been adopted by the shogunate as its official calligraphic school, becoming known as *oieryū*. It then became necessary to write all public documents in this style, which lent a visual uniformity to documents across the country and over time (Aoki 1981:182-83).

[6] See Takigawa 1959, Minami 1967, and Aoki 1981:191-203 for excellent descriptions of the suit inns (*kujiyado*) in Osaka and Edo. The innkeepers formed licensed guilds with limited standing before the shogunate courts and certain obligations to the courts and to commoners who boarded while attempting to litigate. Their contacts, calligraphy, experience in compiling documentation, and knowledge of the complicated bureaucracy were essential for any suitor before the shogunate courts or any petition group coming up to the capital. Takigawa and Aoki also describe the atmosphere in the *kujiyado* neighborhoods of Bakurō and Kodenma as it was captured by comic verse of the time: for example, "Bakurō-chō—where they guide the suckers" (*mukudori ni michibikiwatasu Bakurō-chō*; Aoki 1981:197).

continuances, and even more conciliation sessions. It appears from the final settlement that he "won" his point, but when Henderson leaves him, monetary recompense was still doubtful. Nuinosuke's experience is an object lesson in the arcane court procedures and officers' obsessive concern with exact terminology, proper endorsements, and a full complement of supporting "documentation and evidence" (*shōmon shōko kore ari* announced the accompanying raft of supporting papers).[7] His implacable litigious spirit was no doubt unusual in degree, but he reminds us that petitioning in matters of collective welfare could draw on skills and strategies and experiences of local disputes and litigation before higher commissions.

That there were well-trod ways through the procedural thickets of early 19th-century Japan did not preclude frustration and ultimately more direct action. The overriding difficulty in civil litigation faced by an individual like Nuinosuke was in securing judgment against another commoner in courts which were at best reluctant adjudicators, for whom public decisions were unpleasant last resorts when their efforts to mandate private compromise failed. Petitioning involved its own paradoxes; in fact, it embodied two crucial contradictions that together posed a larger contradiction. On the one hand, petitioning was the accepted method for calling attention to distress and misrule. Procedure, however, dictated that all written pleas must be presented to one's immediate superior (such as villages to village group headmen)—and one's superior was often the very person whose malfeasance was at issue. This frequently provoked the distressed to go outside the hierarchy, to appeal to a distant overlord. This dramatized the demands while compromising the petition's status and exposing the persons to severe punishment. In short, petitioning promoted escalation. On the other hand, if the petition was an accepted, and acceptable, vehicle to secure a hearing, by its very conventions it could set rhetorical limits to protest. Its phrases and forms gave

[7] Nuinosuke's tenacity also implies that claims for present-day Japan as a non-litigious society find cold comfort in the 19th century.

voice to indignation but also constrained anger, forcing it into a standardized vocabulary of hardship and grace. Petitioning, then, embodied a tension between provocation and constraint, and how this was resolved affected the course of all collective action.

In Shōnai in the 1830s, constraint proved stronger than provocation. Throughout the decade, cultivators and townspeople called for domain action in written distress petitions. The steady stream of injunctions, proscriptions, and concessions was a highly visible response to these calls—audible also, as they were read, line by line, to village assemblies across the plain. Largeholders, too, offered periodic acts of charity, such as Akino's 300-*ryō* contribution to the "distressed cultivators" of Kyōden District. And it was the publicity, not the efficacy, of such acts that restrained further agitation. One thousand *koku* of rice distributed across a district of 20,000 persons was a tangible gesture of concern but it could not have filled many stomachs for long. Still, the domain took care not to leave itself open to charges of neglecting the entailments of "benevolent rule." It publicly subscribed to the right to subsistence (Scott 1976) even when it could not insure it; however short its measures fell, they deflected the more serious resort to riot. In Shōnai, the negotiations of correct conduct between ruler and subject, landlord and tenant, were confined to a duel of calligraphic brushes urged by the distant din of disorder elsewhere.[8] The fabric of tributary relationships, threadbare in other parts of the country, was tested but not torn by the difficulties of the 1830s.

AN "IMPOVERISHED LORD" FOR SHŌNAI? THE SHOGUN'S TRANSFER ORDER

For all of its difficulties, Shōnai escaped the very worst of the climatic ravages of the 1830s. The domain actually fared

---

[8] Domain officials were shocked by news of Ōshio's call to revolt, which may have galvanized the debt cancellations in the following year, the most extreme measures they had yet taken (TSS 1974:402).

better than most other regions in the northeast. Indeed, Edo pundits soon tagged Sakai Tadakata as the "Kanda daikoku sama," a reference to one of the popular folk gods of good fortune. The phrase chided the lavish living that he continued to enjoy at his Kanda mansion at a time when many other domain lords had to curtail sharply their Edo expenditures. Given the yawning deficits in domain accounts and mounting rural indebtedness, this was less the reward of conscientious administration than a reckless disdain for logic of the abacus (the behavior of most senior domain elite in the 19th century gives lie to any presumed linkage of immersion in commercial relations, a head for business, and a drive for profit!). Yet Tadakata was to pay for his conspicuous consumption. His extravagance attracted official notice as well as pundits' barbs. It precipitated an even more serious challenge to the domain than the harvest shortfalls it had weathered for a decade.

The first blow was a heavy assessment on Tadakata for repairs to the Tokugawa Mausoleum at Nikkō. Then, on November 24, 1840, still reeling from that exaction, the domain was stunned by a shogunal directive for a triangular rotation of fiefs. After 218 years of Sakai enfeoffment of Shōnai, Tadakata was ordered to Nagaoka, a much smaller domain farther south along the Japan Sea. The Nagaoka lord, Makino Tadamasa, was to move to Kawagoe, just northwest of Edo, and Matsudaira Naritsune of Kawagoe was named the new lord of Shōnai.[9]

The Edo Castle politics behind this directive were arcane (see TSS 1974:406-408, Satō 1975:275-79, and Tsuda 1975:264-65), though they centered on the longstanding am-

---

[9] The shogun had always claimed the right to move and adjust the fiefs of his senior vassals, the domain lords, and 17th-century shoguns exercised it regularly. Even triangular rotations had precedents. But as Bolitho (1974) and others have shown, it was a prerogative much less often exercised in the later Tokugawa period. Documents relating to the movement described here are to be found in Ono 1964:37-142, Naitō 1841, anon. 1841, YKS 1980:935-1019, and SSS 1971:779-92. There are useful discussions in TSS 1974:406-31, Enomoto 1975:234-41, and Borton 1938:99-106.

bitions of a favorite consort of Ienari, the retired shogun, for her son by Ienari, Matsudaira Nariyasu. Nariyasu (also read Narisada) was the twenty-fourth of Ienari's fifty-five children, at least half of whom reached maturity and presented shogunal officials with vexacious problems in finding positions and homes for them. In 1827, when Nariyasu was ten, his mother was able to have him sent for adoption as heir to Matsudaira Naritsune, lord of the 70,000-*koku* Kawagoe Domain. She then began scheming to have the Matsudaira transferred to a larger, more lucrative domain. She was attracted to Shōnai because of its reputation in Edo of having fared relatively well in the last decade and because of the presence of the wealthy Honma merchant family. She seeded rumors of smuggling and lax coastal defenses at Sakata and was able to play on other rivalries within the castle to persuade Ienari to have a transfer order issued in November of 1840.

Tadakata was at the time in Tsurugaoka; when the news reached him by special courier seven days later, his officials were plunged into immediate meetings. They were particularly shocked that the transfer entailed a 50% reduction in official fief value, from Shōnai's 140,000 *koku* to Nagaoka's 70,000 *koku*. Moreover, the transfer came in the unusual form of a personal order (*taimei*) of the shogun. In two hundred years, such a personal order had never been rescinded or directly opposed, and Tadakata's senior advisors quickly concluded that they had no chance of reversal. From the start, their meetings and maneuvers were aimed at raising money to meet the enormous expenses required by the move and attempting to secure some supplemental lands (*soechi*) to cushion the fief reduction.[10] Tadaaki, Tadakata's son and heir-designate who remained in Edo, was used to keep his

---

[10] A third issue that they hotly debated was the disposition of the Sakai family graves: that is, whether to disinter the remains of the earlier lords at the family temple in Tsurugaoka. This was the only ground on which they briefly entertained opposition.

father informed of Edo developments and to pass along gifts and bribes to officials who might be of use within the castle. Honma Mitsuaki was alerted to the news and appeared at the castle on December 1; he was asked to coordinate the move with the domain rural affairs officers (it is his diary which provides details of these castle deliberations; SSS 1971:779-82). Mitsuaki was also questioned closely about his own finances and was ordered to prepare a declaration of current assets. He was able to deflect initial demands of a 300,000-*ryō* moving expense assessment. After several days, this was scaled down to 73,000 *ryō*. Mitsuaki returned to Sakata for family consultations and eventually produced both the asset declaration and a little over 50,000 *ryō* toward transfer expenses.

Other large merchants were not as forthcoming; for example, the two wealthiest merchants of Kamo Port, Akino Moemon and Oya Hachiroji, were each asked for 2,000 *ryō* but pleaded business difficulties and only offered 1,500 *ryō* (YKS 1980:162-63). The domain's initial target was 93,000 *ryō*, and so it had to turn to townspeople and villagers for large assessments. Together with a rapid series of directives dunning the populace for unpaid taxes and all loans, these assessments engendered immediate opposition. This was further fueled by the news that the Kawagoe Matsudaira was to be the new Shōnai fief holder. The family had a national reputation as a line of chronic "impoverished domain lords" (*binbō daimyō*), whose policies were harsh and repressive.[11] The family had already been moved *eleven* times in the previous two centuries!

The fief transfer order, then, was threatening to virtually all domain residents. The domain lord was faced with a severe loss of revenue and the prospect of having to release

---

[11] The standard phrase used to characterize such policies was *karen chūkyū*. The contrasting term was *jinsei* or "benevolent policies." *Tokusei* was occasionally used as a synonym for such paternalistic benevolence, but even in the 19th century it retained its particular meaning of "debt cancellation" (e.g., TSS 1974:359; cf. Hayashiya 1977:26-27, Varley 1967:194-201).

many of his retainers whom he could no longer afford to support. Merchants were faced with a discomforting choice: either follow Sakai to his new location in hopes of preserving business concessions and their loans to Sakai and his retainers, or remain in Shōnai to protect their landholdings and loans to commoners and to negotiate commercial ties with the new lord Naritsune. All landholders, large and small, had good cause to fear a new cadastre that would uncover the substantial underregistration and undertaxation. While senior officials attempted to improve the terms of the move and Honma temporized about moving or staying, other merchants, local officials, and cultivators expressed immediate opposition to the move. Their agitations over the next six months assumed three related forms: direct petitioning at Edo and at other domains; prayer groups at Shōnai temples and shrines; and mass assemblies of rural residents. Honma was soon convinced to back this drive, and gradually, as the political balance in Edo began to turn, the domain itself was drawn to tacit support. This became, then, a most curious "popular protest," and in following its course, we must carefully consider the orchestration of popular participation and the subversion of popular demands.

PETITIONS, ASSEMBLIES, AND PRAYERS

Maneuvering began the day after the transfer order reached Sakai. While domain officials were calculating the costs of the move, a Tsurugaoka doctor quietly visited leading merchants and headmen of the town's wards to propose that they solicit the aid of the head abbot (*bettō*) of the *shugendō* temple complex on Mt. Haguro. Back in 1634, in a political maneuver designed to protect temple lands from Sakai predations, the Haguro abbot had met with the abbot of Kan'ei-ji Temple, which was patronized by the Tokugawa family. He struck a deal whereby Haguro would switch from the Shingon to the Tendai sect in order to place itself under the wing of the powerful Kan'ei-ji Temple (Matsumoto

80

1977:647-48). Now, two hundred years later, the doctor suggested that this direct channel to the shogun be tested, but he was warned off by the town magistrate. Later, the town's moneylenders sent delegates to talk with the abbot, who rejected any such intermediary role as inappropriate, apparently unwilling to risk the temple's interests.

The next move was more daring but no more successful. On December 16, twelve residents of Saigō, a village group to the west of the castle town, left for Edo with a petition to rescind the transfer (see Figure 3). It was headed "With all deference, the humble cultivators of the two counties of Shōnai unite in bringing this written appeal of distress." It began with effusive praise for the "benevolence" of generations of Sakai lords, but pointedly raised the specter of severe

3. A meeting of Kuromori Village residents at their temple
on December 10, 1840 to discuss actions
against the recent transfer order.

hardships in the event of a transfer. With circumlocutions and professions of loyalty, the text (TSS 1974:415-16) read:

> On hearing of the recent order transferring our Lord Sakai Saemon, all of the cultivators of Tagawa and Akumi—young and old, men and women—were filled with anguish and grief. Our lord's family has been here for over two hundred years, and we have relied on the benevolence of generations of his predecessors. In the past, of course, there have been harvest failures, but eight years ago there was a disaster of unprecedented proportions. In the regions beyond Shōnai, there were untold numbers of famine deaths, and beggars from these regions flooded Shōnai in swarms. Yet our lord in Shōnai gave large quantities of rice and money to residents throughout the towns and villages as well as generously extending considerable sums in loans. He arranged to buy rice from other parts of the country for distribution as aid within Shōnai, and well-to-do commoners in the domain provided significant amounts of assistance money. As a consequence, there was not a single beggar or criminal from within Shōnai, which brought tears of thanks to all of us. Even when our lord exhausted his reserves, having acted similarly in previous years of harvest failure, he borrowed large quantities of money from wealthy merchants in other regions. These he extended as loans to Shōnai people so that there was not a single famine death nor was it even necessary for any household in the towns or countryside to pawn or sell one item of value. If such long-standing assistance in rice and cash and loans were to cease, we would be unable to pay our taxes fully and would face grievous losses. And, furthermore, if our kind lord were forced to move, all of the domain's designated merchants would petition to follow him to Nagaoka. Cultivators of the domain have substantial amounts in outstanding loans from these merchants because of the

recent harvest shortfalls. If these were to come due suddenly, there would be enormous hardship. All are
crying out in concern that there can be nothing short of
our lord remaining here. It has reached the point where
everyone in Shōnai, even the children, are making prayers to the gods. All are purifying themselves and making
pilgrimages to Mt. Yudono, Mt. Haguro, Mt. Kinpō,
and Mt. Chokai, and to all of the gods and Buddhas of
the castle town. The people beg tearfully that you permit our lord to remain here as always. With all deference, we humbly bring the above entreaty before you.
The mere cultivators of the two counties of Shōnai now
respectfully seek your kind directive to allow our benevolent lord to remain forever in Shōnai. Your cultivators
join together in beseeching you.

> [from] cultivators of the villages of
> Tagawa and Akumi

[to] the authorities
the eleventh month of Tenpō 11

The group reached Edo and put up at the suit inn Ko-
matsu-ya in Bakurō-chō. However, before they could force
the petition on shogunate officials, they were intercepted by
Sakai soldiers and returned home to the domain. Undaunted,
they circulated posters through the domain during the winter
months, vividly drawing attention to the requisitions of corvée labor to be used in the transfer, the shipment of rice
reserves from Shōnai to Nagaoka, and other ominous measures (e.g., YKS 1980:947).

One of the activists from Saigō Village Group was the
village group scribe, Honma Tatsunosuke, who was no re-
lation to the Sakata Honmas. He came instead from a modest
Tsurugaoka innkeeper house, Kamo-ya, and had been
adopted by the Saigō Village Group headman. The current
Kamo-ya household head, Bunji, became active in mobilizing support in the castle town. There was actually a triangle

of personal links because a woman of the Kamo-ya house had been married to the priest Bunrin (1799-1863), who became chief priest of the Akumi temple Gyokuryū-ji, which was in Eji Village on the lower slopes of Mt. Chokai (Ono 1964:47-49). Bunrin too was drawn in, and his temple became the locus of agitations in the northern half of Shōnai. On January 5, twenty-one persons set out from the temple for Edo, eleven of whom successfully eluded domain soldiers and reached the capital. There they were taken in by Satō Tōsuke, who had been born in Akumi but had gone to study in Edo at the age of nineteen and remained to become a *kujishi*, a lobbyist and facilitator for commoners with petitions and other business with shogunal and domain authorities.[12] Satō's help had been solicited by Shirazaki Goemon, who had been schooled at the Yonezawa Domain school but who moved to Sakata to work under the Honmas in the 1830s. Thus, it would appear that Honma Mitsuaki had moved off the fence and was beginning to maneuver behind the scenes in support of the anti-transfer movement.[13]

Satō devised a strategy for the eleven Akumi cultivators to force petitions on five senior shogunate officials as their palanquins were entering the castle on February 11 (texts: YKS 1980:963-67; see Borton 1938:104). Such petitions were a conventional mode of announcing grievances, but they often drew capital punishment because they violated a cardinal norm by leapfrogging one's immediate overlord. Sharing a final, ceremonial cup of *sake* and resolutely fastening their *hachimaki* cloths about their heads, the men were led to the

---

[12] Henderson (1965:169) and his main source (Takigawa 1959:8-10) draw a clear distinction between the innkeepers of the suit inns and *kujishi* like Satō, who were considered shadowy and unsavory fixers. Aoki (1981:205) interprets the *kujishi* category more broadly.

[13] Mitsuaki was active in several ways. He made overtures to the Yonezawa lord, Uesugi, to whom he had frequently loaned in the past and to whom he now advanced 7,000 *ryō*. Mitsuaki also tried to confuse the transfer with a plan for all largeholders to sign over their lands to Eihei-ji Temple, so that they would have an excuse to avoid contributions solicited by the new domain lord.

Outer Sakurada Gate of Edo Castle, where they crouched among the milling crowds. As, one by one, the palanquins came into sight, they rushed forward in pairs. Extending their petitions on forked sticks, they bowed and called out "With all deference! a desperate appeal by Shōnai cultivators!" (*osorenagara Shōnai no hyakushō gotangan*; see Figure 4). Each pair was beaten off and bound up by the foot soldiers who surrounded the palanquin, until all were in custody. Significantly, however, they were treated very lightly. The arresting soldiers praised them as "model cultivators" (*hyakushō no kikan*). They were remanded to the Sakai mansion and returned to Akumi.

4. Petitioning at Edo Castle: the first group of Akumi cultivators attempt to press their petitions on senior shogunal advisors.

Back home, tales of the leniency shown the Akumi Eleven bolstered the population, and groups set off with similar petitions for the lords of Akita, Sendai, Mito, and other domains. By late March, broad opposition was expressed through mass meetings in several parts of the plain. For four days, from March 29 through April 1, there was an assembly for all Akumi residents on the beach near Sakata, attended by over 10,000 persons. Domain officials were present as observers, but did not interfere and issued only perfunctory warnings. Indeed, when thirty-six representatives brought a petition from the assembly to the castle in Tsurugaoka, they received a polite welcome from a senior elder. The domain maintained correct administrative procedures in reporting this—and other—mass assemblies to the shogunate, along with its efforts to discourage such gatherings, but these reports of about 40-50,000 "utterly stupid cultivators" (*mattaku gumai no hyakushō*; Naganuma 1983:93) gathering to demonstrate for Sakai's "eternal" control of Shōnai were clearly intended to intimidate shogunal officials.

It was apparent that the official domain attitude was shifting to at least tacit support for popular efforts to have the order retracted. Yet I doubt this reflected a sensitivity to commoners' fears or a belief that popular agitation by itself would force a reversal. Sakai's senior advisors were probably more impressed by changing political circumstances in Edo. On February 20, Ienari died. He had officially retired four years before, but had continued to exercise power behind the scenes. Now, his heir and twelfth shogun, Ieyoshi, took over in fact as well as in name. This occasioned the release of considerable pent-up discontent by the domain lords. For example, the twenty-three most prominent *tozama daimyō* (the so-called Outside Lords of the Great Hall, *Ōbiroma tozama daimyō*) drew up a joint message to Ieyoshi that expressed in unusually blunt language their dissatisfaction with such unilateral actions as the Sakai fief transfer:

As we have had no notification from you, and have not been given any information, we humbly offer this com-

munication. . . . Since Sakai Saemonjō [i.e., Sakai Ta-
dakata] comes from a line of hereditary officials, why
has he now been ordered to move and take over Nagaoka Castle? We hereby inform you that we wish to
be told. (Cited in Bolitho 1974:35; see TSS 1974:418)

The domain elite was still wary of the mass assemblies and
uncertain they could be contained. Most alarming were several days of agitations in Nakagawa District around Rokusho
Shrine in Kamifujishima Village (see Figure 5).[14] Called by
announcements posted throughout Karikawa and Nakagawa
Districts, about 7-8,000 people gathered at this shrine on the

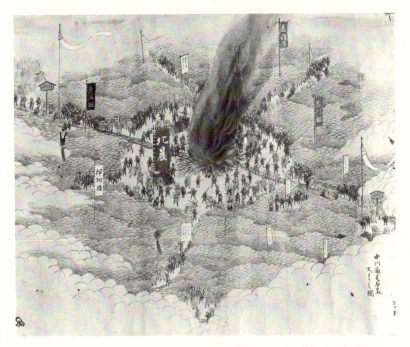

5. Assembly of Tagawa protestors at Nakagawa Yachi, April 1841.

[14] For my discussion of the Rokusho incidents, I have drawn on the recent
work of Naganuma Gensaku (1983:96-107), who has had access to privately
held diaries previously unavailable to researchers.

evening of April 6 to offer prayers for Sakai's "eternal ten-ure" in Shōnai and to "discuss" further action. District offi-cials cautiously monitored the crowds, who were creating a raucous atmosphere with drums and gongs and large conch shells. When they interrogated several of the apparent lead-ers, including Denshirō of Yokoyama Village, the officials were even more alarmed by the specific agenda: to generate support for a petition seeking permission to accompany the domain lord to Edo. Denshirō and the others had learned that Tadakata was due to depart Tsurugaoka on April 12 on his scheduled return to Edo. They feared that once in Edo, he would have to go directly to Kawagoe. For a group of cultivators to join a domain lord's procession would be an unprecedented violation of its rigid protocol. But the leaders had chosen their assembly site carefully; Tadakata's fixed processional route ran along the Tsurugaoka-Kiyokawa road, right through Kamifujishima Village. The officials were polite—agreeing that "the sentiment was admirable" though under the present circumstances "a bit rash"—but firm. They ordered the assembled to disperse, which they did with considerable noise.

But the next day they were back in even greater numbers, marching to the shrine in large groups from villages across the districts. They realized that they would not be permitted to join the procession and began to discuss the alternative: a blockade. That day and the next, materials were gathered and various tactics were devised for barricading the road, destroying the bridges, and removing the domain boats at Kiyokawa, which the lord would board for his trip up the Mogami.[15]

On the 9th, the district deputy and rural magistrate for Nakagawa District called a meeting for all village headmen at 2 p.m. in the compound of the Fujishima Village Group

---

[15] The designated route for *sankin kōtai* was not the usual commercial sea route, but went overland through the interior. Generally in the late Toku-gawa, goods were transported by sea while people traveled overland.

headman. At that time, they repeated their warnings about agitating to accompany or disrupt Tadakata's procession and ordered that Denshirō and other leaders be detained. Yet even while this was in progress, people were spilling out of villages all over Tagawa, streaming to the Nakagawa *Yachi* adjacent to Rokusho Shrine for a mass meeting.[16] Participants' records claimed a total attendance that evening of 55,000 people: 17,000 from Nakagawa District, 15,000 from Karikawa, 10,000 from Kurogawa, 5,000 from Kyōden, and even 8,000 from the shogunate villages around Amarume and Maruoka. If so, that would represent two-thirds of the total Tagawa population! These records have also left us with several memorable vignettes including an image of another Yokoyama Village leader, Genta, in his boldly colored jacket (*kaji haori*) and flowing headwrap.[17] He sat in martial style on a black lacquered camp stool, with banners flying at his side, striking a threatening pose in front of the district granary (which was also in Kamifujishima). He was eventually forced to leave by domain soldiers, and withdrew into the shrine.

The gathering had been carefully orchestrated. A "rules of conduct" was posted on signboards, admonishing the people against arguing with one another, trampling on crops, taunting domain officials, and being careless with fire (TSS 1974:419-21; MCS 1974:232-34). Contingents of men circulated through the crowds to ensure compliance. The leaders had planned for people to gather by district in enormous circles (see Figures 5 and 6). Within each, they were to be

[16] *Yachi* were areas of marsh and scrub forest that were exploited for firewood, earth fill, hunting, etc. By the 19th century, they were few in number and small in area on the largely developed plain. Entry and use were regulated by villages and/or domain.

[17] The headwrap was a *Kumagai zukin*, a long cloth wrap said to be favored by the celebrated bandit of the late Heian, Kumagai Chōhan. The term *fungomi* was also used in the description of Genta's appearance, but its meaning is unclear: *fungomi* was both a kabuki costume often worn by *onnagata* and a local term for straw footwear.

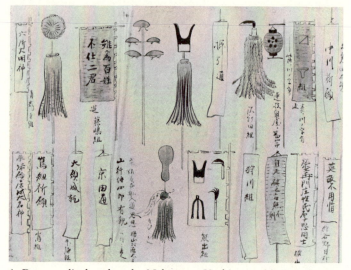

6. Banners displayed at the Nakayama Yachi assembly, April 1841.

arrayed under banners (*aijirushi*) of their village group and village; representatives were to be sent to the center for debate and discussions. The order of village groups around the circle roughly corresponded to geographical location within their district, and the whole scene was keyed to the cosmological structure of the "two dual forces and five natural elements" (*in'yo gogyō*; see Yoshino 1980). There was a North Star (*hokushin*) banner in the open center, indicating the heavenly realm (*ten no hō*), while the populated perimeter was the earthly realm (*chi no hō*). This was reinforced by bannered openings in the circle to the southwest (heaven) and to the northeast (earth). The colors of the village group banners were appropriate to their location (Fujishima Village Group to the east was red, and so on). Sensitivity to such a cosmological scheme for public events was widespread in Tokugawa society, and the intent was similar to aspects of the periodic *okage-mairi* pilgrimages (Davis 1984) and to

Shinto ritual festivals generally (Sakurai 1979:226-30). That is, the event was an empowering act of *hare*, of regenerating *ke*, "the magicoreligious power of everyday life and of agricultural production in particular" (Davis 1984:216). This idiom of "magicoreligious power" was restated in other ways. In addition to the *aijirushi*, other banners displayed drawings of hoes, sickles, other farm implements, and certain crops. Gourds were frequent emblems; Ouwehand (1964:123, 182ff.) and others have drawn attention to their clearly numinous *utsubo* qualities in Japanese folk beliefs. Melons (*uri*) like the watermelon (*suika*) also appeared on many banners (Figure 7) and had similar associations of numinous power (ibid.:208). That such melons ripened while remaining stationary on the ground was a play on *osuwari*, that Sakai should remain in Shōnai.

A third type of banner stated the demand of the assemblies: Sakai's continued enfeoffment of Shōnai (see again Figure 6). Many were phrased in clever word plays, as the following illustrate (see also the character glossary).

1. *nanidozo inari daimyōjin.* One can render this "please remain here, hororable lord" if *daimyōjin* is read *daimyō-sama.* But with *daimyōjin, inari* (written on the banner as "remain here") also recalled *inari daimyōjin,* the popular god of agricultural and commercial prosperity. Thus, the phrase was both an appeal to Sakai and to the Inari folk god.

2. *seiichii inari daimyōchi.* This involved a similar play on *inari* (here written syllabicly) and also on *daimyōchi,* "the domain lord's territory" but also suggestive of *daimyōjin,* the title for addressing gods. *Seiichii* was the highest rank of deities.

3. *hyakushō tari to iedomo nikun tsukaezu.* This can be understood as, "although we are mere cultivators, we do not serve two masters," which was meant to recall the well-known injunction in the Way of the Warrior that the warrior is loyal to only one master.

91

7. An 1841 protest banner featuring melon (*uri*) imagery.

These banners were similar to those flown at the Sakata beach rally a week earlier (see YKS 1980:949-51; Naitō 1841:folios 8 and 16). However, the records suggest that the organizers here were village headmen and ordinary cultivators from within Nakagawa and Karikawa Districts. Support from Bunji, Bunrin, or Tatsunosuke was not evident, nor certainly did the domain find the Nakagawa crowds as benign.

As more and more people arrived at the *yachi* and as the evening wore into night, arguments continued in the center and around the periphery of the circles. Finally about midnight, a petition was drafted that appealed to Tadakata to remain in Tsurugaoka and to send a proxy in his place to Edo (text in Naganuma 1983:101). Many clearly felt this to be inadequate. A large band of about 1,000 men broke into the village group headman's compound and forced him to release Denshirō. Others set upon an advance party that happened along the main road, bearing some of the luggage of the imminent procession. With threats of violence at their back (*uchikorose! uchikorose!*), the porters and guards beat a hasty retreat to the castle.

At daybreak on the 11th, a large contingent of domain officials arrived at the village group headman's compound with several squads of soldiers. All the assembly leaders were summoned for some not-so-gentle dissuasion of further action. Apparently Genta and the others were convinced of the dangers, and returned to announce to the crowds that the officials were accepting the midnight petition for consideration; thus, the objectives of the rally had been achieved, they said, and all should disperse.

The crowd would have none of this and now turned on their leaders for betraying their cause. There was considerable confusion, some shouting threats at Genta and others giving chase to the fast-retreating leaders. When Genta took refuge in the home of the shrine priest, the crowds threatened to tear it down if he were not produced. Finally, he and other leaders were taken into protective custody by the domain soldiers; the still disgruntled set off for Yokoyama Village and attempted to destroy Genta's house. This turn of events diverted the focus of the crowds, and by afternoon they had largely returned home in confusion.

Meanwhile, Tadakata was sending a runner to Edo to plead illness in excuse for his now postponed departure. But the delay was not long. On the 13th and 14th, the domain held meetings in Fujishima with local headmen from all over Tagawa. Several of the most senior advisors made very rare appearances to underscore the domain's determination. They agreed to convey the sentiments of the assembly to shogunal officials, and issued only light disciplinary actions. On the 18th, amid enormous security precautions, Tadakata made his way out of the castle and through Nakagawa on the first leg of his journey. There were no disturbances.

Although intimidated from provocative actions against the domain lord, people in Tagawa and Akumi continued to hold large assemblies (for example, again on the beach at Sakata concurrent with the Nakagawa incidents); these in turn sparked a number of direct petition attempts in April and May. On April 23, thirty-nine persons set out for Edo as "representatives of Tagawa and Akumi," and a week later, another group left Akumi for both Edo and Mito. None of their entreaties was accepted for consideration, but back in Shōnai, the rallies continued. YKS 1980:981-82 and Naganuma 1983:105-107 describe another Nakagawa Yachi rally that resolved to go to Edo "to bring back our lord." Such action was not taken, but after transplanting in late June, groups totaling at least several hundred persons set off for Edo and for other domains in the northeast, in hopes of marshaling their support with another barrage of petitions (TSS 1974:424-25).

As Table 8 suggests, the petitioners were a diverse representation of the villagers. However, much of the funding for these trips was apparently supplied by town merchants. In late March, for example, Bunji and several others arranged a loan of 300 ryō from domain tax collectors and solicited fur-

TABLE 8
Registered Holdings of Shōnai Petitioners to Other Domains,
Spring 1841

Registered Holdings (koku)	No. to Yonezawa	No. to Akita	No. to Aizu	No. to Sendai	Totals
40 – 30	2	6	0	1	9
30 – 20	6	6	2	0	14
20 – 10	3	2	1	2	8
10 – 5	0	3	2	0	5
Fewer than 5	1	12	3	1	17
Unknown				1	1
Totals	12	29	8	5	54

SOURCE: These figures are cited in Igawa 1972:48 and are derived from Naitō 1841. The citation has been checked against the original.

ther contributions of 915 *ryō* from other merchants (TSS 1974:427-28; see p. 423 for earlier contributions by Kamo merchants). These monies were given to rural leaders to underwrite petitioners' travel to Edo, a trip that cost about 3 *ryō* per person at the time.

Besides the petition groups and mass assemblies, a third form of collective action was the organization of pilgrimages to the major shrines and temples on the plain and in the mountains around Shōnai. We have seen how initial efforts of merchants to bring groups to Haguro failed when the abbot refused; a similar attempt to organize an "open pilgrimage" (*manninkō*) to the Tokugawa shrines at Nikkō was discouraged by authorities. But by the spring, both Bunji and Bunrin were encouraging groups from villages across the plain to offer "prayers that Sakai might forever remain in Shōnai" (*goeijō gokitō*). Some of the pilgrimages were of the "naked prayer groups" (*hadaka mairi*) style. The felt efficacy of prayer is always difficult to evaluate, but even to those organizers and supplicants who might not have "really believed" that the gods would answer their prayers, it was widely accepted that the act of supplication (*ogamu*) was a way of gathering up and focusing energy, of settling one's mind and making one resolute. Pilgrimages also had political significance as mobilizations of popular support and demonstrations of strength to authorities that were, nonetheless, legal (they were duly reported to the shogunate).

Meanwhile, the complexion of the political center was changing quickly. On June 5, Ieyoshi retired most of his senior officials and installed Mizuno Tadakuni as his principal advisor to deal with what both feared to be waning shogunal power and an acute fiscal crisis. But the reform decrees that Mizuno promptly began issuing stirred intense opposition among other officials and most domain lords.[18] The fief transfer became an issue of contention in the ensuing power struggle. As a direct order, Ieyoshi and Mizuno saw it as an important test of shogunal prerogative, while Mito and other domains were equally adamant that such an exercise of central power be blocked. The domain lords were also increasingly concerned that full-scale fighting might break out in the Shōnai countryside and in the other affected domains following the transfer. Matters were further complicated in May by the sudden death of Nariyasu, the young lord of Kawagoe on whose behalf the transfer was initially ordered. The Kawagoe Domain elite continued to promote the move to Shōnai, while through June and July the Shōnai leaders stalled and sought allies.

Meanwhile in Shōnai, villagers and townspeople continued their agitations. Young adult males were organized into bands that moved about the countryside to keep feelings stirred up, to collect and distribute expense money, and to encourage the group prayer visits to shrines and temples. It is clear from his journal (Yuza-chō shi hensan iinkai 1978)

---

[18] Tadakuni had been Senior Councilor since 1834, but only now could exercise full power. Known as the Tenpō Reforms, his orders included draconian sumptuary laws, recoinage, forced loans, interest ceilings, and expulsion from Edo of workers from the countryside (Beasley 1972:63-65; Bolitho 1974:216-21; see the satirical print of Ieyoshi and Mizuno in Hayashi 1970:90-91).

that Bunrin was instrumental in coordinating these bands; it is also evident from communications among the bands that enthusiasm to contribute time and money was not universal (YKS 1980:979-81).

These bands fashioned themselves after common folklore images: there were, for example, the "heavens afire, earth afire" gang (the *tenbi chibi renjū*), the red *tengu* gang, and the blue *tengu* gang. The *tengu* was an especially potent figure in the countryside: as "half-man, half-hawk, with a large beak, long wings and glittering eyes, but a man's body, arms, and legs," the *tengu* of the Great Forest embodied the "perilous, ambivalent non-moral forces of nature" (Blacker 1975:182; see Figure 8). It could be called upon to avenge the

8. A *tengu* mask.

97

corruption and injustices of the elite.[19] It is tempting, therefore, to see these *tengu* bands as a casting of popular protest
actions in a powerful, deep strain of folk morality, but I
think that in this case that might be reading too deeply into
the *tengu* imagery. In many Akumi villages, the summer
"lion dance" (*shishi mai*) was known as the *tengu mai*, because
the dance leader wore a *tengu* mask rather than the more
common *shishi* mask (Igarashi 1977:778-80); as in much of
Japan, these dance groups for the summer festival for harvest
success were formed from the larger and all-inclusive young
adult male club in the village. These sodalities, which on
occasion could enforce local norms and punish deviants
(Varner 1977), were probably enlisted by Bunrin to coordinate some of the actions.

Success

What had come to be known nationally as the Three-way
Fief Transfer Order (*sanpō ryōchigae rei*) was finally resolved
on August 17 at a council of the highest shogunal advisors.
After ensuring that Mizuno would be absent, they suspended
the transfer: *kami no shishō (oboshimeshi) ni yori tenpu no sata
ni oyobazu kono mama Shōnai ryōchi tarubeshi* ("through the
benevolence of your lord, a transfer of fief is not necessary
and you are to remain in Shōnai"; Ono 1964:45). It was a
particular victory for the Mito lord, Tokugawa Nariaki,
Sakai's ally and an arch-critic of Mizuno Tadakuni. Capital
pundits, who had followed the maneuvers at the castle with
fascination, quickly turned Tadakuni's setback to satirical
verse.

> Kawagoe mo
> watari tomarite
> sata nagare   (Ono 1964:124)

[19] In the kabuki dance-play "Takatoki," for example, a *tengu* entices the
autocratic Hōjō regent Takatoki into a faster and faster *dengaku* dance in
order to tease and torment him for his harsh rulership.

One could translate this 17-syllable *senryū* comic verse literally as "Kawagoe's transfer was halted as the order was abandoned," but its modest bite depended on the associations among "river fording" (*kawagoe*), "crossing" (*watari*), and "flowing" (*nagare*).

> mizu no yaku
> mito toriage
> nagaretara
> naga no hinobe no
> haru wa kinuran   (ibid.)

An innocuous reading of this 31-syllable *kyōka* comic verse would be "when the irrigation guard opens the gate and begins to let the canal water flow, the lengthening days of spring are approaching." It also yielded a satirical reading: "Mizuno lost his power through the machinations of Lord Mito—even the Nagaoka fief transfer has been abandoned." That is, *mizu no* is Tadakuni, his office (*yaku*) undermined by the maneuverings of Lord Mito. With the permanent postponement (*naga no hinobe*), the safety and joys of spring (*haru*) have come to Sakai.

In Shōnai, the cancellation of the transfer was welcomed by all. Sped by special courier, the news reached Tsurugaoka on August 21, and people spilled out into the streets of the castle town to celebrate (Figure 9). Wealthier townspeople and village officials opened kegs of *sake*, ceremonial rice cakes were pounded, and prayers offered. Many of the revelers broke into the "Daikoku Dance" (*daikoku mai*), a dance referring to Sakai's reputation as the *Kanda daikoku-sama* that was a current rage and would remain popular for several years.[20] The dance was in the form of a "counting rhyme" (*kazoe uta*) of ten lines, beginning consecutively with a number from one to ten. The number's sound was repeated in the line for a cadence effect. Thus,

---

[20] See Ono 1964:123. The *daikoku mai* was also a more general term for celebratory dances invoking *daikoku ten*, the *daikoku* folk god.

9. Celebrations in Tsurugaoka.

ichi ni ima made ita kuni o
ni ni niwaka ni tokorokae
san ni Sakai no jūyaku wa
yottsu yoroshiku hakarite
itsutsu izure no hyōgi ni mo
muttsu muri na koto nareba
nanatsu Nagaoka hikiwatashi wa
yattsu yamu to no gosata nari
kokonotsu koogi mo kimarite
too ni tookoku osuwari osuwari
masu masu Sakai no daikokumai wa
misai na misai na

Again, the song gave a brief rendition of the sudden transfer order to lord Sakai and celebrated the ultimately successful efforts of his senior advisors in having it overturned. No doubt, though, the dancers were animated less by the simple lyrics than by the rhythmic tempo that they sustained.

Thus, the protests dissolved to the strains of festive music, but domain officials were left feeling a bit uneasy. However perfunctorily offered, their various injunctions against protest gatherings and direct petitioning to Edo had been frequently and blatantly ignored over the previous year. Some officials perhaps saw in this a potential challenge to their ability to restore order and begin to govern again. Others, who had actively coordinated some of the actions, were probably more concerned with presenting a correct appearance to shogunal officials. To both, at least some token punitive measures were necessary.

And token they were. Throughout September, village group headmen arranged for the "voluntary" submission of pledges (*kishomon*) by hundreds of village officers and identified activists. Some were individually signed, others jointly presented; all repudiated their activities, apologized contritely, and promised never again to disobey officials and attempt direct petitioning. The domain meted out a few very light punishments (typically, "scoldings" or ten- to fifteen-day house detentions), but then at the end of the year it distributed 12,000 bales of "charity rice."

Still the domain was careful to have the actions memorialized as an autonomous drive of honorable *hyakushō* driven by loyalty and gratitude to their lord (see Satō 1976:180). Bunji, the Tsurugaoka innkeeper activist, began collecting documents relating to the anti-transfer actions to set down an account for future generations of his household. This memoir took the form of a scroll of eighty-seven illustrations with commentary, depicting the entire course of events (anon. 1841). Bunji entitled it "The Floating Bridge of Dreams" (*Yume no ukihashi*), though it is doubtful that he actually did the paintings or script. Hearing of his project, the domain sent around an official to investigate the documents he collected and his finished scroll and insure that it did not carry any suggestion of domain complicity (TSS 1974:431-32).

As such, the "Tenpō Righteous Subjects' Movement" passed into local lore, a tale of brave townspeople and cultivators risking all dangers and rising up in loyal gratitude to support their beneficent but beleaguered domain lord. This version appeared in several retellings in the 1920s and 1930s, at a time of rice riots and rural dissatisfaction with tenancy conditions. In 1921, a local scholar, Saitō Kiyoshi, gathered together documents pertaining to the anti-transfer movement. He added an interpretive commentary and titled it *Tenpō kaikyo roku*, "A Record of the Brilliant Achievements of the Tenpō Era." This was printed under the auspices of the "Akumi County Educational Affairs Committee," a group of prominent, politically conservative Akumi residents who hoped to install it as a school textbook. It was republished in 1927 by a noted scholar of Tokugawa popular revolts, Ono Takeo, with the permission and using the manuscript of the current Honma family head.[21] The events of 1840-41 were glorified as an instance of justifiable action by honorable subjects, in contrast to the more common, and unjustified, anti-lord "peasant rebellions."

Later historians of these events have preferred to emphasize the orchestration of popular opinion and the mobilization of the crowd and to deny that it was a truly popular movement. Kuroda (1939) attacked Saitō's peasant hagiography and insisted that the movement was largely managed by Honma. Igawa (1972) portrayed events as manipulated by local officials and wealthy villagers. Yet this debate about the spontaneity or coercion of mass actions has only obscured a composite movement in which there was pushing and pulling in all directions. Perhaps by the summer of 1841 it was necessary for bands of village youth to whip up flagging commitment to the pilgrimages, but the evidence makes it apparent that Sakai officials and Honma had in fact been pushed toward resisting the order by pressure from below and that the mass meetings and prayer pilgrimages were

[21] It was republished in Ono 1964:37-142. Ono's 1927 volume was Borton's major source for his treatment of this movement.

hardly sustainable by coercion alone. Indeed, the crowds at Nakagawa Yachi were barely containable. (By contrast, we will later examine another Sakai drive to resist transfer; this time, in 1869, there was tight direction from above and only perfunctory and unenthusiastic participation from below.)

Of course the leadership and guidance of district and village-group headmen (whose own positions were threatened) and the machinations of Honma and high officials were indispensable. One can well imagine the difficulties of petitioning in Edo: financing the trip, drawing up and writing out the petitions, knowing whom to approach in what manner— even understanding the Edo dialect![22] Likewise, local actions were intricately involved with events in Edo and other domains; they came at the precise moment when the relative strength of shogunal authority and domain prerogatives hung in the balance. The transfer order and the Shōnai resistance immediately became part of the struggle in Edo by lords like Mito's Nariaki to block Mizuno Tadakuni from reasserting shogunate political hegemony. But whether the order's reversal may be attributed to Nariaki's manipulations in Edo or to the specter of protest and unrest in Shōnai is as futile as earlier measurements of elite orchestration or popular autonomy.

To be sure, the 1840-41 movement was "conservative" in seeking to preserve the existing political-economic arrangements in Shōnai. It had its roots and found its resolution *within* the tributary-mercantile web of the Tokugawa state. Threatened with a reshuffling, it was a spirited, pragmatic defense of a local status quo that played on the state's linkages and cleavages.

One is tempted to interpret it further as demonstration that a moral 'covenant," to adopt Scheiner's metaphor (1978), still bound ruler and subject on this northern plain late in the Tokugawa era. This I would resist because I am

---

[22] One rural Shōnai memo on Edo speech warned that locals going up to the capital might understand only a quarter of the conversation of Edo residents (*Edo kotobazukai no koto*, SSS 1977:873-74).

uncomfortable with his emphasis on a "covenant" entailing the "unilateral protection" by the ruler, the dispensation of munificence "unilaterally by the gracious acts of the more powerful" (ibid.:45). There is danger in accepting the language at face value. It was not identical interests but mutual advantage that forged the collaboration of villagers, merchants, and domain officials. Despite the unctious rhetoric of their pleas, few cultivators had illusions of their overlords' benevolence. Beneath the decorous platitudes of Confucian beneficence was a practical understanding of *tokusei*: rent reductions, tax concessions, available loans, and debt cancellation. These were extended only when persistently requested. Charity might be justified as moral obligation, but it was established in social negotiations.

That, of course, was the bind for the "honorable peasants." They had to seek but could not demand charity and grace. They were drawn by professions of loyalty and cries of indigence onto a stage of deference. But their very deference defied their superiors to respond as 'benevolent lords." Sakai and his subjects, landlords and their tenants, had established a balance of tribute and charity that proved tolerable through the hard times of the 1830s. The very terms by which the cultivators now lauded their overlords in their petitions to the shogunate and other domain lords restated the obligations of proper rule and the limits of legitimate tribute. In placing themselves behind such petitioners, the local elite and largeholders were making it more difficult (although as we will see, not impossible) for themselves to abuse power and prerogative in the future. Villagers now resisted Sakai's dunning of arrears and his fresh assessments of money and labor to move him and his retainers; but even more, they feared the outcomes of confrontations of a new lord to establish new limits of tribute. In mutual defense, both Sakai elite and Shōnai cultivators subscribed to a familiar language of obligation and protest that proved both effective and constraining.

FOUR

. . . And Unruly Mobs: The Ōyama
Disturbances of 1844

IF THE DOMAIN sought to keep alive the memory of the 1840–
41 protests as the zenith of honorable commoner behavior,
it was to castigate a subsequent protest against jurisdictional
transfer as the nadir of unruly mob action. This time, it was
the domain that found itself the target of agitations to prevent its taking over administration of shogunal lands within
Shōnai. It was a dispute that exposed longstanding commercial rivalries between Ōyama and Tsurugaoka *sake* brewers
and, within the Ōyama area, between town and rural brewers. If the former explains the intensity of Ōyama opposition
to the administrative transfer and the harshness of the authorities' reaction, the latter accounts for diffident participation of other shogunate villages in the protest, and insured
its ultimate failure.[1]

SAKE AND SHOGUNATE ADMINISTRATION

As mentioned above, there were three small areas within
Shōnai that had reverted to the shogunate in the 17th century—areas around the small town of Ōyama (25 villages
with registered yields of 10,000 *koku*), around Amarume (24
villages of 10,000 *koku*), and around Maruoka (15 villages of

[1] In documents of the time, participants and officials referred to these
events as the Ōyama Disturbances (*Ōyama sawagitachi*, e.g., OCS:239); historians now write of the *Ōyama sōdō*. My account draws from the original
documents published in YKS 1980:1019-49, Kokushō 1959, MCS 1974:237-
40, and OCS 1957:118-40 (portions of which appear verbatim in TSS
1974:433-42).

105

5,000 *koku*) (see Map 3). There was also a pocket of 14 villages to the north of Shōnai in Akita (2,000 *koku*) that came to be grouped administratively with these to constitute a single and, in the larger scheme of shogunal administration, marginal unit of shogunal territory.

In the spring of 1842, Sakai Tadakata went into retirement and passed the domain lordship and family headship to his eldest son, the thirty-year-old Tadaaki. In Edo, Mizuno Tadakuni was still pressing his reform programs, despite the reversal of the transfer order. He seized on Tadakata's retirement as a pretext for reassuming Shōnai shogunal lands, which Tadakata had been allowed to manage for the thirty-seven years of his lordship. He directed the shogunal regional office for northeastern Japan (in Obanazawa) to establish a site office in Ōyama to which Matsuyama Kumetarō and two subordinates were dispatched. While this action was consistent with Tadakuni's efforts to consolidate shogunal territories throughout Japan, there was clearly a measure of revenge as well.[2] Tadakuni was even more vindictive in appointing Tadaaki as a "sponsor" (*otetsudai*) of the massive Inba Swamp reclamation project that began in 1842 (Bolitho 1974:217-18). In mid-1843, Tadaaki was made financially responsible for the most difficult and costly section of the drainage channel; over 6,000 laborers had to be dispatched from, and supported by, the domain (TSS 1974:443-50; Akiyama et al. 1979:46-53).

But in November of 1843, Mizuno Tadakuni was dismissed, his radical reforms in disarray, the Inba Swamp project suspended, and his policies now repudiated.[3] Several

---

[2] This was the same year as a large uprising in Ōmi that resisted the shogunate's attempts to resurvey its lands in that region—protesting both the survey order and the corrupt manner in which officials conducted themselves. They were attacked, and the survey was ultimately suspended. Documents on this disturbance were also collated by Ono Takeo, as the *Tenpō gimin roku* in the same volume as the *Tenpō kaikyo roku* (1964:263-383; see also Borton 1938:107-20).

[3] Tadakuni made a brief comeback in the following year, 1844, but had lost much of his influence and played no role in the subsequent Ōyama Disturbances.

months later, on March 27, 1844, the new shogunate councilors granted Sakai Tadaaki's request to resume delegated
administration of the Shōnai territories. It was this anticipated return to Sakai administration that touched off immediate protest, particularly in the Ōyama area. The resistance
may be traced both to the substantial benefits of direct
administration to residents in the shogunal territories and to
longstanding tensions between Ōyama *sake* brewers and
Sakai authorities and brewers in Tsurugaoka.

Sake brewing was a commercial activity to which authorities were particularly sensitive because of its effect on both
the supply and the price of rice, from which it was made. It
was thus one of the first products to come under administrative restrictions: the *kabunakama* system of fee licensing of
brewers, who were then organized into local monopsonistic
guilds, and regulation of *sake* production volumes in accordance with rice harvest totals (thus, there were "full years,"
"two-thirds years," "half years," "one-third years," and "no
production years"). Such regulation was as porous here as in
other matters; unlicensed brewing and overproduction by licensed brewers were endemic issues of contention.[4]

For much of the 1600s, *sake* production and trade was controlled by Tsurugaoka merchants, but by the mid-1700s,
they were eclipsed by Ōyama brewers, who established their
small rural town as the largest brewing center on the plain
(see Figure 10). By the turn of the 19th century, there were
about thirty-five brewers in this overgrown village of about
2,900 persons in 670 or so households.[5] About half of their

[4] See OCS 1957:246 for two examples of private agreements among licensed Ōyama brewers to produce fixed volumes over their official quotas
and to share any penalties that might result from disclosure. These examples, moreover, are from the 1830s, when the region faced prolonged rice
shortfalls. The most extensive discussion of Ōyama *sake* is OCS 1957:228-
328, from which I have drawn extensively in this section. See MCS
1974:181-90 and Satō Tōzō 1983:160-77 for materials on village *sake* brewers
in the rural shogunate territory.

[5] Records in 1846 listed 2,911 persons in 667 households, roughly similar
to totals seventy-five years before. Of these households, 542 were registered
as "propertied cultivator households" (*hyakushō*), 109 as "landless cultivator

10. A sketch map (upper left) and listing (lower half) of Ōyama town *sake* brewers.

production was marketed within Shōnai—in and around the castle town, in the many drinking houses of the port of Sakata, and across the Akumi countryside. The other half was shipped through Sakata, principally to Niigata and to Matsumae in Hokkaidō.

Their Tsurugaoka rivals attributed the rise of Ōyama *sake* to an unfair advantage: under direct shogunate administration, the Ōyama brewers were exempt from the domain's levy on *sake* production (which for them would have totaled about 120 *ryō* annually). Instead they tendered a far more modest 23 *ryō* concession payment to the shogunate office. Tsurugaoka brewers pressured the domain into imposing a tariff and a quota on the less expensive Ōyama *sake* brought into domain territory. This did little to stem the flow, and so in 1774 it appointed Kashiwagura Kuemon, a Tsurugaoka brewer and dealer, as the sole importing agent, responsible for collecting and submitting a single, fixed tariff sum. The domain also imposed restrictions on containers (the Ōyama brewers were prohibited from selling their popular portable-sized cask), sales seasons (they were not to sell in domain areas before the first day of the fifth month), and transport (they were banned from using boats or horse carts to carry their *sake* and could only use porters). Yet these also were to little effect. A detailed report by frustrated Tsurugaoka brewers in 1794 claimed that over four times the allowable amount of Ōyama *sake* was flooding dealers and taverns of Sakata and Tsurugaoka (OCS 1957:246). It suggested that Kashiwagura was proving to be a more effective export agent for the Ōyama brewers than import regulator for the domain. No doubt it was correct: the Ōyama brewers promptly used Kashiwagura as negotiating agent to deflect the substantial increases in duty payments that the report called for with minimal compensation payments to Tsurugaoka brewers and to domain officials (OCS 1957:248).

---

households" (*mizunomi*), with a few temples and mountain priest households (OCS 1957:222-23).

The tide was reversed in the early 1800s. In 1803, Kashi-wagura was removed, and in 1805, with resumption of Sakai administration over Ōyama and the other shogunate lands, more effective control was imposed on the Ōyama brewers (YKS 1980:800-802). They were further battered by the series of disastrous rice harvests in the 1830s. These dampened demand for their *sake* and even threatened their supply of rice; at one point in the decade, the domain banned all rice sales to brewers and later rationed such sales. By 1833, for example, Ōtake Saburō's debt totaled 851 *ryō* and he had to secure a 200-*koku* rice advance from the large landholder Akino to brew that winter (OSC 1957:300-302). Ōyama brewers were also drawn into a lengthy dispute to prevent Sakata town magistrates from imposing crippling sales restrictions (ibid.:251-53).

Though beleaguered, Ōyama remained a brewers' town; in 1843, eleven of the twelve town officials were licensed brewers—two ward headman, five elders, and five cultivator representatives. They had thus welcomed the return of direct shogunal administration in 1842. Their tax burdens were lowered, and Matsuyama, the assigned office head, proved very helpful in having some of the sales restrictions removed and in promoting sales outside Shōnai. Town carpenters, coopers, and other artisans who depended on the brewing houses were again no longer liable for any of the miscellaneous domain levies on trades and crafts. And landholders in the area enjoyed the return of a substantially lower land tax burden: under direct administration, the basic land tax rate was lower, there were fewer ancillary levies, and they were permitted to tender taxes with rice vouchers and cash.[6]

---

[6] This differential no doubt explains the noticeably lukewarm support that Ōyama residents had given to the anti-transfer actions of 1840-41. In fact, on hearing of the transfer order, Sumii Yazaemon (Kaga-ya), who had been the largest *sake* brewer in Ōyama in 1788 but who was forced to the verge of closing down in the 1830s, had sent his son, Manpei, to Kawagoe to introduce his firm, and Ōyama brewers generally, to the prospective new lord. Upon his return, Manpei and several other Ōyama youths were arrested and later died in the Tsurugaoka Jail.

It is thus not surprising that Ōyama area residents reacted sharply to the news that reached them on April 1, 1844 (perhaps intentionally to coincide with the busy transplanting season, the official transfer of administration had been set for June 13). In short order, the large brewer Kaga-ya, three fellow brewers and town officers, and the headman of the village on the town's northern border had established a headquarters at the village group granary. They composed a petition of protest for circulation throughout Ōyama, Amarume, and Maruoka villages. Signed by the "three village officers" of seventy-three shogunate villages, it was presented to Matsuyama within a week (text in Kokushō 1969:124 and OCS 1957:122). When Matsuyama declined to accept it, they drew up a much longer petition to carry directly to Edo (text in YKS 1980:1019-21). It complained of onerous taxation and discrimination in boundary and irrigation disputes with domain villages. It noted that the seven decades of harsh Sakai policies since the late 18th century had caused a precipitous decline in the Ōyama town population ("from about 1,000 households to about 700") and a similar depopulation of the shogunate countryside. It hinted that there had been improvements under the recent return to shogunal administration but warned that further decline was now imminent. It was signed by "the village officers, representing all the ordinary people" (komae ichidō murayakunin sōdai).

Six persons representing the three shogunate territories were appointed to make the petition trip to Edo. However, antagonisms within and between these three areas soon complicated the drive. Initial plans to leave by boat from the small port of Yunohama were blocked by the Yunohama headman's refusal to allow them a boat. They were then to go up the Mogami along the inland route, but the representatives from Amarume dropped out, ostensibly because of parents' illness,[7] and only four made the journey. Indeed, the

---

[7] In this case a pretext, but not always. Direct petitioners risked death or long imprisonment, and those with vulnerable family situations could bow out on those grounds.

Ōyama leaders soon discovered that two village headmen in Amarume, Tamimasu and Kiyosuke, were secretly cooperating with the domain. On the evening of April 16, they summoned Tamimasu to the Ōyama Granary and had him violently beaten; he was then forced to write a note summoning Kiyosuke, who was also beaten severely when he appeared. Several days later, crowds attacked the houses of two other suspected domain informants in Ōyama itself. Meanwhile, the four remained in Edo throughout April and early May, and it was not until May 18 that they were successful in forcing their petition upon the Senior Councilor Doi Toshitsura and, three days later, upon a Superintendent of Finances. Both rejected the documents, and the four were turned over to the Obanazawa regional office.

With their Edo initiative a failure and the transfer looming on June 13, the Ōyama leaders realized that only direct action could now prevent it. They asked village officers to bring *all* their villagers to Ōyama in advance of that date to create a human blockade (text in OCS 1957:124). When the Yunohama officers refused to announce this directive in their village, they too were attacked and their houses destroyed. As the day of transfer approached, the domain tried to dissuade people from gathering at Ōyama by stationing officials along principal roads and at ferry landings. Still several thousands made their way to town, camping out at several temples and on the high hill behind the town. They made up cotton banners with village name and insignia, prepared lanterns and torches, and rang the temple bells and blew on conch shells to arouse the crowds. As planned, they formed a human wall around the shogunal office; they blockaded the approaches into town with bamboo barricades and destroyed the bridge on the main road to Tsurugaoka. Domain officials responded by surrounding the town with several companies of soldiers, dressed in full battle gear and armed with bows, rifles, and other weapons (YKS 1980:1027). The domain's liason officer with shogunal territories, Hayashi Motozaemon, attempted to negotiate with Matsuyama, but the latter was now very coy about supporting a forcible transfer. The troops were kept on the periphery of town during the day and night, and the next morning negotiations between Matsuyama and Hayashi resumed. They finally agreed to postpone the transfer pending fresh instructions from Edo, and on the condition that the barricades be dismantled, the troops were withdrawn to Tsurugaoka.

Several months passed before two high shogunate magistrates arrived in Ōyama on August 11; a decision had been made in Edo to complete the transfer and punish those who had protested in the spring. They were put up at the house of Tanaka Tarozaemon. Though a branch household of the Ōyama Village Group headman, Tanaka Tokuemon, and the largest brewer in town, Tarozaemon had secretly shifted to the Sakai side; this was probably after the June demonstrations, when perhaps he realized the futility of further resistance. Tarozaemon helped the Edo magistrates devise a trap for luring the protest leaders. First they pretended to apprehend those like Kiyosuke and Tamimasu who had informed on the protestors, detaining them at the Ōyama Granary. They then sent out word that they would entertain any petitions about the transfer that people wished to present. As soon as Sumii, Saburoji, and the other leaders came forward, they were arrested and locked up in Tarozaemon's private storehouse. This was followed by a general roundup; OCS (1957:127) lists twenty-one arrests, including Tokuemon, the village group headman. Moreover, each of the seventy-three villages was required to send one resident for confinement as guarantor of village behavior.[8]

The shogunate officials decided to try the arrested at a temporary court in Shiono Town, to the south of Shōnai on the coast of Echigo. Shiono was also a shogunate territory,

[8] Volunteers were obviously scarce. Futakuchi villagers finally resorted to lottery (*kujitori*), but signed a written agreement that Bunzō, who was chosen, would receive a daily "allowance" (*tema*) of 300 *mon* and that in the event of death or serious punishment, his family would receive a "condolence payment" (*chōkin*) of 100 *ryō* (text in YKS 1980:1021-22).

administered by Yonezawa Domain, and that domain provided a large force of soldiers to convey the prisoners from
Ōyama. The leaders were carried in penal baskets (*tomaru
kago*), the others were led manacled (Figure 11). The inter-
rogations were unrelenting; Kichiemon, a brewer from Ara-
machi, was said to have committed suicide at Shiono.
Moreover, as the sessions progressed, more and more village
officers and other suspects were summoned before the court,
until over 3,000 had made the trip. As it was October, just
at harvest, many sought exemptions from appearing, but to
no avail. The nature of the trial, if that indeed is an appropriate term, is not clear, but the submission of a unified tes-
timonial document by the "defendants" suggests that they
did not view the verdict as a foregone conclusion. The document laid out in detail their complaints about Sakai and his
administration. It reiterated the various extra levies and duties that the domain assessed over and above those during
direct administration. It accused the domain of artificially inflating its land tax calculations. It complained of discrimination in land and water disputes between domain and shogunate villages, of utter disregard of property and person by
domain warriors (trampling through fields and *yachi* and as-
saulting any who complained), and of arbitrary arrests and
unwarranted punishments by domain officials (text in YKS
1980:1025–28).

The trials at Shiono continued through the end of 1844;
their conclusion coincided with the transfer of administration
to Sakai on December 26 and 27. Five of the leaders, including Sumii, were led off to Edo, where they died in jail before
final conviction, not an uncommon fate in the Edo jails at
the time. Twenty-three others were detained at the Tsurugaoka prison. Sentencing was withheld until June of 1846;
over fifty persons were transported under guard from Tsurugaoka and Ōyama to the regional office in Obanazawa,
where over 3,500 punishments were meted out. About 3,400
of these were rather stiff fines, assessed on a sliding scale.
Village headmen were fined 5 *kanmon*, other village officers

a

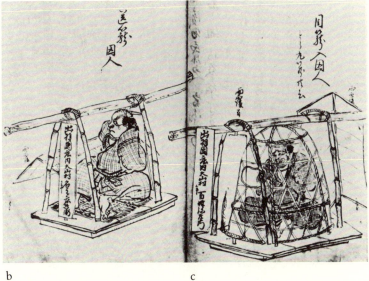

b   c

11. Conveying the arrested Ōyama protestors to the
Shiono hearings. a. Prisoner manacled and led by soldier.
b. Prisoner carried in a transport basket (*okuri kago*). c. A leader,
Kaga-ya Yazaemon, transported in a penal basket (*tōmaru kago*).

3 *kanmon*, and all registered cultivators 2 *kanmon* per 100 *koku* of registered holdings. Twenty-three sentences were even more severe, ranging from imprisonment to expulsion and banishment; all of these twenty-three also suffered confiscation of property. Those who were banished lost house and land, while the most serious offenders had all assets, fixed and moveable, confiscated. Most of these twenty-three were from Ōyama town itself, including village officers and several brewers, who lost their brewing licenses as well. Others were headmen, cultivators, and priests from villages around Ōyama and Maruoka; none was from Amarume. Also punished were Matsuyama, his two deputies, and nine Sakai officials (see the listing of punishments in YKS 1980:1046-49 and OCS 1957:134).

Needless to say, the incident left commercial relations between Tsurugaoka and Ōyama thoroughly embittered, but it served to neither's advantage. In Ōyama, Tarozaemon's complicity in luring the agitators to their arrest had divided the town. A new set of town officials was installed, drawn largely from brewers who had not been among the protest's leaders. The domain tightened its regulation of Ōyama *sake*, and the town's brewers lost forever their prominence in the local economy. Even their exports to Niigata and Matsumae faltered with stiffer competition from Ōsaka area brewers. In 1843, the thirty-seven Ōyama brewers produced *sake* from 2,468 *koku* of rice; by 1865, its thirty-four brewers used only 750 *koku* of production rice.[9] Interestingly, though, Tsurugaoka town brewers did not seem to benefit greatly from this. Rather, the only real increases in 1843-65 were realized by the smaller village brewers, a point consonant with Smith's model (1973) of "rural-centered growth" in late Tokugawa Japan. It is also a commentary on the inability of Ōyama area activitists to forge a unified front among sho-

[9] See the table on TSS 1974:442, but also the text on page 440. The table has several misprints. See OCS 1974:302-304 for details of Tokuemon's decline.

gunate areas against the transfer order; they were deceived by village officers and residents in Amarume, an area of small village brewers who had suffered from and remained suspicious of those in Ōyama town (OCS 1957:276-79).

Indeed, to most present-day historians of the Ōyama Disturbance, it was the town brewer elite which was the principal force behind the anti-transfer actions. While this is undeniable, it does not follow that the thousands of villagers and townspeople who manned the barricades on June 12 and 13 were compelled to lend their support to a local elite threatened by a predatory domain. In many cases, *sake* brewing in the Tokugawa countryside proved a lucrative business, a basis of paddy land accumulation, and a vehicle of patronage by offering work to local cultivators during the winter off-season.[10] It would be wrong, though, to overestimate the Ōyama brewers' control of the local economy. Labor demands were not great; most houses appear to have had two to five full-time employees, with perhaps four to ten persons added during the winter months; thus the direct *sake* labor force in Ōyama probably did not exceed several hundred. (And wages were low; in 1849, winter work in the breweries paid 50-200 *mon* a day.) While several of the houses accumulated substantial paddy lands in the villages around the town, most had rather modest holdings. In 1846, the medium-size brewer, Haneda Yojibei, yielded 150 bales of rice from his parcels, almost all of which were let to or mortgaged from ten cultivators. His acreage seems to have been about five hectares. At the same time, though, he had outstanding loans of 726 *ryō* and owed a large quantity of rice; merely the interest due on the rice was over twice his annual yield.[11] In short, resistance from the Ōyama brewers was a

[10] Because of the cold-temperature fermentation process, brewing was done over the winter months, from late October through early March.

[11] OCS 1957:299-300. If the houses were not getting their rice from their own lands, where did it come from? Three other sources were more important: purchases from cultivators and rice dealers; loans of rice from domain granaries, repaid in *sake* or cash after sales; and consignments of rice

defensive reaction by a sagging commercial interest, not the aggressive demands of an entrenched and expanding elite.

Small landholders had their own reasons to oppose the transfer. Evidence from Futakuchi Village (in the Ōyama shogunate area) reveals that while the domain did not replace cash or rice voucher payment of taxes, it did manipulate the tax rice-cash conversion formula to its considerable advantage. Under shogunal administration in 1842 and under Sakai administration in 1847, Futakuchi had a total rice assessment of about 160 *koku*; in both years, it only tendered about 42 *koku* of that in rice, paying the balance in cash. This cash payment, though, jumped from 70 *kanmon* in 1842 to 105 *kanmon* in 1847 (and 138 *kanmon* in 1864; TSS 1975a:56). Having enjoyed a fixed conversion rate for several decades, shogunate villages now faced escalating taxes (the increment of which was retained by the domain and not passed along to the shogunate).

As with the earlier agitations against a transfer directive, one need not celebrate an autonomous popular uprising to deny a reductive interpretation of elite manipulation. The Ōyama Disturbance was a composite movement that drew definition and direction from the petitions of a few aggrieved town brewers and from the barricades of many more aroused villagers. And it stymied the domain through the summer of 1843 because of the collusion of local shogunal officers in blocking the transfer. Yet it failed, as much because commercial interests were divided as because domain and higher shogunal authorities acted in concert. This allowed a much harsher disposition of the protesters by the authorities. Domain interests as well as shogunal prerogatives were at stake this time, and Sakai elders could enlist high shogunal officials

---

from cultivators, landlords, temples, and individual retainers (who would then receive *sake* in exchange at a negotiated rice-to-*sake* rate, typically 2:1 or 5:3). This was a very different supply pattern from that of rural brewers like Tōzō of Futakuchi Village, who depended almost entirely on his landholdings. It was perhaps the vicissitudes of their supply, rather than vagaries of market demand, that left the town brewers at a commercial disadvantage.

in going to considerable lengths to deal with the protesters. Hearings at two different locations (Shiono and Obanazawa), the conveying of prisoners, the 3,500 fines—these formed a response far in excess of the shogunate's meager revenue from these miniscule holdings.

A final note to this episode again illustrates how national figures intersected local events but also how pulses of popular actions in Shōnai were curiously out of phase with peaks of intensity elsewhere. In 1843, Suzuki Shigetane, a follower of the noted National Learning (*kokugaku*) scholar Hirata Atsutane, passed through Shōnai on his way to Akita, where Atsutane had been remanded by the authorities. Returning to Edo, Shigetane passed again through Shōnai and stopped in Ōyama in late June 1844, just after the showdown at the shogunate office. He stayed with the brewer Ōtake Saburō (Mitsuakira), whose interest in National Learning scholarship went back to 1821, when he traveled to Ise to study with Arakida Suehogi. Shigetane remained in Shōnai for about six months, lecturing on the Man'yōshū and Atsutane's thought in both Ōyama and Tsurugaoka. Ōtake had been on the verge of bankruptcy through the 1830s but he managed to finance construction of a small house in his compound in which Shigetane established a school, the *Sakaki no ya*. Shigetane returned to the area at least seven times in the next fifteen years to lecture to an ardent circle of warrior and merchant followers that included a rice dealer, doctor, Shintō priest, and several minor domain officials from the castle town, a Buddhist priest from Sakata, and a member of the Akino family of Kamo. Seemingly diverse, it was not unlike the composition of other cells of Hirata nativism. Shigetane adopted one of Ōtake's sons and even became implicated in an abortive effort by the Ōyama brewers' attempt to stimulate sales by moving into the Edo market in the late 1850s. They funded him lavishly to promote their *sake* with leading wholesalers. He proved a poor agent, most of the *sake* was lost at sea in a storm, and the venture proved calamitous to the already sinking fortunes of the Ōyama brewers (OCS 1957:261-70).

Ōtake Saburō does not appear in any of documents of the Ōyama Disturbances, nor did Shigetane have any apparent contact with its leaders. Rather the web of contacts suggests intellectual ties that spanned and diluted commercial and administrative rivalries. The point is significant because Hirata's thought, with its ritual and scriptural support for reverence of the Emperor, was a central text of the new "Restorationism" discourse. In the 1850s, members of the *Sakaki no ya* circle plotted with others against the domain establishment, but in 1844, Hirata's thought was tangential to this ill-fated burst of local protest. Shōnai in the 1840s was not immune to the new political discourse and economic forces that posed radical alternatives to the present arrangements, but in this domain, the coalescence of collective popular action for the first time in two centuries was catalyzed by strains *within* the existing web of tributary and mercantile relationships.

FIVE

Restoration in Shōnai

THE 1850s saw factional strife among the warrior-retainers of Shōnai Domain that replicated the larger struggles in Edo between supporters of the shogunate and advocates of stronger prerogatives for both the court and the larger domains. By the early 1860s, though, such dissent was neutralized, and the domain elite had closed ranks behind the shogun. In the mid-1860s, while the shogunate was paralyzed by indecision and Edo wracked with intrigue, Sakai officials within the domain took several steps to tighten control over the population and to increase their call on both agricultural production and commercial activity. The measures were obviously unpopular with villagers and townspeople alike, but significantly, they provoked none of the disturbances and rioting that was widespread elsewhere in Japan, even in the most volatile year of 1866. With generous financial assistance from Honma, the domain was able to mount strong military resistance to the new Restoration forces in 1868. It was only after Sakai's surrender and the partition of Shōnai that popular discontent assumed organized form in what has come to be known as the Tengu Disturbances of 1869-71. These actions were directed at local representatives of the new central leadership who had been sent to Akumi to establish direct control over Sakata Port and the Akumi countryside. Despite several attempts to control these agitations, they were unable to establish order in Akumi. In 1871, Ōkuma and other Meiji leaders were forced to the highly unusual step of reconstituting Tagawa and Akumi under the old domain elite. It was a most unexpected "restoration" in Shōnai.

A Tightening of Administration

Suzuki Shigetane regularly visited Shōnai from 1844 to 1857, and his lectures on Atsutane's variant of National Learning and "reverence for the Emperor" (*sonnō*) found an attentive audience among a small group of retainers, merchants, and priests. Some of Sakai officials stationed at the Edo mansion also developed similar leanings from the more radical capital currents. Together, they formed a "revolutionary faction" (*kaikakuha*) that plotted in 1858 to replace the domain lord with a Sakai sympathizer of their Restorationist cause (TSS 1974:469-77). By the early 1860s, most had been eased from office or dispatched to the Hokkaidō coast guard, and domain leaders lined up behind the shogunate in its final years. In 1863, Suzuki Shigetane was assassinated in his Edo home; that same year, Shōnai was one of thirteen domains assigned to police the Edo wards. A year later, it was ordered to join the abortive shogunate expedition to punish the rebellious Satsuma Domain. To finance their preparations, Sakai elders assessed its population 49,400 *ryō*, and exacted an additional 40,200 *ryō* from its designated merchants (of which Honma contributed the lion's share, 30,000 *ryō*; TSS 1975a:54). Sakai warrior-retainers continued their police patrols of Edo through the worst of the rioting of 1866, and the domain sent 1,000 soldiers to join in the burning on Satsuma Domain's Edo mansion in 1867.

During these years, domain authority rested with those of its officials in the Edo mansion, where the Sakai lords remained, seldom venturing back to Shōnai. In 1861, the 21-year-old Tadatomo became lord. When he died a year later, Tadazumi, a younger brother then 10 years old, was chosen to succeed. Over the next few years, two middle-rank retainers, who had distinguished themselves in the Edo police patrols, worked themselves to the side of the young lord: Matsudaira Chikahiro (1839-1913) and Suge Sanehide (1830-1903). Both were to remain in effective control of the domain, and later prefecture, during the popular protests to come.

Fearful of the disorder in the capital but confident of their ability to administer back home, domain officials in Shōnai moved to reassert political authority and economic control over population and production. In September of 1864, in appreciation for the domain's policing of Edo, the shogunate added its 27,000 *koku* of Tagawa and Akita lands to Sakai's fief grant. The domain, which had administered the territories since the contested transfer in 1844, now began to eliminate all differences of taxation and impose its full schedule of duties on the villages, including tax in rice rather than cash or voucher. This prompted a petition from village officers in Ōyama Village Group to their village group headman that recalls the objections expressed twenty years before and prefigures many of the demands of the next decade. They sought continued permission for their villages to pay 70% of the basic tax in Sakata rice vouchers, to be exempt from the domain's rural public works levy (*gōfushin mai*) and to pay instead toward a separate village group fund, to be excused from the domain's mandatory rice borrowings (*tanebujiki-mai*), and to pay all assessments for village expenses in cash rather than in rice (text in TSS 1975a:58). The domain apparently agreed to continue tax payment in cash and voucher, but made the tax rice-cash conversion formula even more onerous. There were, however, no violent eruptions like those twenty years before.

Then, in the autumn of 1866, a very poor rice harvest and a sharp rise in the price of rice fueled many rumors of unrest through Shōnai. On October 9, the domain granted "reductions" (*teatemai*) on the year's tax totaling 10,000 bales, later increasing this by another 3,000 bales, a very modest sum when its total revenues exceeded 150,000 bales. On November 2, posters announced a protest gathering to be held in Tsurugaoka, and on the evening of the 5th, several hundreds of townspeople were joined by people from the countryside at the castle town's main shrine, Sannō, to agitate against the

123

rising prices of rice and other commodities. Talk turned to breaking into the storehouses of several prominent rice dealers, and at least one was attacked.[1]

In November and December, there were other large gatherings on the plain, and some of them turned nasty. In Amarume and Kiyokawa, groups of cultivators attacked the houses of several village group headmen and village headmen, demanding the elimination of ancillary levies and a 50% reduction in that year's basic land tax (Igawa and Satō 1969:17). In mid-November, 360 poor households in the small port of Kamo requested rice loans from the two resident designated merchants, Akino Moemon and Oya Hachiroji; they sought one bale per household per month for the five winter months, November through March. The rural magistrate argued that this would be impossible to meet because it would set a dangerous precedent for other areas. Akino and Oya, however, discussed the demand with village officials and considered three responses: loaning rice to the households, selling it to them at a reduced price, or distributing "charity rice" (*hodokoshi mai*). They eventually decided to offer 300, then 400, bales of charity rice.

1866 was a year of great ferment throughout Japan (for example, see Totman 1980:219-24). Aoki (1971) has graphed it as the peak year of commoner unrest, and even if his typology exaggerates and homogenizes, there were large organized actions in a number of regions. Sippel (1977) has given us a finely grained picture of the rioting in Bushū, an area of Musashi to the west and northwest of Edo that included the Matsudaira domain of Kawagoe. There, for six days in late July, rampaging mobs spread through three hundred villages and towns, attacking wealthy merchants and landlords, destroying their property in their storehouses and burning their ledgers. It may have been an "outburst," but it was not feverish "mass vandalism"; Sippel insists in-

[1] There is a brief description of this gathering in the diary of a domain official, Shigeta Matagen (cited in Igawa 1972:52).

stead that it was "a punitive and relatively disciplined attack on the property of selected rich households" (ibid.:301).

Shōnai historians, too, read the "semi-proletarian" composition of the crowd at the Sannō Shrine and the rural house attacks as indicative of the national "millenarian conditions" (*yonaoshi jokyō*) of the year (e.g., Igawa 1972:52, Satō 1981:24). Yet these actions pale before the force and scale of the Bushū mobs or those in Kami-murayama (Aoki 1972). In their search for a Shōnai past of radical collective protest, both Igawa and Satō have exaggerated the intensity and duration of the 1866 actions.

On the contrary, I find it more reasonable to suppose that the greater shocks to Matsudaira, Suge, and other domain leaders were the disorders that they witnessed in the streets of Edo. The mutedness of the 1864-66 protests back home only emboldened them to harden their policies further. In 1866, for example, they received permission from the shogunate to increase domain claims on commodities passing through the port of Sakata by revising upwards its schedule of port taxes (*minato yakusen*) and adding a number of goods to its taxable list (TSS 1975a:58-60). In doing so, they ignored both the pleas of the Sakata merchants and ship chandlers and the protests of merchants in upriver interior domains. Then in May of 1867, domain officials began a revision of the land registers (*mizuchō aratame*) throughout the domain (see TSS 1974:489-90, TSS 1975a:60-61, MCS 1974:244-46, and Igawa 1966). Over the decades, land sales and loans with land collateral had created well-known discrepancies between registered holders and actual owners; these continual transfers resulted in much land within villages under non-resident cultivation and/or non-resident ownership (both termed *irisaku* in the documents of the time). In revising the land books, the domain hoped to trace the collateralized and purchased parcels and to register the present owners; it planned to survey these parcels and determine their actual rents (*sakutoku mai*). Then, it proposed to levy a new tax on these non-resident holdings: 8% of the

125

rent for owners resident outside the village group of the parcel and 5% if resident within the village group but outside the village.[2]

The announced objective of the 1867 revisions was to discourage vast absentee holdings and so protect the self-cultivating smallholder, who remained in domain ideology the production base of the political-economic order. There were no doubt more practical objectives too. The domain was both adding a new ancillary tax and identifying the large landholders, who were thought better able and, once registered, more liable to pay the taxes due. As usual, the rigor of implementation fell short of the force of its promulgation, as comparison between the 1867 registers and 1876 post-Land Tax Revision registers makes clear. There were no on-site surveys; rather, village and village group officials were summoned to the domain administrative hall. They came with their registers in hand, and sat about making sufficient revisions of their books as to satisfy the rural magistrates, who gazed over their shoulders. The new non-resident holder levy not only drew the predictable resistance from largeholding merchants; the 5% levy on non-resident holdings within a single village group also incited smallholders, many of whom let out and/or tenanted parcels in adjacent villages.[3]

The Boshin War and the Fall of Shōnai

No doubt the domain would have pursued the land register revision with even more diligence had not its attention been diverted by imminent dangers to the shogunate, to whom

[2] This levy, *irisaku yonaimai mai*, was the third such levy on non-resident landholders. The first dated to 1796 and was 13% of declared rent. The second was instituted in 1838 and was approximately 7% of the registered rent (TSS 1974:490).

[3] See MCS 1974:245, in which the villages of Yokoyama Village Group protested that they considered themselves in this respect to be a "single village."

the Sakai lord, Tadazumi, was firmly committed. With the palace coup in early January of 1868 and the shogunate's defeats at Toba and Fushimi, fighting between Restoration forces and shogunate supporters broke out in what is known as the Boshin War.[4] After Keiki's surrender and the fall of Edo Castle on May 3, strong resistance to the new authorities remained in the northeast, especially in Aizu, Sendai, and Shōnai Domains. Shōnai began maneuvers in May; soon it dispatched forays south into Echigo and sent larger forces up the Mogami River to take over the Shinjō Basin. In June, it met with twenty-five other northeastern domains at Sendai to draw up an alliance agreement; they were joined by six Echigo domains in an Alliance of Northeastern Domains (Ōu reppan dōmei). Fighting between the Shōnai army and a force from Akita Domain to the north broke out on August 23, and Shōnai remained on the offensive for several weeks.

To finance these extensive military operations, the domain turned again to its designated merchants and to the cultivators. From the former it sought "military expense" contributions (gunyōkin). Honma had already given the domain 93,400 ryō and rice vouchers totaling 16,000 bales in May; now, he offered his services in buying weapons from a Dutch merchant.[5] From the latter they demanded both men and materiel. Those villages within 8 kilometers of the castle town were to present men for induction into commoner army squads. All villages were assigned quotas, by muradaka and household numbers, for cash contributions toward munitions and for a wide range of supplies. Jōzenji, for exam-

---

[4] See Bolitho 1979 for some of the developments in northeastern Japan and Sheldon 1975 (who uses the term Civil War, not Boshin).

[5] This was the agent Eduard Schnell, who was selling arms to a number of domains in the northeast (see Bolitho 1979:266). Honma used his cousin Kōsō as an actual contact with Schnell (Satō 1976:193-95). As Table 3 indicates, from 1841 through May of 1868, the main Honma house had offered "contributions" (sunshikin) of 144,720 ryō and had left another 357,572 ryō as "uncollected loans" (saikakukin). These sums were significant even to Honma; the main house's total net income in 1867 was 268,347 ryō (of which 182,306 ryō was from moneylending (kin'yū).

ple, a village in Arase District with 42 households and a *muradaka* of 236 *koku*, was assessed 1,692 person-days as coolies and laborers, 11 men impressed into the commoner militia, 15 *ryō* toward munitions, 18.1 *koku* of rice, unspecified quantities of pickled vegetables, 9 bedquilts, 14 sets of nightwear, and 273 pairs of straw sandals (TSS 1975a:69-71, Igawa 1972:54).

Frustrating the domain's military operations was the need to deploy some of its units against its new subject population. Tanabe Gihei, then a domain rural affairs officer (*gundai*), was sent to the Shinjō Basin to administer this new territory. He related in his diary numerous mass gatherings of cultivators in that area; there were attacks on village officials' and merchants' houses throughout the summer and early fall (Igawa 1972:54-55). In response to claims that harvest prospects were poor, the domain on October 12 authorized a 50% reduction in basic land taxes in the Shinjō area and agreed to investigate further claims of especially hard-hit villages—to which several villages immediately petitioned for relief from all taxes (*munengu*).

Meanwhile resistance to the Meiji forces was collapsing. With the fall of Aizu-Wakamatsu Castle on November 4 and the surrender of Yonezawa and then Sendai Domains, Shōnai faced the brunt of the Meiji attack. Two days later, Sakai's advisors presented a formal document of surrender to the Meiji expeditionary army. The domain withdrew its border guard units, and on November 11, the Meiji army under Kuroda Kiyotaka entered Tsurugaoka and Sakata. As initial conditions of surrender, all Sakai forces were pulled back to Shōnai, where their weapons were confiscated and stacked in great open piles in front of the castle. The young 16-year-old lord, Tadazumi, was taken from the castle for confinement at Zenryū-ji temple near Ōyama, and his father, the retired lord Tadaaki, was held outside of town at Shōryūji Village (TSS 1975a: 42-43). A military affairs officer (*gunyōkan*) and a general administration office (*minseikyoku*) were set up in Sakata.

In the midst of its retreat and the stationing of Restoration forces in its castle town and chief port, the domain faced further agitation from its villages. Harvest prospects were poor in Shōnai as well as Shinjō. When word of the domain's concessions in Shinjō spread into Shōnai, an alliance of Akumi villages presented a similar request for a 50% tax reduction (*gonengu han toritate*) in December. The domain's offer of much smaller "reductions" (*teatemai*) proved unsatisfactory to the villages. On the 4th and 5th of January, posters (*tafefuda*) appeared at Hachiman Shrine in Ichijō Village (Arase District) and in front of headmen's houses in surrounding villages. They announced a meeting to be held on the 9th at a well-known gathering spot (Nikkō River's Shinkawa) to draw up a "united cultivators' agreement (*hyakushō ittō gi sadamekaki*) that would reaffirm the demand for 50% reduction. Both the contents of the poster and the gist of the grievances were relayed to higher authorities in memoranda from a lower domain official (texts: TSS 1975a:67-68). The domain, though, apparently stuck with its earlier offer.

Pressed from below, the domain was also buffeted by the swift actions of the new Meiji authorities in consolidating their control. On November 22, Sakai Tadazumi was shifted to confinement at a temple in Tokyo, and the Sakai headship was passed to his 13-year-old brother, Tadamichi. On January 19, the new lord was granted continuance of the house name and line, but his fief was reduced from 170,000 *koku* to 120,000 *koku*. Then, on February 5, the Sakai's 246-year control of Shōnai appeared at an end, as Tadamichi was reassigned to Aizu-Wakamatsu Domain (at the time, also valued at 120,000 *koku*).[6] Thirty years earlier, the movement against such a transfer order began in the countryside with local officials but soon received widespread popular support. This

---

[6] Shōnai was to be divided between Satake of Akita and Horiguchi of Shibata Domain. Tanabe Gihei calculated in his diary that Shōnai's actual tax base was four times that Aizu-Wakamatsu (TSS 1975a:73-74). This was an exaggeration, but the order, like that of 1840, did carry a substantial reduction in fief.

time, the resistance that was to engulf the plain through 1869 was spearheaded by senior domain officials and the Honma brothers and drew only reluctant participation from the populace.

A THIRD ANTI-TRANSFER PROTEST

Immediately upon hearing of the transfer order, domain elders mounted a two-pronged campaign to have it reversed. Within a few days, senior retainers set off for Kyoto, and later Tokyo, to lobby Iwakura Tomomi, Sanjō Sanetomi, and other influential figures in the new state council (*gisei-kan*). Among the lobbists was Tanabe Gihei, who recounted his efforts in his diary (YKS 1978:1018-19; see TSS 1975a:74-76). TSS (1975a:84) calculates that during the spring of 1869 about 30,000 *ryō* was sent to Kyoto and Tokyo as private gifts to facilitate a hearing.

While the retainers were attempting to deflect the order with high-level negotiations, a direct petition drive (*jikisho*) seeking reversal was started among the villages in late March. Suddenly, there were village delegations streaming off to the main shrines and temples in the towns and in the mountains around the plain to offer prayers for Sakai's "eternal" rule in Shōnai (*goeijō no gokitō*). Village representatives were sent to Tokyo with petitions for the new government. Like petitions of 1840-41, two surviving examples (YKS 1978:1017-18 and TSS 1975a:77-78) are both effusive in praise for the boundless benevolence and kindness (*kōon*) of the long line of Sakai lords and melodramatic in their depictions of the hardships to the common people that would surely follow upon Sakai's forced transfer.

However, other sources make clear that this was not a spontaneous outburst of popular sentiment for the existing order, but a demonstration carefully orchestrated by middle-level domain officials. For example, Tanabe's diary (TSS 1975a:80; YKS 1978:1018-19) describes the visit of a group of "representatives" to the capital. They remained in Tokyo for fifteen days, though their petition presentations required only four days. Ushered about by village group headmen, they spent most of their time seeing the sites, from Yoshiwara brothels to the famous temples. Toward the end they were hosted at a banquet at the Sakai mansion, thanked by some minor officials, and each given 2 ryō toward his expenses.[7]

To finance these efforts, the domain began in late March to require contributions from its retainers and to solicit money from the countryside through village group headmen and village officers.[8] If the example of Futakuchi Village is any measure, this money was not easily forthcoming. Futakuchi's quota was 38 ryō the headman himself, Tōzō, ended up paying 30 ryō, with the balance allocated among the other households. In fact only 4 of that 8 ryō was ever collected (TSS 1975a:84).

The domain had better success with contributions from its designated merchants, who continued to offer financial support to the domain. Honma records (TSS 1975a:85) indicated that most of the 30,000 ryō that went to the capital in the spring of 1869 was raised from these merchants—indeed much of that from Honma himself (see Table 3). As TSS (1975a:55) observes, this was in contrast to the designated merchants in most other defeated domains, who quickly shifted their substantial loans and gifts to the new national authorities.

As the domain mounted this dual campaign of high-level lobbying and simulated "popular" protest, the new Meiji leaders were trying to shore up their own control of the northeast region by enlarging their three civil affairs offices

[7] For further details see also TSS 1975a:79-80 for a section of the travel diary of Chōjirō, one of the petitioners to Tokyo.

[8] See the messages from the former pressuring the latter in TSS 1975a:83-84. Senior officials were apparently not wholly confident of the drive because they simultaneously began preparations for a move. They started dunning villages for outstanding taxes and loans, and began shifting rice reserves from village group and district warehouses to its central stocks.

(*minseikyoku*) at Sakata, Ishinomaki, and Aizu-wakamatsu. On March 10, they appointed as head of the Sakata Civil Affairs Office Nishioka Shuseki (1848-1923), a young doctor from Saga, who was to work with the military affairs officer, Funakoshi Yōnosuke. A full complement of samurai from other domains was brought in as initial staff. A wooden sign at the gate announced that the former Sakai fortification in the center of Sakata now housed both the Military Affairs and Civil Affairs Offices. The reduction in Sakai's fief meant that all of Akumi was placed under Sakata jurisdiction, and from June 1 through June 9, all of the administrative staff and military units made a show-of-force tour of the Akumi countryside. Nishioka ordered an inspection of land registers, which were reluctantly produced by the village officers.

Still, its hold was tenuous. Its demand for an end to the group pilgrimages to pray for Sakai's continued rule in Shōnai was ignored. The Sakata notable appointed by Nishioka as town affairs officer was sending regular intelligence reports to Sakai officials through intermediaries (TSS 1975a:97). And the town's leading financier, Honma Mitsuyoshi, remained a major contributor to Sakai.

Of these problems, it was perhaps the position of Honma that drew the attention of the new central authorities. From early on, they seemed to harbor both the political ambition of separating him from Sakai and the economic aim of securing his loans and contributions. In 1868, their efforts to extract funds from wealthy merchants (as *kaikei kitatekin chōtatsu*) had yielded about 3 million *ryō*, chiefly from Kinai merchants. By the spring of 1869, the Meiji leadership was casting its efforts farther afield, and on June 20, it summoned both Mitsuyoshi and his younger brother, Umanosuke, to Tokyo (SSS 1971:948-49). Significantly, this was about a week after Sakai's transfer order was stayed; on June 13, the Civil Affairs Office at Wakamatsu had been converted to Wakamatsu Prefecture, and another individual was appointed governor. No doubt both Honma and Sakai officials suspected a link between the stay of transfer and Honma's summons. After consulting with Matsudaira, Mitsuyoshi decided to appear.

The Honma brothers arrived in Tokyo on July 4. Three days later, pleading illness, Mitsuyosji sent his brother to meet the Financial Comptroller of the nascent government. Umanosuke deflected requests for substantial loans, but the Honma brothers remained in Tokyo. Negotiations continued into July, with Mitsuyoshi always sending his brother and remaining in close communication with Suge and other Sakai officials in Tokyo (Mitsuyoshi reports on his time in Tokyo in some detail in his diary, SSS 1971:948-83; see also TSS 1975a:99-106). To all requests for financial assistance, Honma responded coyly, importuning that while he himself had few resources to offer, if he were approached as a domain official, through his domain lord, he would do all he could to be of assistance. When he finally offered 10,000 *ryō*, he was abruptly refused and told to return to Shōnai. He quickly raised his offer to 50,000 *ryō*, which was deemed acceptable on July 17.[9]

Throughout Honma's time in Tokyo, domain officials continued to orchestrate shows of support for Sakai, but it was proving more difficult to recruit villager "volunteers" for the trip to Tokyo; their reluctance was no doubt due to the approximately 15 *ryō* in expense money each person cost the village group budget (TSS 1975a:87). District officials blamed the village group headmen for "negligent leadership," and in June and July the village group headmen were

---

[9] Honma delivered this sum in four installments between September 24 and October 4. The terms of the loan called for a 10% annual interest, but Honma agreed to return half of the interest. Moreover, he had to accept as collateral the 50,000 *ryō* in "gold bonds" (*kin fuda*) that the several Mogami River basin domains had just been forced to borrow from the government (TSS 1975a:105-106). TSS (1975a:104) notes that this was a large sum. Only twenty-nine persons throughout the country were asked to loan more than 10,000 *ryō* in the year from early 1868 to early 1869; only six gave 50,000 or more.

forced to requisition villagers for the trip. The headmen also had to apply constant pressure to ensure a daily flow of supplicants to all of the main mountain and town shrines, offering prayers for Sakai's continued rule. In the sixth month (lunar calendar), for example, the twenty-one villages of Ōyama Village Group were responsible for sending people on alternate (even) days to arrive at Ōyama's Boō-ji Temple before 7 a.m. The village group headman found it necessary to draw up a detailed schedule, by which Harima-kyōden Village was to send two persons on the 2nd and 6th, three persons on the 4th, 8th, 10th, 12th, 14th, 16th, 18th, and 20th, and one person on the 22nd; Futakuchi Village was to send a total of six persons, three each on the 2nd and 24th, and so forth (YKS 1978:1019-22).

No doubt both Honma and domain officials hoped that his loan would permit Sakai to stay in Shōnai, but Meiji leaders remained adamant in moving him. This sent domain elders and the Honma brothers into further conferences to determine just how much they could feasibly raise within the domain. Their fears were confirmed on July 23, when Sakai was reassigned to Taira as governor (*chiji*) of Iwaki Domain and ordered to assume the position by mid-September.

This apparently convinced most senior officials that further efforts to block the transfer were futile, and they began moving small groups of retainers to Iwaki. By late August, almost half of the 16,000 retainers and their dependents had left for Iwaki. The elders tried to doctor land registers by replacing the names of all landholding officials and merchants with the names of the cultivator tenants (who were not told of the changes and so would continue to pay them rent). For its part, the Sakata Civil Affairs Office issued a directive prohibiting commoners around the castle town from taking advantage of the move by buying up samurai belongings at "distress sale" prices (text in TSS 1975a:110).

Still, Honma and Suge persisted in lobbying for a change of heart. They focused their efforts on Ōkuma Shigenobu, now in charge of international financial matters as a vice-comptroller of the Foreign Office. Honma Mitsuyoshi stayed in Tokyo; no longer coy, he repeatedly called at Ōkuma's residence for an audience. It was not until his thirteenth visit, on August 17, that he was allowed in to see Ōkuma, who told him at last that a large contribution just might secure a reversal. In his diary, Honma linked this to the government's acute financial crisis; at that very moment Ōkuma and others faced stiff demands from the Western ambassadors for a more stable currency, and the prospects of gold specie from Sakai must have seemed useful (SSS 1971:965; see Lebra 1973:17). After a week of contacts, Honma thought that 50,000 *ryō* would be acceptable to the government, but on the 28th, this was flatly rejected. The next day, the domain was informed that a far larger sum, 700,000 *ryō*, would be necessary as a "contribution" (*kenkin*). It agreed immediately, and on the 31st, Sakai was named governor of Shōnai Domain.[10]

These developments also unfolded in the midst of sharp debates among the Meiji leaders about disposition of the entire domain and domain lord system (Beasley 1972:325-35); for example, the "return of domain registers" (*hanseki hōkan*) order was issued on July 25. Ōkuma was probably persuaded by political as well as economic calculations. One reason for moving Sakai in the first place had been the Meiji leaders' concern to secure and control the two crucial ports along the Japan Sea coast, Niigata and Sakata. Yet Ōkuma came to realize that moving Sakai at this juncture would seriously disrupt Honma's operations and the opportunity to enlist his financial power in the new Meiji economy. Thus, Ōkuma urged that Sakai be allowed to remain in Shōnai, but in a countermove, upgraded the Sakata Civil Affairs Office to Sakata Prefecture, a direct government prefecture. It was as-

[10] SSS 1971:967. On September 30, the domain was officially reassigned its 120,000 *koku* of lands in 301 villages (which it had in fact continued to control). The next month, it was given the choice of being renamed Tsurugaoka or Ōizumi Domain; it chose the latter and assumed that name on October 24.

signed 255,000 *koku* of territory throughout the Mogami basin, including about 101,000 *koku* in Shōnai—the 235 villages of Akumi plus 73 Tagawa villages that were former shogunate territory (TSS 1975a:172, table 7). The former office head, Nishioka, became vice-administrator (*gonsanji*) in charge of the prefecture's Shōnai lands. Thus, Shōnai was partitioned, with the central authorities administering Akumi to the north of the Mogami and the old Sakai Domain elite in control of most of Tagawa.

The initial problem for Matsudaira and Suge was of course the 700,000 *ryō* due the government; they had promised Ōkuma to pay at least 300,000 *ryō* by late autumn. Honma himself pledged 300,000 *ryō*; for the balance, the Sakai leaders again began assigning quotas to individual retainers, merchants, large rural landholders, and village units. And again the large landholders and village officers ended up paying most of the village quotas (see TSS 1975a:119-28 for details of the drive). The actual totals raised remain something of a mystery. The 300,000 *ryō* was paid, but the 400,000 balance (together with similar balances owed by Morioka and Kanazawa Domains) was forgiven by the government the next spring, following the urgings of Satsuma leaders and over the objections of Ōkuma and Itō. Yet rumors persisted for years that at least part of the 400,000 had been collected and quietly kept by senior domain officials—rumors that eventually reached, and agitated, both Ōkuma and the rural Shōnai population.

With the success of the anti-transfer movement, all pretense of domain solidarity dissolved. The small landholders and ordinary townspeople, reluctant participants all along, were again restive. Nezumigaseki Village Group in the southwest corner of Tagawa, for example, had been a battlefield during the Boshin War and consequently suffered more than the usual number of assessments. At mass assemblies at the end of the year, they harangued village officers: "where were the promised reimbursements for cash and tools and supplies taken for the troops, for the wages of those conscripted as bearers, for the costs of quartering the soldiers?" (They sought returns of assessments by Meiji forces as well as the Shōnai side!) They were hardly satisfied by the officials' explanations that actually about 1,035 *ryō* had been sent to the village group, but that this only covered "various expenses," leaving nothing to be returned to individuals. Incensed, they brought direct petitions to domain officials. The latter indignantly refused to honor claims against their enemy, but did agree to pay a further 750 *ryō* for domain requisitions. This was to be small consolation to the Nezumigaseki residents, because instead of returning this, the domain simply credited it as a contribution from the village group toward the 700,000 *ryō* fund. This experience was a portent of many similar incidents in the next several years.

But even among large merchants and samurai, unity was soon strained. It was, in fact, only a small group of young, middle-level retainers who seized control of the administrative positions of Ōizumi Domain. They were led by Matsudaira Chikahiro, who became the new administrator (*sanji*); Suge Sanehide, the new vice-administrator (*gonsanji*); and Tanabe Gihei. All three had become powerful in the mid-1860s as advisors to the very young lord, Tadazumi. They eased aside most senior elders and reduced the fiefs of their enemies, whom they accused of failing to fight for the domain during the Boshin struggle. They cited the central government policies of reducing fief grants and emphasizing salaried posts to consolidate their position and reward themselves and their supporters; Suge, for example, gave himself a 1,000 *koku* stipend.

At the same time, they moved aggressively to control commercial activities and establish new monopolies. At the very moment when they were due to make payment on the 300,000 *ryō* levy, Tanabe Gihei was negotiating through Honma to purchase an American steam freighter to ship rice and *sake* directly from Kamo to Tokyo, bypassing Sakata (Honma persuaded the major firms of Echigo-ya and Kado-ya to sign as ostensible owners; SSS 1971:1013-14). In spite

137

of government edicts prohibiting direct contacts with foreign businessmen, Suge (who remained in Tokyo) and Tanabe negotiated contracts with Western agents to supply raw silk thread. They received a 150,000 *ryō* advance for thread of that value to be delivered within three years, a risky venture because there was virtually no sericulture in Shōnai at the time! They also contracted to buy and reprocess Western salt, another industry alien to Shōnai. The domain went on to promulgate commodity standards and set prices on all essential goods within Tagawa, and attempted to license all trade within the domain. This naturally antagonized the merchants who had supported the anti-transfer actions (TSS 1975a:156-64). And in 1873, when the domain began a forced agricultural project, opposition divided its own samurai ranks with the emergence of a "Reform Faction" (*kairyō ha*) that was to prove an annoying thorn in its side for several years. It was the coalescence of these agriculturalist, merchant, and ex-samurai grievances that would lead to the Wappa Disturbances in 1874. But first we must consider the difficulties that the Meiji authorities faced as they attempted a direct administration of Akumi.

The Tengu League Disturbances and Related Challenges to Sakata Prefecture

As these fissures were opening in Ōizumi Domain, across the river Nishioka and the new Sakata Prefecture faced equally fractious eruptions of rural and urban opposition. Protesters in the Akumi countryside created an ongoing organization that drew support and several leaders from merchants and townspeople in Sakata, who themselves were provoked by a new prefectural rice sales plan. Agitations began in the Akumi countryside in late 1869 for reduction and/or elimination of the many ancillary levies and for return of the money and supplies requisitioned during the Chōshū Uprisings and the Boshin War. These actions—assemblies, petitioning, trips to Tokyo, attacks and confrontations with officials—lasted for about twenty-eight months, until March of 1872. They came to be known as the Tengu Disturbances (*Tengu sōdō*), and composed the third of Shōnai's four 19th-century collective protests.

In autumn of 1869, rice harvests were again discouraging, and villagers in the three Akumi districts (Arase, Yuza, and Hirata) began petitioning for tax reductions. When these were turned back by village group headmen, "a large number" of cultivators met at Sakata's Sannō Shrine in early November and presented directly to prefectural officials an eighteen-clause petition that went well beyond considerations for poor harvest (text in Igawa 1970:529-30 and YKS 1975:397-99). As Table 9 summarizes, they articulated three general grievances: they sought abolition of ten categories of levies ancillary to the principal land tax, including several whose ostensible purposes were clearly outdated; they wanted procedural reforms in the assessments of several other ancillary levies; and they wanted changes in several village and village group-level posts.

The prefecture's first response was to order village officers to prevent any residents from coming to town (YKS 1978:1022-23); this had little effect. It then agreed to abolish four of the ancillary levies (Table 9: #1a, b, c, d) and offered to distribute 5,700 bales of "charity rice" to the three Akumi districts. This did not satisfy the petitioners, who then created a more permanent organization. They constituted themselves as the Tengu "League" (*tō*) to insure anonymity, with leaders known as the big *tengu* (*ōtengu*) and followers known as the little *tengu* (*kotengu*). They opened a meeting house (*kaisho*) in Sakata, where up to several hundred people rotated in constant attendance, and spread rumors about the countryside that the new national government would exempt all ancillary levies. Villages throughout Akumi were enlisted in the Tengu League, contributing movement expense money (*undō hi*) in proportion to registered village yield.[11]

---

[11] Igawa 1969:15 cites records of Makisone Village, which made four contributions to the Tengu League in 1869-70. These amounted to 19% of total

TABLE 9

Grievances of the Tengu League in Its Eighteen-Clause Petition
to Sakata Prefecture, December 1869

1. Abolition of certain ancillary levies:
    a. *[uma] kaiban daimai* [rice equivalency levy for feed grasses for domain horses; 0.369005 *koku* per 100 *koku* of registered yield]
    b. *gō takaichibu fumai* [rice equivalency levy for porterage in domain lord's procession to and from Edo; 0.01 *koku* per 100 *koku*]
    c. *komononari iro watarihakobi age mai* [rice surcharge for miscellaneous non-rice tribute items; 0.17543 *koku* per 100 *koku*]
    d. *furinin kyūmai* [levy for rice supply of domain retainers' house servants; calculated at 4 bags per servant per year]
    e. *Yokoyama kayakari daimai* [rice equivalency levy for thatch-cutting for castle buildings; 0.35866 *koku* per 100 *koku*]
    f. *osamekata tedai nai yaku goteate mai* [special allowance to district officials and village group headmen for various rice tax inspection duties; 0.0044708 *koku* per 100 *koku*]
    g. *Sakata gokura mai nezumikiri koshiraenaoshi tawara sadame goto-ritate mai* [levy to cover rice lost to rodents and insects in domain warehouses, losses in moving rice sacks around warehouses, and costs in replacing worn and damaged sacks; 0.33954 *koku* per 100 *koku*]
    h. *sakutoku yonaimai* [surcharges on land rents of non-resident holdings; 8% if outside village group, 5% if within village group but different village, etc.]
    i. *ōjoya yashiki yonaimai* [surcharge for maintenence of village group headman's house]
    j. *kimoiri uradaka daimai* [rice equivalency allowance for village headman]
2. Reform of procedures for levying other ancillary taxes:
    a. *gotanebujiki mai* [suspension of 30% annual interest charge on forced seed and food rice borrowings from domain; borrowings were 7.2 *koku* per 100 *koku*, thus annual interest was 2.15 *koku*]
    b. *gō gofushin sashidashi mai* [rural public works levy; formula was 2.8 *koku* per 100 *koku*; request was that only actual project costs be assessed, up to formula maximum]
    c. *kumimura kenkin daimai* [levy for expenses of village group and village officials traveling on business within Akumi and to

TABLE 9 (*cont.*)

Sakata; request was that these be assessed only on presentation of itemized expenditures to all *hyakusho* of village]

  d. *sankumi tayamori kyū* [levy for stipend of watchman at house maintained in Tsuruoka for Akumi officials on business; 0.339545 *koku* per 100 *koku*]

  e. *kimoiri ichibu kyū* [stipend allowance for village headman; 1 *koku* per 100 *koku*]

  f. *kaisai yado muramakanai daimai* [essentially similar to 1(f)]

3. Abolition and/or reform of several local offices:

  a. abolition of secretary/scribe to village group headman

  b. rotating appointment of irrigation guards, etc.

On December 12, cultivators again assembled to discuss a course of action, this time at Shinkawa. They decided to petition the prefecture again for the fourteen demands not yet granted. Moreover, each district this time prepared a separate set of local demands. In Arase District, sixty-nine villages demanded return of numerous items that had been requisitioned during the Boshin War.[12] Cultivators in Hirata District sought an extension of the tax deadline and the option of paying two-thirds of the total in cash (TSS 1975a:175-76). In Yuza District, actions were more direct. Cultivators from the twenty-nine villages of Ishitsuji Village Group attacked the house of the village group headman, Konno Mosaku, to demand repayment for money assessed for munitions in 1868.

Thus what began as isolated petitioning for temporary tax reductions escalated after initial rebuffs into a broad, continuing protest coordinated across the Akumi countryside. There was a similar and simultaneous pattern in those ex-

---

village expenses for that period. Tengu activities are reported in YKS 1978:1022-27 and in the daily records of Abe Korechika, a Sakai liason officer in Sakata (Abe 1869-70; unpaginated). I have used Abe's records extensively in this section.

[12] They were quite explicit in their listing: 224 bed quilts, 130 cotton sleeping robes, 29 sets of eating trays and bowls, 2 pots, 65 pillow blocks, 2 pillow block covers, 7 mosquito nets, 1 wood bucket (portions of this document cited in Igawa 1969:16, Igawa and Satō 1969:12, n.4).

shogunate areas of Tagawa that had been placed under Sakata Prefecture (Amarume and Karikawa). In December, "all *hyakushō*" (*gohyakushō ittō*) in these Tagawa villages submitted a petition that called for: (1) payment of the basic land tax in five cash installments; (2) a 50% tax reduction for 1869 due to wet weather damage; (3) permanent elimination of three types of ancillary taxes and of all village group assessments; and (4) distribution of charity rice (YKS 1978:1027). That is, we have seen that after resuming administration of these villages in 1865, Shōnai Domain attempted to reintroduce tax payment in kind, and it added several new ancillary levies (for example, compare the itemization of Nishikonogata Village for 1863, 1868, and 1869 in Igawa and Satō 1969:10). The villages were asking, in effect, for a return to shogunate conditions.

To their later regret, this petition was rebuffed by the village group headmen, who refused to pass it along to prefectural headquarters. The petitioners then circulated an announcement through the villages that produced a gathering of about 2,000 people at Hachiman Shrine in Amarume on December 18. That night, groups attacked the houses of three village group headmen (in Amarume, Seki, and Kadota), setting fire to the fences and breaking into the main houses and storage buildings. In the next two evenings, chiefly in the Karikawa area, five village group headmen, seven village headmen, and three other prominent villagers had their houses attacked.[13] Six weeks later, villagers in the Karikawa area continued their resistance by refusing to pay virtually all of their tax obligations. They tendered only 165 *koku* of the 803.2 *koku* basic land tax and none of the 436.2 *koku* in ancillary levies (YKS 1975:175–76).[14]

There were intriguing similarities in the assemblies, griev-

---

[13] Reports of these incidents are included in Abe (1869) and in the diary of Satō Kiyosaburō, an Amarume cultivator (Amarume kyōiku iinkai 1979:165–66).

[14] The prefecture faced protests from rural areas outside Shōnai, as well (see Igawa 1972:60–61).

ances, and petition language of the Tengu League movement in Akumi and these concurrent agitations to the south around Amarume. They suggest organizational links between the two adjacent areas, although there is no evidence of actual communication and coordination. On both sides of the Mogami, demands were extensive but specific, carefully delineated but stopping short of any radical reordering of existing tributary obligations. Nor, in contrast to 1869 disturbances in the Aizu region (Vlastos 1982), were there efforts to institute a political program of local elective offices. Once again, the subversive *tengu* imagery proved an effective idiom for mobilizing the Akumi countryside, but as in the demonstrations thirty years before, it was more a convention for anonymity than an emblem for an avenging popular justice.

In both Akumi and Amarume, village and village group headmen were the immediate targets of protest, not Nishioka and his staff. The headmen were the officials held responsible for the ancillary levies and for failure to return requisitioned items. For the moment, at least, it was the prefectural authorities to whom the appeals were addressed. There is even some indication that the prefectural officials, all new to Shōnai, reacted tentatively and defensively, with little understanding of the demands and less than full confidence in the village and village group officials. Among the more useful documents of the time are several explications of local taxation which the perplexed prefecture ordered local officials to prepare (for example, the three examples in Satō Tōichi 1967).

For their part, these embattled village and village group headmen had little confidence in their new supervisors, and they mounted their own petition drive concurrent with the Tengu and Karikawa agitations. They identified themselves as the "cultivators' representatives" (*hyakushō sōdai*) of eighty-five Tagawa and Akumi villages, but most in fact were village and village group officials, including Konno Mosaku and others whose houses had just been attacked. In

143

a December 1869 petition they asked to be returned to Sakai jurisdiction (i.e., Ōizumi Domain). The text of this petition (TSS 1975a:181–82) was strikingly similar to the 1869 fief transfer petitions, hardly surprising as many of the signatories were the same. The reasoning was patently disingenuous; they bemoaned being placed under Sakata jurisdiction after having supported Sakai in his efforts to remain in Shōnai. In "deep appreciation" of Sakai's "long and benevolent rule," they looked forward to helping their lord meet the 700,000 *ryō* requisition, and asked to be returned to the domain so that they might continue to contribute. Perhaps more to the point, the local officials were highly alarmed by the violence to their property and lacked confidence that the prefecture would or could take effective protective action. At least Ōizumi still had an armed retainer band.

The authorities in Tokyo reacted to these assorted challenges by strengthening the prefectural leadership. On January 4, 1870, they appointed as governor Ōhara Shigemi, son of the Meiji counselor, Ōhara Shigenori. He immediately rounded up eleven Tengu leaders, but this only prompted from the movement a "wave petition" drive; each member village in succession sent three persons to the Sakata jail to seek the leaders' release. On March 28, about 4,000 supporters assembled at Hachiman Shrine in Ichijō Village to ratify their outstanding demands. The next day, large numbers tried to force their way into the prefecture offices, an action which resulted in the arrests of 30 more persons.

At this point, the prefecture softened its position somewhat. While arguing that it was difficult to introduce changes in the current year, Ōhara offered to reconsider the elimination of ancillary levies pending an investigation. He claimed that Nagahama and other Tengu leaders had been jailed not for direct petitioning but for collecting money in the villages for movement expenses before taxes had been paid; he agreed to release them to house detention in September. And finally, he agreed to "partial" late tax payment (which is to say, he would not press penalties on current outstanding amounts).

Throughout 1870, the besieged prefecture increased its efforts to enlist the Honma family to its side. In February, it appointed both Honma Mitsuyoshi and Umanosuke to several prefectural posts. For their part, the brothers seemed ready for some accommodation. In his capacity as agricultural production officer (*shinōgata seisankakari*), Mitsuyoshi immediately submitted a proposal for a number of reforms in taxation and rural administration, including:

1. tax reductions and concessions (*teatebiki*) according to harvest conditions;
2. a reorganization of tax books and land registers to disentangle "private and public matters";
3. continuation of rural public works levies and mandatory seed and food rice borrowings but a write-off of all currently outstanding sums as "indigent people's welfare" (*kyūmin sonae*) in the former case and as "rural welfare assistance" (*gō sonae*) in the latter;
4. abolition of village group headman posts and establishment of a district office (*gōchū kaisho*) with three to four village headmen elected by all district residents to yearlong tours as coordinators at the office;
5. elimination of all village posts beyond the three main positions; and
6. combination of the prefecture's agricultural and financial affairs offices (YKS 1975:399-400; see TSS 1975a:185-86).

On the whole, Mitsuyoshi's proposals represented more a tightening of rural administration than a concession to cultivator demands. They were not implemented, but the prefecture continued to solicit Honma assistance. In July, Mitsuyoshi was appointed agricultural promotion officer (*kannō kakari*). Again he submitted detailed recommendations, this time calling for the creation of local posts under his supervision (*shitakakari no hito*) to promote "conscientious" farming; sixty-three persons, mostly from village headman ranks, were appointed to these posts (SSS 1971:890-93). Honma himself traveled through the Akumi countryside for a week in early September to put the hierarchy in place, but there is no evidence that it ever functioned.[15]

Its crisis in rural control was not the only reason for involving the Honmas in prefectural administration. There was yet a fourth coalescence of opposition to prefectural initiatives that can be linked to the rural Tengu activists. This was in Sakata itself, where Ōhara faced stiff resistance from many Sakata merchants to a new rice sales policy, the so-called *Tokyo kaimai* policy. That is, the central government was then trying to commute all rice fief stipends into cash salaries, and it ordered that tax rice from all prefectures was henceforth to be sent to Tokyo for sale directly by the government and not sold locally. In March of 1870, Ōhara notified the Sakata commodity dealers' council (*sōton'ya*) that henceforth all but 10,000 *koku* of the prefecture's rice would be shipped for direct sale in Tokyo. In other words, only 10,000 *koku* would be sold locally through Sakata dealers. The dealers' council responded urgently (YKS 1975:518-19), advancing several reasons why the existing "local sales" (*chiharai*) practice should be continued. First, Sakata dealers would lose the broker commissions (*kuchigane*) and warehouse fees (*kurashiki*) that they received from the large commercial houses which sent ships to Sakata to pick up their purchased rice. They would also lose the profits when auctioning the tax rice vouchers that they bought from the prefecture. With a drop in the number of ships calling in Sakata, they forecast a steep rise in the prices of the salt, cotton, pottery, and other commodities imported by sea from Osaka and Tokyo. Finally, the petition argued that the Sakata econ-

---

[15] See the partial diary entries of his trip in YKS 1978:1028-31 and his July and September memoranda on proper agricultural practices [*nōji kokoroe oboe*] in YKS 1975:361-66; the latter are valuable accounts of contemporary cultivation methods. Honma may have modeled his hierarchy of agricultural promotion officers on the "agriculture overseers" (*nōgyō metsuke*) that the domain had tried to create in 1842 (Naganuma 1983:76).

omy was centered on the rice trade and this new policy would work a terrible hardship on all townspeople.

The prefecture was alarmed by this reaction, though officials acknowledged many of the arguments. In March, Ōhara sent his vice-administrator, Ōta Kotarō, to Tokyo to seek a temporary stay of implementation. He was successful, and the prefecture announced that, at least for 1870, the previous local sales procedures would remain in effect. The central government, though, was apparently less persuaded by the merits of Ōta's arguments than by a 100,000 *ryō* loan that it privately negotiated with Honma as a quid pro quo for the postponement (Igawa and Satō 1969:12). In return, Honma secured the appointment of Ozeki Matabei and Koyama Taikichi, as sole agents (*haraimai goyōtashi*) to handle the local sales; both were rice merchants backed by Honma capital. This proved a lucrative concession; in 1870, Ozeki and Koyama handled over 45,000 *koku* of Sakata tax rice, worth about 428,000 *ryō* and 2,000 *kan* in copper coin.[16]

The apointments of Ozeki and Koyama, of course, outraged the other Sakata dealers, who immediately called for dismissal of leading prefectural officials and a return to the original local sales procedures by which most of the larger dealers had been "designated merchants" (see the draft of their petition in YKS 1975:449-52). Many of these dealers were also active in the Tengu agitations, most notably Nagahama Gorokichi, who had been head of the dealers' council since 1867 and whose arrest as one of the Tengu leaders sparked the "wave petition." As landholders themselves, many of the dealers shared the concerns of rural cultivators that the ancillary levies were assuming an ever larger percentage of tribute burdens and that this represented ever more egregious diversions of funds by local officials.

Thus, the partition of Shōnai and the attempt to govern its northern half directly proved quite taxing for the new

---

[16] At the same time, Honma shrewdly continued his contributions to Sakai and the Ōizumi elite (see Table 3).

government. The prefecture tried to deal with the urban and rural unrest by delegating to the largest merchant and landlord some policy responsibility in agricultural affairs and by appointing his 'satellite" merchants as sole rice sales agents. But this only aggravated the fears of non-Honma dealers in Sakata, the suspicions of rural residents toward village and village group officials, and the lack of confidence of these officials in the new prefecture's ability to support them. This tenuous administrative hold was further undermined by open disputes among the village group officials, as illustrated by two incidents from Karikawa and Amarume.

Karikawa Village Group

This was the village group with virtual non-payment of taxes in 1869, following the autumn attacks on houses of local officials. The next spring, the village headmen jointly petitioned the prefecture to allow extended payment in two installments of rice vouchers and a third in cash (YKS 1975:399–400, Igawa 1970:537). Both the village group headman, Takahashi Yōnosuke, and the current chairman of Tagawa-area village group headmen, Saitō Junnosuke (who was Kiyokawa Village Group headman), passed it on to the higher authorities. However, they added an attachment in which they acknowledged such a request to be counter to prefectural policy, but pleaded that they had done everything possible to dissuade the proposal. No doubt they were prompted by the memories of the attacks of the previous year when they did *not* pass along the petitions (TSS 1975a:187). The prefecture was already wary of Takahashi's abilities, and sought to dismiss him and place Saitō in charge of both village groups. This prompted the intervention of the Ōizumi official posted to the prefecture in Sakata, Toda Jisaku, who argued that such an action would be the first taken against a village group headman since Ōhara assumed office, and so the prefecture should move with caution. Moreover, the idea of adding Karikawa Village Group to

148

Saitō's responsibility was dangerous because Saitō already had his hands full—as a post station, Kiyokawa was a busy place and had always been rather troublesome. Toda counseled a reprimand (YKS 1975:421; Igawa 1970:537-38). Toda's intervention suggests that it was less Takahashi's abilities than his loyalties to the prefecture that were at issue, and it proceeded to dismiss him in June.

Kamiamarume Village Group

Another of the houses attacked in December of 1869 was that of Kenmochi Gentarō, the Kamiamarume Village Group headman. Perhaps in fear of an even more contentious tax collection period and perhaps to avoid responsibility for tax shortfalls, he promptly resigned, citing ill health. Wada Shūzō was named as a temporary replacement. But in late January, just when taxes were due, Kenmochi had a change of heart and announced that he was recovered and ready to resume office. Wada, however, had no intention of relinquishing the post, and it was decided that they would share the post. This proved an untenable compromise. Trouble began when Kenmochi summoned the village headmen and ordered that the village group's books and records be returned to his house from that of the village group secretary[17] in Seki Village, where they had been taken before the attack in the autumn. Hearing this, Wada wrote in alarm to the prefecture that Kenmochi was going to use his house as the village group office without even minimal repairs to it (it was, Wada added indignantly, "barely liveable"—even "the door doesn't close"). In June, the thirteen village headmen filed a request for Kenmochi's removal from office (*kyūyaku todoke*). In apologizing for its delay, they explained that they would have filed it immediately after the autumn attack had that not been the tax payment season; out of consideration,

[17] *shoyaku*, one of the subordinates of the village group headman whose salary and expenses were resented by villagers.

149

they had waited until now. The prefecture realized that the instigators of this were the village group secretary and four village headmen who were close supporters of Wada and that this was but a continuing dispute between the village headmen and Kenmochi (TSS 1975a:188-89, Igawa 1970:538-39).

Thus, Ōhara and his prefectural staff were in difficult straits. They lacked the undivided commitment of local officials to their efforts, they did not themselves have the force necessary to override the widespread resistance, and their occasional concessions were not supported by the central ministries. Rural unrest was widespread throughout the country, and many local officials turned to Tokyo for permission to accede to petitioners. Meiji authorities refused most and indeed regarded with much suspicion any local officials who unilaterally offered concessions. Knowledge of the rural and urban resistance and of the local administrative rivalries in the Sakata Prefecture did not escape the central authorities. They had been apprised of these various troubles in a June 1870 report by Iwao Sukenojō, a police inspector sent to investigate conditions in Shōnai.[18] The embattled Ōhara thus faced a restive populace below and critical reports of his performance to superiors. He expressed bitterness toward such meddling hardliners as Iwao in an exasperated letter to his father that summer (TSS 1975a:193-94). By late 1870, government leaders had lost confidence in Ōhara, and on October 23, he was forced to resign. As part of a reorganization of much of northeastern Japan, Sakata Prefecture was amalgamated with other prefectures in the Mogami River basin to form Yamagata Prefecture in hopes that consolidation would enable more effective control. A new governor was sent in, the 23-year-old Bōjō Toshiaki, who had been head of police for that region and a critic of Ōhara's "lax" attitude. Iwao remained in Sakata as chief administrator of the

---

[18] A partial text is in TSS 1975a:191-92; the complete text is in Ōkurashō 1962:388.

new prefecture's branch office, but much of the staff moved to the new capital at Yamagata City. This reorganization did not produce the desired results. Bōjō and Iwao began forcefully, rearresting Nagahama and the other Tengu leaders, but they quickly discovered the vulnerability of their position. Predictably, the arrests only pressed Tengu supporters into demonstrations for their release, and in March, most were let off with light sentences (YKS 1975:643). At the same time, Bōjō found it necessary to go to the ministry to seek another year's suspension of the Tokyo rice sales plan. Finally, faced with another presentation of Tengu demands for elimination of ancillary levies, he convened a conference of local officials from throughout the prefecture on March 8. Expected to last a single day, it was prolonged by fierce debate and stretched out to March 17. The conference apparently impressed him with the depth of tax grievances, because ten days later he issued a sweeping directive (the *zatsuzei menjō futatsu*, YKS 1975:640) that suspended all ancillary levies on agricultural production. It eliminated the requirement of adding the extra *nobimai* to bales of tax rice, and in place of the village group and district granaries, it called for the establishment of reserve stocks in each village.

Whatever joy that produced in the countryside was short-lived. The directive was immediately overruled by the Home Ministry, which dispatched ten of its officials to the prefecture on April 4. Infuriated, the Tengu League held mass assemblies in Akumi; soon after, Bōjō again promised a "radical revision of the tax system" (*tenka ippan zeihō gokaisei*). In late spring, he wrote to the Home Ministry for such permission, but he was refused.

Bōjō, it seems, was trapped. Like his predecessors, he had tried to entice Honma Mitsuyoshi into the administration by appointing him to several posts, but this time, Honma chose to remain out of the public arena. After his tax reform was overruled, his key subordinates in the Sakata Office resigned; whether they objected to his actions or the ministry's retraction is unclear, but their departures only added to the office chaos. Bōjō raised further suspicions with his ministry superiors by arguing vigorously against the direct Tokyo sales of Sakata rice, but whatever goodwill that earned him among port dealers was lost by his efforts to eliminate their council and centralize town administration under the prefecture. Finally, reprimanded severely by his ministry, he accepted responsibility for the persisting agitation and resigned at the end of 1871.[19]

For yet a third time, the ministry reshuffled regional administration, this time as part of a nationwide reorganization in late 1871 that consolidated the country into three metropolitan districts (to) and seventy-three prefectures (ken). In this reorganization, Shōnai's disposition was exceptional. On December 14, against the tide of consolidation, Akumi and those parts of Tagawa from the former Sakata Prefecture were hived off of Yamagata Prefecture and joined with Ōizumi Prefecture to create the "Second Sakata Prefecture," which now approximated the old boundaries of Sakai Domain—that is, the plain and surrounding mountains of Shōnai.[20] More significantly, in almost all cases in this national consolidation, governors and senior staff of the new prefectures were appointed from outside the local region. One of the very few exceptions was the Second Sakata Prefecture, where the former Sakai leaders of Ōizumi were retained as its staff—Matsudaira as administrator, Suge as vice-administrator, and most of their subordinates from Ōizumi.

There are several possible interpretations of Shōnai's

[19] His term ended in failure but not disgrace. After being removed, Bōjō went abroad to study in Russia and France and served in the legation in Paris before returning in 1875 to join the Ministry of Education and, later, the army (Igawa 1970:555). It was a peripatetic career common in these early Meiji years.

[20] After the Abolition of Domains and Establishment of Prefectures (haihan chiken) in August-September 1871, Ōizumi Domain had become Ōizumi Prefecture. The Second Sakata Prefecture was now valued at 235,029 koku—the 389 villages of Tagawa (160,087 koku) and the 272 villages of Akumi (74,942 koku).

marked deviation from national policy. Igawa (1972) traces it to the close relationship which Sakai and his retainers had forged with Saigō Takamori after the Boshin War and especially after Saigō had turned critic of the Restoration leadership. Saigō, Igawa has suggested, used his influence to keep Sakai's retainers intact and in power. It was reminiscent of support an earlier Sakai lord received from Mito's Tokugawa Nariaki in the 1840-41 anti-transfer protest, but this Saigō-Sakai alliance was far more surprising. It was Suge and Matsudaira who had led the savage attack on the Satsuma domain mansion in 1867. Saigō, though, was soon disenchanted by the central bureaucratic initiatives of other Meiji leaders, and strongly resisted their efforts to consolidate the many domain forces into a single national army, a policy equally unappealing to the Sakai people. The first high-level contacts between Saigō and Sakai were in 1870. In mid-December, the retired lord, Tadazumi, had traveled with some seventy retainers to Kagoshima, where they trained under Saigō's military officers for five months (TSS 1975a:44-45). Satsuma, it is worth noting, was one of the few other exceptions to administrative consolidation.

Equally important, though, Ōkuma and other leaders saw clearly how the first Sakata Prefecture and its successor, Yamagata Prefecture, had been stymied in efforts to bring the Akumi countryside and Sakata port under effective control. They acceded to the reconstitution of Shōnai and the retention of the Sakai band as an unpleasant but temporary political expedient. And unsettling it must have been for the central leaders in the next few years; the prefecture avoided the military capitalization assessments ordered by the Meiji government, continued to resist a Tokyo direct rice sales policy, and refused to follow central directives on its assumption of old domain debts and on handling of the prefecture's own mounting debts, which reached 510,000 ryō in 1871 (TSS 1975a:214-23).

In the longer term, however, their gamble proved sound. Within four years, the rebellious and autonomous tendencies of the local Sakai elite were tempered by the creation of a national army and a more effective Home Ministry. At the same time, their ability to govern was sorely tested by a series of popular protests that came to be known collectively as the *Wappa sōdō* or Wappa Disturbances.

SIX

Initiative and Inertia:
The Second Sakata
Prefecture

THE RESOLVE of the new prefecture was immediately tested when it faced in early 1872 what proved to be a final flareup of the Tengu League in Akumi. On the evening of February 18, about 2,000 people gathered at Aozawa Village (Arase District) to ratify four familiar demands:

1. elimination of all ancillary levies, as Bōjō had agreed to the year before;
2. release from prison of Nagahama and ten other Tengu leaders;
3. repayment of all assessments from the Boshin War; and
4. a moratorium on tax collections until the above conditions were met.

Matsudaira responded harshly. Citing the national government's recision of Bōjō's directive, he jailed sixteen leaders and remanded four others to their villages.[1] Predictably, this only incited further actions. A week later, there was another large assembly, this time for two days at Hachiman Shrine in Hirata Village. The crowd resolved to send a petition to Yamagata Prefecture and, if that proved unsuccessful, to go directly to Tokyo. On the 29th, an estimated three to four thousand persons set out for Yamagata, shouldering rice,

[1] See Matsudaira's report on the assembly to the Treasury Ministry (TSS 1975a:210), which is interesting for its faithful and explicit reporting of the petitioners' demands. Officials were generally quite conscientious in recording and reporting demands and petitions, even when they contained sharp criticism, in order to justify retaliation. One is reminded of an aphorism attributed to Dean Acheson: "a memorandum is written not to inform the reader but to protect the writer."

155

salt, pots, and other supplies for the journey. Forewarned, the prefecture dispatched two large squads of soldiers to intercept them, arresting about forty persons. It sent other contingents to all of the principal exit points from the plain to stop those who might try to go directly to Tokyo. Fearing that some had already left for the capital, the prefecture ordered some officials to Tokyo in early March.

There are no surviving records of agitations in Tokyo, nor are there any later documents which refer to the Tengu League, then over two years old. Igawa (1969:20) is probably correct in inferring that the movement was effectively suppressed by this show of force. Nonetheless, the cultivators' demands for tax relief and the objections of ordinary merchants to the prefecture's rice agents continued to breed sporadic protest.

Ever wary of Matsudaira and his staff, Ōkuma delegated the governor of Akita Prefecture, Suzuki Onosuke, and the governor's aide, Otome Mitsumasa, to investigate conditions in Shōnai in the aftermath of these events. In separate reports, they warned Ōkuma that Matsudaira and Suge had ignored the 1871 order to disband domain forces and were actively purchasing munitions and training daily. Suzuki's report went on to detail the Tengu protests of that spring, concluding that even if Matsudaira and his subordinates could restore order, the cultivators would continue to harbor considerable resentment.[2]

Gaining confidence from its suppression of the Tengu League and undisturbed by the suspicions it aroused in Tokyo, the prefectural elite intensified its economic program begun in 1869 with the purchase of the steam freighter, contracts with foreign agents, and stronger licensing and controls on local commercial activity. In 1872 and 1873, it undertook three major initiatives that, together, promised an integrated prefectural control over agricultural production and marketing.

[2] Suzuki's report: W 1981:1; Otome's report: W 1981:2-3.

156

First, it sponsored an extensive tea and mulberry scheme for its former warrior-retainers. Such government encouragement of agricultural or commercial ventures for ex-samurai was common in early Meiji, but Shōnai was unusual both because prefectural leaders directly coordinated the projects and because they required the participation of all warrior-retainers. The centerpiece of their plans was the clearing of Ushiroda Forest, an upland area of scrub forest on the east side of the Aka River (see Map 3). On September 19, 1872, they mustered their 3,000 retainers on the edge of Tsurugaoka. Arrayed in their customary military formation, six battalions of thirty-four bannered squads, they were paraded out of town and marched the six kilometers to Ushiroda. They erected temporary shelters, surveyed land blocks that were then assigned to each squad, and began the work of clearing the brush and tree growth (Figure 12). By late November, about 110 hectares had been cleared. Several of the leaders traveled to Shizuoka to study tea and mulberry cultivation and silkworm techniques. Adjacent uplands in Kurokawa, Mawatari, and Takadera were also cleared, so that by the following spring, when mulberry and tea bushes were planted, the total area had reached about 300 hectares. The original site at Ushiroda was christened Matsugaoka, a reference to Tsurugaoka and to Sakata's Kamegazaki Castle through a saying, *tsurukame ni matsu o haisuru* ("a pine placed on a crane and turtle"), that played on the crane (*tsuru*) and the turtle (*kame*) as metaphors of longevity—that the Sakai band should forever remain in Shōnai.[3]

Clearly the prefectural leaders intended the Matsugaoka scheme as a link with the silk thread factory they had established in Tsurugaoka and the foreign sales contracts they had signed. It is no small irony that they were Shōnai's first capitalist entrepreneurs. But Matsudaira and Suge also saw political advantage in keeping the retainer band together in such a secluded location. A strong communal ethos was fostered

[3] See TSS 1975a:228-38 for details of the scheme.

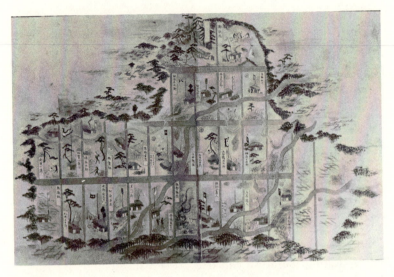

a

b

c

d

12. Scenes from the Matsugaoka Project. a. Sketch map of land blocks assigned to retainer squads. b. Land clearing by the Shira sqauad. c. Transporting roof tiles from Tsurugaoka Castle to Matsugaoka. d. A squad photograph (late 1870s).

at Matsugaoka, and constant physical and spiritual training stressed martial readiness and loyalty to Sakai.

The spartan living and hard physical labor in service of Lord Sakai did not prove universally compelling. First grumblings came from the brigade formed by shogunate officials in the early 1860s from the unattached samurai then roaming the streets of Edo. This brigade of about 1,500 soldiers had been assigned to Sakai and folded into his retainer band (as the *shinchōgumi*). They were led back to Shōnai in 1869, and one can well imagine their lack of enthusiasm for pulling stumps and hefting hoes in the cold, wet Shōnai autumn. Many simply deserted, though they were pursued and punished. More serious for prefectural leaders were the mounting complaints from its own retainers, especially, it seems, from those whose fiefs and stipends had been reduced during the Ōizumi Domain period. These dissidents came together in what they styled as a "Reform Faction" (*kairyōha*), and they were to play an important role in the events of the next few years.

The leaders of this Reform Faction included the 30-year-old Ōtomo Sōbei and three brothers; Kanai Tadanao, 44 years old at the time; Kuwahara Shintoku, about 40 years old; and the youngest, Honda Inri, then 36 years old (figure 13). The father had been a middle-level retainer of Sakai. He arranged for his younger sons, Shintoku and Inri, to be adopted into other retainer households; Tadanao succeeded to the Kanai headship in 1866. Tadanao had received a certificate at the Naganuma Military Academy in Edo in 1855, and in the 1860s was posted to Shōnai's assigned territory in Ezoland (Hokkaidō) as magistrate. His 400 *koku* fief grant ranked him as one of the senior officials. When Oizumi Domain was set up, he was appointed as a hearing officer (*kōgisho hanji*) and later, in Sakata Prefecture, an administrative officer (*gondaizoku*), attached to the General Affairs Section. Kanai and his brothers, however, found themselves increasingly disenchanted with Matsudaira and his supporters. A local historian, Satō Jisuke, believes this stemmed from their father's participation, and death, in the 1867 attack on Satsuma's Edo mansion. The Kanai brothers, Satō has reasoned, continued to regard Satsuma as their father's arch-enemy, and were distressed when Matsudaira and the other retainers switched over to staunch support of Satsuma and Saigō (Satō, personal communication).

In March of 1873, Kanai Tadanao and twenty-nine other Reform Faction supporters challenged the prefecture with a petition sent directly to the Ministry of Justice. In it, they charged Matsudaira and Suge personally and the prefectural officials generally with ten counts of "serious misconduct" and "wicked behavior." These included failing to circulate government directives, forcing participation in the Matsu-gaoka project, maintaining an armed samurai militia, open-ing petitions sent to other offices, and accumulating private profits from public tax collections. Only in Shōnai, they al-leged, were they denied the "rights of freedom" that people throughout the country now enjoyed.[4]

The Matsugaoka scheme also antagonized cultivators throughout the plain. They not only suffered special requi-sitions of corvée labor and materials, but were also outraged to discover that over 90% of the interest charges on their mandatory rice borrowings (the *tanebujikimai*) in 1873-75 was diverted to subsidizing the Matsugaoka area projects.[5] Many

---

[4] *kaidai itchi banmin jishu no ken o e[ri]* . . . The text of the March petition appears in TSS 1975a:271 and W 1981:21. A nearly identical petition with twenty-nine signatories and dated May 7 appears in Ōkuma monjo 1:155-57; it is probably a resubmission. The Meiji leaders, notably Ōkuma, indeed had some reservations about the Matsugaoka scheme. In July, the Ministry of Justice dispatched an investigator, Hayakawa Kyōku, although no action was taken against the prefecture for the moment. Expectably, though, Saigō Takamori wrote in strong endorsement of the domain's projects (see his message of May 1873 to Matsudaira in TSS 1975a:233-34). The prefecture's designated merchants also voiced their support, and Honma proffered con-tributions of 15,000 *ryō* in 1872 and 10,000 *ryō* in 1873.

[5] This amounted to 1,538 *koku* and 44,518 *yen*; YKS 1962:66. These in-terest charges were of course an ancillary levy to which they had been ob-jecting for several years. The prefecture was later to argue that as Ōizumi Domain, it had received permission from the Ministry of Finance to use this interest money for school construction and commercial promotion, so its diversion was proper.

a. Matsudaira Chikahiro.

b. Suge Sanehide.

c. Mishima Michitsune.

d. Honda Inri.   e. Mori Tōemon.
13. Some of the principals in the Wappa Distrubances.

of those actually laboring in Figure 12 are cultivators requisitioned from Tagawa villages.

The prefecture's second initiative—a major reorganization of landholding—proved equally provocative. In 1872, it devised a plan to purchase all arable lands from the registered holders at what it termed the "rental" value of each parcel; this was a computation in cash of each parcel's putative yield minus all taxes and a fixed cultivator's share. It then intended to sell each parcel back to the holder, with a property certificate, at a "total land value" calculated from the full yield at market prices (see Satō 1981:47-52). This differed significantly from several of the reform plans that were being floated in the national government at the time (cf. Beasley 1972:390-400, Niwa 1966). It was shrewdly conceived to benefit from either conscientious on-site surveying (which would uncover the widespread underregistration and undergrading) or mere calculations from existing land registers

163

(which in effect overstated the tax burden on most parcels, thus lowering the value at which they would be appropriated from the holders and inflating the value at which the holders would have to redeem them).

In the autumn of 1872, it began preparations for an on-site survey (*chiken torishirabe*) to serve as a basis for this appropriation and resale, but this soon floundered. The following spring the prefecture revised its procedures, ordering each village to prepare a register (*chibiki chō*) that listed all landholders and parcels and that specified the yield, taxes, and rent of each parcel; on-site surveying was encouraged but not enforced. There was to be a final column in the registers—the parcels' cash values (*chidaikin*)—but this was to be left blank and filled in later by prefectural officials (TSS 1975a:245)! Throughout the summer, work on these registers continued despite promulgation in August of a national Land Tax Reform Law that mandated quite different guidelines and principles. In the autumn, the prefecture began issuing land certificates.

Given the formula of land purchase and resale, it was difficult for even large landholders to evade some financial hardship, and the program thus invited broad hostility. Its unpopularity was heightened by its preservation of the gross inequalities of tax rates among villages. Yet another provocation was a special tax surcharge that was ordered by village group headmen and many village officers, ostensibly to recoup their expenses in preparing the survey registers; it was set at 1.5% of registered holdings. Alleged irregularities in assessment and expenditure of these funds was soon added to the litany of charges against them.

The prefecture's program was not fully implemented. In early 1874, the Meiji government ordered a postponement of and redemption and certificate exchange in prefectures like Sakata that had begun their own programs. By this time, the prefecture was faced with rising unrest and would have been hard pressed to complete its program. As we shall see, it was not until the autumn of 1875 that the land tax survey was begun again, this time in accordance with the national law and in a very different local political climate.

The prefecture's third initiative of 1872-73 was a revision of land tax procedures—again, in a manner highly profitable to itself, flouting national guidelines, and incurring the enmity of cultivators, landholders, and those merchants who were not included in the new system. In the fall of 1872, the Meiji leaders had promulgated several taxation reforms, including a Tax Payment Law, Directive #222 of September 14.[6] This directive permitted cash payment of all principal and ancillary taxes on land; it further provided that if cultivators chose to pay in kind, they need only submit bales of 0.4 *koku* volume.[7] With the adoption of the Western calendar on January 1, 1873, the government also allowed land tax payments in up to three installments through March of the year after harvest. Taxes had been due by the end of the twelfth month, typically in early February by the Western calendar. The government recognized that December 31 would be too early for most cultivators to finish threshing and hulling.

Matsudaira and Suge, however, decided not to circulate these laws, and gave a peculiar interpretation to "cash equivalency tax payment" (*kokudainō*). In an explanation of tax procedures (*Tōken kokudai osame tetsuzuki sho*; W 1981:139-41), Matsudaira claimed that he had wanted to permit direct cash tax payment but Shōnai was a "snow country" (*yukiguni*) and it would be too difficult for cultivators to pay a *cash* tax by the year-end deadline. Instead, the prefecture was

---

[6] *nengu toritate hō*. See SSS 1981:814-19 for copies of the texts of this and related directives.

[7] Commonly known as "4 *to* bales" (*shi to iri tawara*). That is, they no longer had to add extra rice to each bale, the *nobimai* that in Shōnai amounted to 0.10–0.12 *koku* per bale. To be more precise about the law, unrest in lands under its own jurisdiction had led the government to permit cash taxes to those cultivators; with Directive #222, it was extending this option to former domain lands. The price for purposes of determining tax obligation was to be the nearest town's average market price from October 1 to November 15.

adopting a "contractor cash tax system" (*kaiuke kokudainō sei*). Landholders were to continue to pay taxes in kind; this rice was then sold by the prefecture, which tendered a cash tax to the central Treasury Ministry. In the same document, Matsudaira added that any changes in specifications of tax rice bales or an institution of a Tokyo rice sales policy would be severe hardships on domain finances. The explanation of procedures ignored the persistent demands for elimination of ancillary levies.[8]

In essence, the prefecture was introducing yet another variant of the old practice of designated merchants (*tokken shōnin sei*). Six Tsurugaoka merchants and four Sakata merchants were selected as broker-contractors for cash tax payments.[9] The cultivators were to bring in the customary bales of 0.52 *koku*; indeed, on November 27, 1873, Matsudaira informed local officials that all expenses of handling the rice until it was received at the harbor would be borne by the taxpayers! As a formality, each village group headman[10] would submit

[8] Hattori (1974:175-76) cites a newspaper account of December 4, 1874, describing similar prefectural deception and collusion with large merchants in the Sanriku area (now Miyagi Prefecture).

[9] *kokudai jōnō ukeoinin* was their official term, but the older term, *goyō-tashinin*, was more commonly used. The contractors are listed in Satō 1963:77. We might wonder why Honma was not one of the ten. Kashiwagura's (1961) explanation is that the family's principal business remained moneylending and exchange and not rice dealing per se. In 1867, for example, its agricultural income (including selling its tenants' rice) was 25,094 *ryō* in gold, 1,550 *momme* silver, and 28 *kan* 528 *mon* in copper coin, but this was only 9.35% of its total income, the bulk of which was derived from finance. That is, the designated merchants would pay the tax due the central government by the prefecture (that is, they would advance money to the prefecture) in exchange for a monopoly on receiving and selling all tax rice collected in the prefecture. Honma preferred to remain one step removed and lend money to the designated merchants.

[10] In November of 1872, there was yet another administrative reorganization. The districts (*gō* and *tōri* in Shōnai) were renamed *daiku*, and the forty village groups (*kumi*) were consolidated into twenty-one *koku*. The village group headmen were renamed *kocho*. They remained resident in their areas of jurisdiction, overseeing the village headmen. I will continue to use the term "village group headman" for this level of posts. See MCS 1974:250-53 for further details on the changing administrative grid.

a request to one of the prefecture's designated dealers to sell the village group rice and pay the cash tax for them.

To cultivators and taxpayers, these commercial initiatives and tax rearrangements only added layers of encumbrances to their obligations. This is seen graphically in the listing of taxes due in 1872 and 1873 in Ōyodokawa Village. This was a settlement of thirty-eight households in the southwest corner of the plain between Ōyama and Tsurugaoka, and was to be one of the centers of the agitations that would begin in 1874. Table 10 and Table 11 follow the classification of taxes in a document prepared by the village headman; the tax rates are percentages of village registered yield.

For both years, various ancillary levies added about 21% to the principal land tax rate of 55.2%, so that about three-quarters of all putative production in the village was appropriated as taxes. At first glance this seems to have been an onerous burden, but it is much less so when measured against actual yields and acreage. That is, the registered village yield in Ōyodokawa was 570.9144 *koku*, of which 534.5989 *koku* was in paddy land parcels. Registered acreage was 52 hectares, of which 45 hectares was paddy land. However, judging from the land survey three years later, *actual* acreage and yields were roughly double the registered acreage and yields. This at least partially explains why indignation focused not on the total tax burden, and not on the obligation to pay a principal land tax, but rather on the noisome and numerous subsidiary levies.

And an enormous laundry list they comprised. In 1872, there were five categories of levies beyond the principal land tax, calculated to the thousandths of a percentage point! Within the category of "prefectural expenses" were ten separate items; within "village group and village expenses" were twenty-six separate items. Most of these were minuscule in amount, and many had long outlasted their original tax objective; for example, the last domain lord procession to Edo had been six years before. While there was some reduction in the number of items and some changes in terminology in 1873, the totals remained virtually unchanged.

167

TABLE 10

Itemizations of Taxes and Levies, Ōyodokawa Village, 1872

Total taxes and levies (categories A-F) as a percent of registered village yield	76.157%
A. Principal land tax	55.200%
B. Inspection surcharge rice	2.208%
C. Levies for "prefectural expenses" (10 items)	4.293%

    1. levy in lieu of porterage in *sankin kōtai*
    2. rural public works
    3. rice threshing wages
    4. thatch cutting wages
    5. guard salary, village group official house in Tsurugaoka
    6. Tsurugaoka Granary storage loss levy
    7. expenses of district officials in rice inspection
    8. Kamo Granary guard salary
    9. Kamo Granary maintenance levy
  10. Kamo Granary annual storage losses levy

D. Interest on forced rice borrowings	2.160%
E. Levy for miscellaneous expenses of granary officials	0.639%
F. Village group and village expenses (26 items)	11.657%

    1. reserve fund to repay borrowings from district officials
    2. principal and interest on domain loans to village
    3. levy for feed grasses for domain horses
    4. miscellaneous commodities levy
    5. village headman salary (1% of village registered yield)
    6. village groups reserve rice
    7. rice equivalency levy to district level officials
    8. rice equivalency levy for straw bales to be supplied to the district officials' office for public works projects
    9. (another) miscellaneous commodities levy
  10. village group headman's scribe stipend
  11. village share of land tax on village group headman houselot
  12. village share of land tax on permanent seed rice granary

TABLE 10 *(cont.)*

13. village share of headman's tax exemption
14. village elders' stipends/expenses
15. village elders' official business servant/labor costs
16. main canal intake guard stipend
17. charge for straw bales used in canal repairs
18. indemnity for land used in construction of Kuranowaki Branch Canal
19. Kuranowaki Branch Canal intake guard stipend
20. indemnity for land used in construction of tertiary level canals
21. tertiary canal watchman stipend
22. village messenger stipend
23. village expenses
24. levy for land used in construction of the new canal
25. "national levy" requisition
26. allocation for Meiji reserve seed rice supply

NOTE: These figures, categories, and items are translated from a summary from the villages' tax ledgers prepared by village officers for the village groups headman. These ledgers were discovered by Ōtomo in his investigations of May 1874, and included in his report to his ministry. They were used by Numa in assessing misappropriations by village and village group officials.

SOURCE: W 1981:10-12.

From such a listing we can understand how village and village group headmen could come to embody excessive, arbitrary, and anachronistic taxation. We can also appreciate the frustrations of residents prevented access to the particulars of the account books.

On the other hand, these local officials' motivations remain quite puzzling. This proliferation of ancillary levies must have demanded intricate bookkeeping for seemingly paltry gain. One would have expected from the depth of feeling expressed in the Tengu League and the Karikawa agitations against these levies that their totals would have been much more burdensome than this and other similar listings demonstrate. Why did the village and village group headmen

169

TABLE 11
Itemizations of Taxes and Levies, Ōyodokawa Village, 1873

Total taxes and levies (categories A-F) as a percent of registered village yield	75.747%
A. Principal land tax	55.200%
B. Inspection surcharge rice	2.208%
C. Ancillary levies	6.306%

   1. interest on forced rice borrowings
   2. required contribution to reserve rice stock
   3. rural public works fund levy
   4. guard stipend, village group official house, Tsurugaoka
   5. Tsurugaoka Granary rice storage loss
   6. rice inspection officials' expenses
   7. Kamo Granary guard stipend
   8. Kamo Granary maintenance levy
   9. Kamo Granary annual rice storage loss

D. (Additional) Kamo Granary levies	0.688%
E. Village groups and village expenses (18 items)	9.251%

   1. interest and principal of loans to village and village group
   2. village headman salary (1% of village yield)
   3. village group headman's scribe stipend
   4. land tax for seed rice granary site
   5. village elders' expenses/stipends
   6. village elders' servants/laborers (official use)
   7. main canal intake guard stipend
   8. rice equivalency levy for straw bales to be supplied to the district officials' office for public works projects
   9. indemnity for land used in construction of Kuranowaki Branch Canal
  10. indemnity for land used in construction of Kuranowaki Branch Canal
  11. Kuranowaki Branch Canal intake guard stipend
  12. tertiary canal watchman stipend
  13. village messenger stipend
  14. village expenses
  15. indemnity for land used in construction of

TABLE 11 *(cont.)*

tertiary level canals
16. "national levy" requisition
17. reserve fund to repay borrowings from district officials
18. rice equivalency levy to district-level officials
F. Special temporary levies   2.094%
   1. requisition for land tax survey expenses
   2. principal and interest of village membership share in village group rotating reserve association

NOTE: These figures, categories, and items are translated from a summary from the villages' tax ledgers prepared by village officers for the village group headman.
SOURCE: W 1981:12-13.

persist with such obviously contentious procedures? To be sure, we will see that their closely held account books could mask a variety of pecuniary sins, something villagers had always suspected. However, it was not until the Wappa agitations in 1875 that "fraudulent" *(fusei)* dealings became a central concern of collective actions. The contrast, in any case, with prefectural officials is striking.

THERE WERE, it seems, two diverse strata of political elite in Shōnai during these years. On one level were the ex-samurai Sakata prefectural authorities, confidently and aggressively attempting to shape the local economy to their own commercial advantage. Their active mercantile policies and incipient capitalist ventures belie any characterization of their actions as mere "feudal reaction" (e.g., Igawa 1969:13) to a new age in which they had no place; they would have no permanent place, but for very different reasons. Below them, locked in uneasy alliance, were the village group and village headmen, increasingly isolated from their constituent populations but resolutely clinging to the past prerogatives of their positions. "Progressive" leaders and anachronistic subordinates? An unlikely combination, but an explosive one, especially

171

when agitators found critical leverages in the suspicions of the central government about Matsudaira and his supporters, in the rhetoric of the new Meiji regime, and in the mistrust between the two levels of local political elite.

I have suggested how the Tengu protests of 1869 assumed a less radical form than those of the same year in Aizu. Shōnai in these first years after the Meiji Restoration also had a very different political complexion from Kawasaki, the locality that Waters (1983) has studied. In Kawasaki, a local archivist warned Waters, "nothing happened" in the Meiji transition—no class struggles, no millenarian uprisings, no later "violent incidents" by the Movement for Freedom and Popular Rights. Waters sensibly turned the warning into a research agenda and tried to understand why the transition in Kawasaki was so smooth. At the center of his interpretation stand the local leaders, who "continued to regard themselves as guardians of the region's prosperity, and paternalistic protectors of ordinary peasants" (1983:125). Their conscientious stewardship of regional affairs cushioned economic and political change in Kawasaki.

In Shōnai, "something" was most definitely happening, and it was happening because the initiatives of the prefectural authorities and the inertia of the village and village group officials incurred antagonism and suspicion in all quarters— from the national leaders, from renegade "Reform Faction" ex-samurai, from non-designated local merchants, and from landholders and cultivators of all scales. It was the convergence of these several lines of opposition on these two rather strange and mutually wary partners in local political authority that I believe to be central to interpreting the pattern of conflict and the course of protests in the two years to come.

SEVEN

Cash Taxes, Suppressed Reforms, and Falsified Expenditures

THE PREFECTURE'S attempts to revise landholding and taxation had only rekindled the long-standing grievances of both large and small landholders—the endless, arbitrary levies, the secret books and registers, the diversion of public tax monies, and the requirement of payment in rice for both the principal land tax and most ancillary levies. It was this last grievance, together with rumors of the prefecture's suppression of Directive #222, that spurred calls for the option to tender all land taxes in cash. This demand was voiced in a growing number of petitions to the prefecture in the winter of 1873-74. These first appeared in the Yamahama and Kushibiki Districts of Tagawa but soon spread across Tagawa and north into Akumi. When headmen and district officers refused the cultivators, they carried their requests to Tokyo. Finally in June of 1874, the central government dispatched a ministry judge to offer a resolution. However, his compromise to permit future cash taxes did not satisfy the Tagawa cultivators; indeed, it only spurred them to a mass mobilization of fellow Tagawa residents. In July a much more far-reaching plan for a rice marketing cooperative surfaced, and throughout August villagers across the plain organized to challenge, bluntly and sometimes physically, their local officials. Even when the prefecture eventually curbed these August agitations with mass arrests, Tagawans remained undeterred, shifting tactics and finding new leaders. In hindsight, though only in hindsight, the spring petitioning and summer assemblies may be seen as the first two of an eventual four phases of what we now call the Wappa Disturb-

173

ances. They are the phases that this chapter is concerned with.

EARLY PETITIONING: WINTER AND SPRING, 1874

It is now frequently argued that the conversion of taxes in kind to cash taxes in early Meiji was disastrous to most tenants and smallholders in the Japanese countryside—that they were thrust unwittingly and unwillingly into the jaws of the market, that the large-scale landlordism of the mid- and late-Meiji can be attributed to this market vulnerability. Perhaps in retrospect this is a justifiable judgment, but it was certainly not the way in which the Shōnai cultivator-taxpayers evaluated their situation in the early 1870s. Their demand for the right to tender cash taxes was a demand for directly marketing all of their own production. A particular source of indignation was the rates by which tax rice was converted into cash—that is, the rice prices used by the prefectural and local officials to calculate rice equivalencies for levies nominally expressed in cash and to determine the cash value of the principal land tax and other levies expressed in rice. These, they protested, were artifically manipulated to be continually disadvantageous to taxpayers. In 1873, the prefecture had computed the cash value of the principal land tax at about 50% below the autumn market rice price, thus realizing a substantial profit when it sold the rice through its designated merchants. The petitioners preferred to take their chances with direct sales on the market—especially, they argued, when they could reap additional profit by holding rice off the market until prices rose in late winter and spring.

In late 1873, oral requests from cultivators to tender cash taxes percolated up the administrative chain, from village headmen to the village group headmen to the prefecture's rural affairs officials. The latter urged their subordinates to deflect them, but by January and February of 1874, requests took the form of written petitions and could be less easily ignored. Two examples are worth examining in some detail to gain a flavor of the interactions. They demonstrate that from the outset there was a diverse cast of activists from a wide range of Tagawa villages. They further reveal the catalytic role of the Reform Faction ex-samurai, Honda Inri, in fashioning a coordinated movement from isolated expressions of discontent.

The first is that of Suzuki Yaemon, a smallholder in Katakai Village with a registered yield of 22.3 *koku* in 1867 and registered holdings of 1.01 hectares in 1876 (W 1981:25-29, 51-53; see Satō 1981:60-62). In addition to the rice he grew, however, he also bought about 40 bales per year for a small *sake* brewing business. Moreover, in 1873, he had taken on 760 bales of tax rice from forty-six other households, planning to sell the rice, take a small commission, pay the taxes in cash equivalent, and return the rest to the households. Apparently all but three of the twenty-four households in Katakai had for some years been consigning at least part of their rice to him.[1] Two of those three were households with less than 0.1 hectare of paddy land; the third was the village headman, with 1.6 hectares of land. In later testimony, Suzuki described going in late January to Itō Gisaburō, the village group headman, to try to pay his 1873 taxes in cash. Itō would only give him permission to pay his dry field portion in cash. Suzuki petitioned again on February 2; this time Itō told him to bring the cash equivalent of whatever amount he wished to pay by the next day. Suzuki wanted to convert 800 bales, for which he would need about 1,000 *ryō*, an enormous sum to assemble overnight. Indeed, it was not until the morning of the 4th that he was able to bring the sum to Itō. Itō refused to accept it. He told Suzuki that if he had brought it the day before, he would have accepted it; now however he had already made arrangements with Hirose Iemon, one of the designated merchants in Tsurugaoka, to

---

[1] See Takeda 1977:157-64 for details of early Meiji bulker-traders in Akumi (*kedashi* was the local term).

pay the village group taxes. Suzuki asked if Itō might use Suzuki's cash to reimburse Hirose, but was turned down.

Two days later, Suzuki took his complaints to Honda Inri, with whom he had had previous business dealings. Then on the 7th, Suzuki and several relatives were called before Itō, who explained that the prefectural officials had turned down Suzuki's request. When Suzuki insisted on presenting a written petition, Itō reminded him that he would have to go through the proper channels. On the 8th, Honda himself went to see Itō on Suzuki's behalf, but was given the same perfunctory reply. Later that evening, Honda called on Itō's superior, Ikeda Teisaburō (formerly the district deputy of Kushibiki District). Ikeda refused to discuss the Suzuki case, however, unless Honda came to the prefectural offices the next day. There he was told that because of market fluctuations, cash tax payments were prohibited, and an exception could not be made in Suzuki's case. When Honda questioned Ikeda further about just how cash taxes were complicated by such fluctuations, Ikeda got up and left the room without responding. Honda then took the matter to Inoue Saburoemon, a prefectural hearings officer (*chōshōgata*). Inoue indicated that if Suzuki would address a written petition to Matsudaira and submit it to his headman, he (Inoue) would take it up when it reached him. On the 17th, Suzuki presented such a petition that recounted the above events and emphasized that prefectural actions were counter to the Treasury Ministry's directive; he closed with a request for a judgment of "the merits of the case" (*kyokuchoku*; W 1981:25-26, where the date is a typographical error).

At the same time as Honda was helping Suzuki press his request, he was working with several others, notably Satō Hachirobei of Ōyodokawa Village (W 1981:32-34; Satō 1981:67-68). Satō was the second largest landholder in his village, with 5.7 hectares of paddy lands registered in the 1876 land survey. After paying his taxes, Satō had come to

Honda to complain about the high assessments for the land survey expenses—30 *sen* per *koku*.[2] Honda mentioned that he had just been talking to Suzuki, who was agitating for a cash tax. Honda observed that last autumn the rice price had been about 10 *ryō* per nine bales, while by February it had risen to 10 *ryō* per five bales; one could realize a substantial profit if allowed to sell rice freely (and one would find the burden of assessments to be much more tolerable). He offered to help Satō with a petition. Satō had heard that cultivators in the Ōyama area had been allowed partial cash taxes in 1872 and 1873, and used a copy of one of their requests to draw up his own draft, which he brought to Honda. A final petition was drawn up on February 5 at the Torinabe Teahouse on the southern edge of Tsurugaoka. Satō, together with Shirahata Goemon of Kamishimizu Village, set about collecting signatures, and a large gathering was held at the teahouse on the 19th.

The 39-year-old Shirahata Goemon was an intriguing character. He had been born in 1835 to Shirahata Niemon, a smallholder with 1.2 hectares in registered holdings in 1873. At the age of twenty-two, Goemon had been adopted by a cultivator household in another village, but he enjoyed business and soon returned to his family of birth to work as a fish peddlar. In 1873, he had only a small shack next to the main house, and was little interested in the earliest talk about cash tax payment among the villagers. However, as he explained under later interrogation (W 1981:34-35), his peddling took him around the countryside and into Tsurugaoka, and Suzuki's petition was the talk of all the teahouses he frequented. Given his peddling, he was persuaded by fellow villagers to represent them in bringing a petition to the vil-

---

[2] The *yen* had been introduced as a unit of currency in 1871 to replace the gold *ryō*. Initially, 1 *yen* was to equal 1 *ryō*, and both currencies and standards remained in local use. 100 *sen* equaled 1 *ryō*; thus, the survey surcharge was 0.03 *ryō* per registered *koku*.

lage group headman, who was a customer of his. When this was turned back, he went to Honda through an introduction from Satō Hachirobei.[3]

News of Directive #222 and drafts of Suzuki's and others' petitions circulated quickly through the Tagawa villages in mid- to late-February, prompting village assemblies and putting pressure on village headmen. Sample petitions were passed around for individuals and villages to copy. One such draft by Honda Inri began by stating rather directly that although there had been no prefectural notification, the petitioners were aware of the national decree permitting cash tax payments.[4] It complained of the high surcharges for the land survey costs, and argued that if the signatories were permitted to follow national directives, even they might profit enough from rice sales to help offset the burdensome surcharges (*migi sōrōba watakushi domo ganzen tabun mashikata mo kore arisōrō*; W 1981:30).

This widening activism was viewed with alarm by prefectural officials. To them it was not spontaneous popular initiative but rather agitation and coercion by a few malcontents, who refused to pay their taxes and who threatened those who refused to sign their petitions (and even those who had paid their taxes) with village ostracism and attacks on their houses. Officials decided they would have to crack down but realized that already the number of "village representative" signatories had reached twenty to thirty persons. So they decided to make examples of a few prominent petitioners. From February 22 to 25, seven individuals were rounded up, including Shirahata and Satō Hachirobei (W 1981:31-32). All were interrogated and jailed in Sakata.[5] At

---

[3] Goemon's life story was subsquently embellished by his eldest son into a somewhat apocryphal tale for later generations—the *Shirahata Goemon ichidai ki*, the "Story of the First Shirahata Goemon" (partially rendered in TSS 1975a:274-77; for full text, see Satō n.d.).

[4] The opening words were *watakushi domo . . .* , a humble "I," but nonetheless an unusually direct opening phrase (W 1981:30).

[5] One was released without charges after several weeks of questioning,

the same time, the prefecture issued firm warnings to all Tagawa village group headmen that no cash tax would be permitted (W 1982:31).

Curiously, Suzuki was not arrested, but he did not escape another sort of ordeal at the hands of the prefecture. On March 3, he was summoned before the interrogators, and appeared with an ex-samurai as spokesman. He continued to challenge the official explanation that tax rice from Kushibiki and Yamahama Districts was used for samurai fief payments and this had to be in rice. "Why these two districts?" he asked. "Because these districts are close to Tsurugaoka." "But there are other districts around Tsurugaoka as well," he protested, and intimated that he would go to Tokyo and ask the Justice Ministry for a judgment. His two interrogators replied that he was free to appeal to whomever he wished, but that for the moment he should pay his tax in rice; if he was successful in his appeal, the rice could always be returned to him. Suzuki was obliged (*shitagatte yamuezu*, W 1981:52) to sign an agreement to bring in the full amount by March 10.

However, he was only able or only chose to bring in 660 bales of the 800 bales by the 10th. Several days later the prefecture decided to confiscate his property, and Itō and the Katakai village officers searched and itemized his property and served notice to Suzuki's relatives—Suzuki himself had gone into hiding (W 1981:26-27). At the same time, the head of the tax office ordered that the village officers arrange for immediate payment of Suzuki's outstanding balance. On the 18th, the headman called together Suzuki's relatives, who agreed to the need to sell his house.

The next day, though, these relatives were surprised by Itō's announcement that he was having Suzuki's house torn

and three others were released into custody of relatives due to sickness, not surprising given typical prison conditions. However, Satō, Shirahata, and one other were detained for 145 days and only released in mid-July under an order by Matsudaira Masanao, a central government official dispatched to Shōnai.

179

down. They immediately appealed for a stay, promising that they would pay 30 bales and the village's assistant headman (*soeyaku*) would contribute 100 bales by the next day. The prefectural officials refused to compromise, but were faced with additional pleas when they put up at the village headman's house that night. The headman admitted that he had sold Suzuki's house for 23 *yen* to Jiemon in nearby Komaki Village. Suzuki's relatives immediately called on Jiemon, who was persuaded to sell back the rights to them, but this, too, was denied by the village group headman. The next morning, the 19th, the prefectural officials sounded the conch shell, calling on all residents of the surrounding four villages to assemble to dismantle the house and carry the materials to Jiemon's compound. Not a single person answered the summons. Later in the morning, Itō repeated his order. Still no one responded, and he was forced to return home that night. At noon the next day, Itō was back with more than seventy hired laborers from Tsurugaoka, and finally managed to have Suzuki's main house (a sizable structure, 20 meters by 12 meters in size) demolished by the afternoon of the 21st. Leaving the materials at the site, he dispersed the laborers for the day. That afternoon, Suzuki's relatives again assembled to importune the headman to speak with Itō. They appealed to Itō to leave standing Suzuki's storehouse and his *sake* brewing equipment and barrels, arguing that he had old and sick family members to support, and promising to pay all his outstanding taxes by 10 a.m. of the 22nd. Itō finally agreed to this, and the 130 bales were produced. Suzuki returned to Katakai briefly that evening, but fearing arrest, went back into hiding.

Already in the events of January, February, and March, we can see certain features of subsequent protest. From the outset, the demand for cash tax engaged a spectrum of Tagawa residents. Clearly village brewers and petty rice agents like Suzuki and smallholders like Satō felt they stood to gain by such an option, but the early participation of the peddlar Shirahata and smallholder/tenants like Maeno Nisuke of

Kamishimizu (39 years old, with only 0.26 hectares of paddy land) demonstrate how broadly the issue struck a responsive chord. From the outset, too, these Tagawa residents sought advice from Reform Faction ex-samurai like Honda Inri. They used the Kanai house as a meeting place, sharing experiences and tactics and circulating drafts of petitions; the Kanai house was in Baba Ward of Tsurugaoka, on the east side of the castle and directly in front of its main gate!

The focus of agitation was a specific economic issue, but one with obvious political overtones. It challenged the prefectural leaders' plans to control the regional economy and drew attention to their disregard for national directives. The petitioners found district-level subordinates to be evasive and arbitrary. Yet the prefecture could not assert its authority decisively even at this early stage; Itō was publicly embarrassed when surrounding villagers refused his orders to assist in dismantling Suzuki's house. That he was the village group headman and that he was staying at the village headman's house during the incident highlighted the visibility and vulnerability of the men in these posts as rural executors of prefectural authority.

Even as the prefecture was attempting to make an object lesson of Suzuki, a group of five cultivators set off for Tokyo with Honda Inri. They went as delegated representatives of residents in sixteen villages, and managed to lodge a petition with the Home and Treasury Ministries (W 1981:36-37). It complained of the prefecture's failure to circulate Directive #222 and sought ministry intervention in securing the right to pay cash equivalency taxes (*kokudai jōnō*). Its language was very similar to the January and February petitions; it was titled as a "distress petition" (*tangansho*) that asked simply for a correction of administrative wrongdoing. While it lacked a deferential *osorenagara* opening and did not resort to images of indigent people (*kyūmin*), it was still far less assertive than, for example, Kanai's list of charges against the prefecture a year earlier. It was refused by both ministries on the pretext that it had not been endorsed by the prefecture (*ten-*

181

kan kore nashi). Privately, however, it was influential. An internal Home Ministry memorandum two days later encouraged an investigation.

Their visit to Tokyo coincided with a grave political crisis in the capital. There had been a major break in the oligarchic central leadership in the autumn of 1873 over the issue of an invasion of Korea. Those favoring an invasion (the so-called *seikanha sangi*, including Saigō, Etō Shinpei, Gotō Shōjurō, and Itagaki Taisuke) had resigned or been forced from their positions. Gotō and Itagaki returned to their native Tōsa to organize ex-samurai into a "Self-help Society" (*Risshisha*), which was to be a precursor of the Freedom and Popular Rights Movement. Both men were implicated in later Shōnai developments. Saigō returned to Kagoshima, where his supporters continued their military training and maneuvers. Etō returned to Saga (which had pursued a tax rice sales program similar to Sakata's; TSS 1975a:286) to lead an uprising that was quashed by government forces under Ōkubo Toshimichi. Ōkubo had become Home Minister in 1872 after his return from abroad with the Iwakura Mission; now he came to the fore in this post-1873 configuration of power. His close supporters were Itō Hirobumi and Ōkuma Shigenobu, the latter now becoming both councilor and Minister of the Treasury.

We have seen that it was Ōkuma who was particularly alarmed by Sakata Prefecture's links to Saigō, and in the spring of 1874, he again sought direct intelligence on Shōnai conditions. The April 10 report from his agent, Ōe Taku confirmed the continued military strength of the ex-domain retainers, their close connections with Saigō, the improper land survey that had given rise to much unrest (*yue ni shita ni fuhei o narasu hito sukunakarazu*), and the prefecture's failure to circulate the government directives on cash tax (W 1981:4-5; cf. Satō 1981:85-86). At the same time, Ōkubo received an even more detailed report ("an itemization of a secret investigation," *tantei kajō mokuroku*) from Ōtomo Senshū, whom Ōe apparently left behind in Shōnai for further inves-

182

tigations. In the 36-clause confidential report, Ōe conveyed the persisting rumors that Matsudaira and Suge had embezzled the 400,000 *ryō* balance of the 700,000 *ryō* sum assessed Sakai for reversing his transfer order (W 1981:5-6). He went on to express serious doubts about their loyalty to the government, and recommended removing Matsudaira, Suge, and nine of their subordinates (the "Ōu rebel leaders," *Ōu no zokkai*, W 1981:8). Ōtomo also sent the next month a follow-up report, with copies of several documents, including a complaint from Kamishimizu and Takazaka Villages (Maeno, Itagaki, etc.) about the requisitions of supplies and labor for the Matsugaoka mulberry scheme, which the prefecture had made "in the name of the Emperor's wishes" (W 1981:7-13).

While Ōkuma was receiving these reports from his investigators, Ōkubo at the Home Ministry was requesting an explanation from Matsudaira of the charges in the petition that Maeno and the other representatives had presented in March. Matsudaira responded with a lengthy and forceful defense (dated April 23, W 1981:135-39). Shōnai, he argued, was a rice area with no other significant products; there were few who were rich and many who were poor; transport and shipping were difficult during the harsh winter months. Thus, cultivators trying to sell rice and pay a cash tax would be at the mercy of unscrupulous large merchants, the only ones who would benefit from such a system. The disputes that would inevitably erupt would only weigh further on the prefecture's efforts to administer fairly. The prefecture's contractor tax system, on the other hand, was designed to protect the cultivators.

Matsudaira continued that Satō Hachirobei and the others were arrested in late February not because they petitioned but because they were stirring up the countryside. Behind them stood the seditious Honda Inri and a few other rebellious ex-samurai. These malcontents had resisted the Matsugaoka scheme, gone into business on their own, and soon found themselves bankrupt. They then formed a "conspiracy" (*totō*) with other "wicked people" (*kanmin*) and went about the countryside instigating trouble (W 1981:138-39). Matsudaira specifically pointed to the phrase in the cultivators' petition about "common people venturing to beseech the benevolence of the Emperor" as the thinking of Honda and not that of the common people. Finally, Matsudaira responded to the matter of the account ledgers of Ōyodokawa Village, copies of which Honda had passed to Ōtomo. Matsudaira claimed that these were unofficial accountings and were not to be seen as the official tax ledgers (*sōzei wappa chō*); they did not exclude those levies that had recently been phased out.

Matsudaira's point-by-point defense might have been accepted as a plausible defense by a fellow administrator, yet it apparently did little to assuage Ōkubo's suspicions, which continued to be fed by Ōtomo's reports. In May, Ōkubo asked for further explanations from Matsudaira, who merely summarized the arguments he had raised in his earlier reply (report of June 2, W 1981:39).

At this point Ōkubo was proceeding cautiously. An internal conference memo of mid-June (W 1981:38) agreed that the prefecture had ignored the national orders on cash taxes but noted that without prefectural endorsement, the ministry had no jurisdiction to take up the Maeno petition (the "people's suit," *jinmin kōso*). Still, Ōkubo decided to send out another of his officials, Matsudaira Masanao, a middle-level ministry secretary (*shojō*). Arriving on July 16, he spent eight days headquartered at a Sakata temple, hearing testimony from prefectural officials and from activists like Satō and Shirahata, both of whom he ordered released. Sakata administrator Matsudaira claimed under questioning that he had indeed passed along the Directive #222, and that it was then suppressed by subordinates. During the hearings, a directive went out to all village group headmen, under his seal, ordering that henceforth all national laws on cash taxes and regulations on official bale volumes should be honored. Before returning to Tokyo, Matsudaira Masanao summoned

184

officials and cultivator representatives to the forecourt of the temple to hear his decision, which was notable for treading a middle course (W 1981:129). He ruled that a cash tax should be instituted, but only from the current year, and that rural administrative units and their assessment procedures should be reviewed and reformed. He decided that the three most onerous ancillary taxes (mandatory rice borrowings, public works levies, and surcharges on non-resident holdings) could be levied as usual, while only a fourth (the levy in lieu of porterage in the official processions to Edo) was to be discontinued.

THUS, in the winter and spring of 1874, requests for a cash tax were rebuffed and petitions met with arrests; yet this only sparked a wider mobilization of large and small landholders, who by spring were bypassing the prefecture and going directly to the national ministries. Given the focused demands of the petitioners, one would expect that Matsudaira's decision would have been received as a vindication and a victory, and that agitations would quickly subside. Instead, his July hearings only prompted a broadening of demands and a wider mobilization of the rural populace. Two matters now assumed prominence. One was reimbursement for the two tax years after initial issuance of Directive #222; the other was repeal of all ancillary local taxes. Behind both was an indignation as strong as the desire for monetary restitution.

This was apparent, for example, in the later testimony of Satō Shichibei of Hirakyōden Village. He told how he met some angry fellow cultivators on July 21, on his way to Sakata to appear at the Matsudaira hearings for a second time. They were angry because they had heard that "proof" had been presented to Matsudaira that villagers had been notified of Directive #222 back in 1872 by their village group headmen. They knew this to be false. When they challenged their village headman about this, he had admitted that he had been pressured into writing such a declaration for his village group headman. He expressed regret to the villagers and wrote them out a apology and confession. It was this statement of apology that they wanted Satō Shichibei to present to Matsudaira Masanao. He agreed, but Matsudaira refused to accept it, saying obliquely that the prefecture's handling of the directive was a matter of general knowledge and that it was not necessary to accept the apology officially. This refusal to acknowledge formally the duplicity rankled.[6]

Then on the 23rd, Satō Hachirobei, speaking as the designated representative of villages in the three districts of Yamahama, Kushibiki, and Kyōden, tried to raise the matter of ancillary levies at the hearings. Matsudaira Masanao "politely" explained that village and village group levies were outside the official prefectural ledgers and therefore technically not the responsibility of the Treasury and Home Ministries to supervise. He advised them to address any grievances to their local officials. Still, several cultivators gathered together examples of village ledgers—with some difficulty, because village headmen refused them access to their records. They brought them to Sakata only to be told that Matsudaira had just left for Tokyo.

Finally, in the days of the Matsudaira hearings, Tagawa cultivators frequently stopped off at the Kanai house in passing through Tsurugaoka on their way home from Sakata. There they swapped experiences, including their requests to Matsudaira for reimbursement of the profits which the prefecture had made by selling their 1872 and 1873 tax rice. Matsudaira had put aside such queries, saying that the taxes had already been entered in the national accounts and there was nothing to be done. The cultivators were disgruntled, and in the evening conversations after the daily hearings, they were encouraged by several of the Reform Faction exsamurai to press for reimbursement.

The Matsudaira hearings were thus of little consolation to the petitioners, who only renewed the long-standing call for

[6] For this and the next two paragraphs, I have used W 1981:46-58.

186

abolition of all ancillary levies and added a demand for return of all "overcharged taxes" of 1872-73. It was also in the aftermath of the Matsudaira hearings that a proposal surfaced among these activists for a Tax Rice Cash Conversion Company (*kokudai kaisha*). This proposal and these demands, together with the mass assemblies and actions they provoked in August and September, constituted a second phase of the popular protest that has come to be called the Wappa Disturbances.

THE TAX CASH CONVERSION COMPANY, AUGUST-SEPTEMBER, 1874

The plan that emerged in the aftermath of the Matsudaira hearings called for the establishment of a cooperative shareholder company to sell members' rice and provide them with necessary commodities and supplies. Company by-laws were composed to spell out the particulars.[7] It was to be capitalized at 300,000 *yen* by issuing 1,500 shares at 200 *yen* each. The planners intended that villages across Shōnai would join by purchasing several shares collectively. The company would be headquartered in Sakata, where it would operate rice granaries. Rice inspection and granary management was to be handled jointly by three representatives from each member village and salaried company employees. The by-laws continued that the warehouses would be open every afternoon from four to six p.m. for sales of salt, cotton cloth, iron implements, and other commodities and then from six to eight p.m. for purchase and sales of rice.

The genesis of the idea for the cooperative is not clear, but I suspect that again Honda Inri was a critical stimulus. He had gone back to Tokyo in mid-June of 1874 and returned to Shōnai about July 23, after being told of the Matsudaira hearings. It is very possible that he had learned of other such

[7] The text of this *kisokusho* is in YKS B19:1064-65 and W 1981:62-63. The membership agreements (*kanyūsho*) are collected in W 1981:146-72.

187

schemes while in the capital, though it is hard to establish specific precedents. Satō (1963:45) has suggested a parallel with the "Cooperative Company" (*kyōdō kaisha*) in Yamaguchi Prefecture, which was formed a year earlier and was also designed to sell members' rice at favorable conditions, pay their taxes in cash, and return the difference. He has not established, however, that Honda or the others knew of the Yamaguchi scheme.[8] Still, Honda testified after his arrest that he was the central figure in the plan: "in order to plan for such matters as the convenience of agriculture and the ease of commerce, I became a principal in wanting to put together the cash tax equivalency company."[9]

The fact that Honda spent the night in Sakata at the merchant Mori Tōemon's house upon his return from Tokyo suggests the possibility that Mori and other Sakata merchants contributed much to the operational details of the planned cooperative. Perhaps they drew upon the ideas of Honma Gunbei, whom Mori had known. Gunbei was from a branch household of the main Honmas and had pursued Western studies in the late 1850s, becoming an English teacher in Kagoshima in the mid-1860s. There he had authored and printed up a plan for an international trading company.[10]

I suspect, too, that the tax procedures of the ex-shogunate villages in Tagawa also served as a model. As we have seen, these villages had been able to pay most of their tax obligations in cash or rice voucher for over one hundred years, but this did not mean that individual households sold their pro-

---

[8] Indeed, the Yamaguchi cooperative was organized by the Enterprise Promotion Bureau (*kangyō kyoku*) of Yamaguchi Prefecture, which came under sharp popular criticism in 1874 for its involvement. As a result of this, the cooperative was set up as a *bōchō kyōdōkai* (Satō 1963:45).

[9] *nōmin no benri shō no kōtsu nado o hakari, jibun nushi to nari kokudai kaisha torimusubitaku* (W 1981:77; see also Satō 1963:78, 85).

[10] *Sashū shōsha happen* (Kudō 1981:26-27; Satō 1976:198-99). Gunbei was poisoned by Shōnai Domain officials in 1868 when he visited Sakata to raise capital for his venture.

duction and tendered coin or vouchers. Rather, villages would contract by unit with one or several rice dealers in Kamo or Sakata, through whom they would sell village output (or at least enough to meet tax obligations, which within the village were calculated and gathered in rice).[11] Familiarity with these joint arrangements was surely a stimulus, even if not a template, for the form of cooperative economic organization envisioned by these activists.

The Cash Conversion Company plan was explained to a wider circle of local supporters in late July at a secret meeting at Ryūan-ji Temple in Kamishimizu Village.[12] These supporters then fanned out to organize mass meetings at the main temple or shrine of each village group to explain the plan and solicit members. These assemblies, in late July and early August, touched off six weeks of organized and occasionally violent disturbances and demonstrations that we will now explore in some detail. In contrast to the Tengu League, which arose in Akumi, the most intense agitation was now in the five districts of Tagawa (see Map 3). While it was particularly centered in those plains areas around Tsurugaoka, there are at least some surviving materials from all of the thirty village groups in Tagawa.[13]

[11] One can interpret this in two ways—either it represented a "traditional" solution by subsistence-oriented peasants to provide at least a modicum of insulation from the market, or it suggests an emergent entrepreneurial appreciation of the advantages of scale in joint sales.

[12] During the summer, the planners had been using the temple when not meeting at the Kanai house. This was not because it was more secluded; indeed the Ōyama Village Group headman, Yoshida Hatsutarō, had his residence in the village. Rather, it was because Kamishimizu had an unusually large number of activists. In addition to Shirahata and Maeno, these included: Itagaki Giemon (age?, 1.9 hectares); Itagaki Kinzō (34, Giemon's son); Satō Yokichi (39, 0.9 hectares); Satō Naokichi (36, 1.3 hectares); Igarashi Sakubei (age?, 1.2 hectares); Katō Kosaku (age?, 0.9 hectares); and Maeno Kan'emon (age?, 1.3 hectares). That is, they tended to be those with minimal or modest registered holdings. The village temple priest supported the cause by helping to compose and write out many of the petitions.

[13] The most comprehensive published collection of materials relating to the events of late July, August, and September is in W 1981. These docu-

The meetings of all villagers within a village group were called to explain the idea of the Cash Conversion Company and to solicit members and sell shares. This support was readily forthcoming in the form of an "agreement" (*yaku-jōsho*) signed by several representatives of residents of a single village, who pledged that they would market a certain volume of rice through the company. Calculations from the surviving agreements suggest that an overwhelming majority of villages in Tagawa subscribed in August and September and that most villages committed a majority share of their production. This would have meant that over 200,000 *koku* would be marketed through the cooperative. These agreements and the subsequent actions also clearly demonstrate what the more fragmentary evidence of the Tengu League only suggested: lines of antagonism within the villages were more political divisions, pitting most villagers against their largely isolated headmen, than conflicts between economic strata. Harima-kyōden Village was typical. The two chosen representatives were both large landholders—Giemon, a large Ōyama landlord with over 30 hectares, including 32 *koku* in Harima itself, and Yasubei, with over 75 *koku* of Harima lands. The village headman, Yasuemon, with over 79 *koku*, refused to join.[14]

The planned cooperative offered a strikingly new economic arrangement for direct, collective rice marketing by large and small cultivators across the Tagawa countryside. But the ratification assemblies also quickly became occasions

---

ments fall into three categories. There are reports by village and village group headmen to the prefecture about what was typically termed the "cultivators' agitations" (*hyakushō sawagitachi*); these contained first-hand experiences, hearsay, and copies of petitions and announcements of the agitators themselves (W 1981:173-221). A second category is the reports to the prefecture by its inspectors and armed patrols dispatched about the countryside during these months (W 1981:222-93). Finally, there were the written testimonies taken by prefectural interrogators from those protesters who were arrested (W 1981:76-126).

[14] Satō 1963:45, where Giemon is incorrectly identified as Moemon; see W 1981:157-58.

for venting much broader, long-standing grievances against local administration and taxation, directed principally against village headmen and village group headmen. In meeting after meeting across the plain, the headmen were charged with improper and arbitrary taxation, with misappropriation and embezzlement, and the meetings often ended with direct confrontations. This was the start of six weeks of widespread collective actions that engulfed Tagawa through August and September and that were directed against the headmen— their houses were attacked, they were detained and beaten, those who fled were pursued, their account books were con- fiscated and made public, they were forced to repay what were judged to be improper levies and expenditures.

Yet it is equally significant that these six weeks of actions did not generate a radical political reform program commen- surate with the economic plan of the cooperative rice mar- keting company. This broad-based popular protest contin- ued to focus on specific "economic" issues; there was no abstract and florid language of political rights or millennial retribution. This is not to argue that this phase, and those before and after, can be reduced to strictly utilitarian moti- vations, a drive for profit and restitution. There was an equal measure of indignation and outrage in their efforts to expose the egregious excesses of local and prefectural administra- tion. To appreciate this, let us consider the happenings in one particular village group.

KUROKAWA VILLAGE GROUP

Kurokawa Village Group in Kushibiki District lay at the southern edge of the plain, a couple of kilometers from Tsu- rugaoka and just below the uplands of the prefecture's Ma- tsugaoka mulberry and tea scheme. On July 31, over a thou- sand people from its twenty-three villages met at Kasuga Shrine through the efforts of Kenmochi Torazo (1848-1902) of Tsubaide Village, who had joined the circle of activists at

Ryūan-ji earlier in the summer.[15] The 26-year-old Torazo outlined the proposal for the cash conversion cooperative and announced that "officials of the Imperial Court" (tencho oyakunin) were circulating through the countryside to explain its operational details. The assembled people agreed to invite them to come before them. Honda was at the time in Akumi, while Ōtomo and Uranishi were appearing before other assemblies in Tagawa. On August 5, Kenmochi and a number of others, dressed formally in hakama, went to the village group boundary to greet officially Ōtomo, Uranishi, and their party, which also included Ishikawa Buntarō of Takazaka Village. They were put up that night at an activist's house in Takenokami Village, and the next day addressed an assembly of village group residents at Kasuga Shrine. Ōtomo read out the by-laws of the cooperative and encouraged their support. He promised that if they joined the cooperative, he would work for a repeal of all ancillary levies, and he raised the issue of the domain's profiting from its sales of the 1872 and 1873 tax rice. Finally, he suggested that there were serious misappropriations in recent local taxing, and urged the crowd to demand access to the ledgers from their village headmen. All agreed to support the cooperative and drew up commitments (the yakujōsho).

About ten days later, some fifteen hundred people gathered at Miyanoshita Shrine below Kasuga, and from there forced their way into the house of the Nakagumi Village headman, Saitō Chōzaemon. They demanded to see his records and ledgers. The next morning, another group of about two hundred similarly besieged the Kurokawa Village headman, Kobayashi Zensaburō. When Kobayashi refused them, they moved off to another headman, Akiyama Shoemon. Akiyama claimed that all of his records were stored at the

---

[15] Kenmochi was the eldest son of a household with only minimal landholdings (0.16 hectares of paddy in 1876). Documents pertaining to Kurokawa, on which my account is based, are to be found in Matsunaga 1972:343-46 and W 1981:173-81, 183-84, 225-28, 232-33, 239-40, 242, and 258-64. See also Satō's discussion of these materials in Satō 1981:123-30.

home of the village group headman, Yatabe Kyōho, so that afternoon the crowd pushed their way into Yatabe's compound with a long list of ledgers to inspect. Yatabe was forced to make copies of some of the documents in his possession, but insisted that many others had been taken to Tsurugaoka to the office for all Tagawa village group headmen.

Hearing this, part of the crowd led several of the village headmen off to the Tsurugaoka office, where they demanded access to the record boxes on the second floor. At some point in the evening, several men from Nakagumi tied up the village officers and made off with some of the books. This set off some violence and vandalism by others. The village group headman on duty could not control them, and the melee continued until the next morning, when prefectural soldiers were summoned. Soldiers were also sent around to several of the Kurokawa villages to cool tempers. Though they were soon withdrawn, agitators at Kanai's house issued a warning that if ever any cultivators were arrested, they would send out the *shinchōgumi* against the prefectural squads, a reference to the recalcitrant brigade that remained unhappy about the Matsugaoka Project.

About the same time, Tsubaide villagers caught their headman trying to carry off the records of four villages to the Tsurugaoka office. They relieved him of them and brought them with others to the Kanai house. In several days of studying them, they discovered among other apparent embezzlements that he had collected "village group expenses" of 3,499 bales of rice, which he had sold for about 7,000 *yen* though his recorded expenses only came to 3,466 *yen.*

On the morning of August 17, Kenmochi appeared at another gathering of about 800 persons at Kasuga Shrine. He announced that the Nakagumi Village headman, Saitō Chōzaemon, had fled to Yatabe's house with the village books, and called for a group to go after him. A prefectural official who had been dispatched to Yatabe's house sent a warning to the gathering that if they had any requests they were to send one representative per village to Yatabe's compound. That afternoon, though, more than seventy persons showed up at his gate. Some of them entered the compound and asked Yatabe to bring out Saitō so that they might question him. Yatabe replied that he was in the middle of a conference with Saitō; two or three delegates could enter to talk with him, but he wouldn't send Saitō out. The crowd found that unacceptable, and informed Yatabe that all would go over to Saitō's compound and await his return. The prefectural official later ventured out and followed the crowd over to Saitō's place, where he spent the night trying to persuade them to disperse. Finally, at five in the morning, he returned to Yatabe's.

By daybreak, the crowds surrounding Saitō's compound began shouting to be fed (takidashi). His wife refused, but his relatives eventually produced three bales of polished rice, which they cooked up and distributed. The people still refused to disperse, and instead returned to Yatabe's compound, where they milled about until the next evening (August 19).

On the 20th, they again assembled at Kasuga and discussed going up to Uenoyama Village. Uenoyama, a small settlement of ten households, had signed a pledge to join the cooperative at the August 6 meeting, but its residents had refused to join the subsequent demonstrations. Kenmochi headed up a party that asked the village's participation as well as a contribution of 10 ryō and 3 sho (about 6 quarts) of sake from each household. They accosted the headman and extracted a written promise of support.[16] On the 23rd, Kenmochi and supporters were back in Uenoyama, where they found several of the houses abandoned and those who remained unwilling to agree to the contributions he demanded.

---

[16] That same evening, another group approached the official who held the key to the Kurokawa Village Group granary and forced him to hand it over (though there is no further reference to actions against the granary).

194

Threatening expulsion from the village group, the Kenmochi group withdrew.

On August 31, a large crowd again forced its way into Yatabe's compound; about forty of them pushed into the small administrative office beside the main house. This time they demanded reimbursement for the "excess" 1872-73 taxes. Yatabe explained that these allotments had just been calculated for all village groups and villages and that he was in the process of dividing Kurokawa's share among the headmen. As no such decision had been made by the prefecture, we must conclude that this was a stalling action by Yatabe or a reimbursement that he and his village headmen were making themselves. The crowd, though, declared that since they had paid their 1872 and 1873 taxes in rice, they wanted any reimbursement in rice, not in cash. They told Yatabe that he could draw from the village group or prefectural stocks. Yatabe protested that he had just "gratefully" received Kurokawa's allotment in cash. There was, nonetheless, no such distribution in either rice or cash.

The crowd also began challenging him on levies that he and his headmen had made for which they could find no notation in the tax ledgers. "Where are the directives that justify them?" "Why, for example, do you assess a village group reserve rice levy (kumi sonaemai)?" "How specifically were the land survey levies spent?" They went through their lists column by column, questioning items about which they had no doubt long harbored suspicions. They were seldom satisfied by Yatabe's explanations. When they finally declared they were going off to interrogate Saitō Chozaemon and another headman, Ueno Matsuzo, about village tax collection procedures, Yatabe advised them smugly that they would find neither at home. This only further angered them, and they forced Yatabe to provide a written promise that he would produce them within three days. Yatabe immediately set out for Tsurugaoka and Sakata, where they and other headmen had sought refuge.

That evening at seven, over 1,000 persons gathered at

195

Ueno Matsuzo's compound to await his return; again Kenmochi Torazo was among the leaders. They began to harass his wife, threatening to confiscate the house, storehouse, and lands if her husband did not return the land survey expenses. Leaving behind Ueno's brother-in-law, his wife and other household members fled. Through the night, the villagers forced him to produce and cook up eight bales of rice; they helped themselves to salt, *miso*, and other supplies from the storehouse.

Early the next morning, part of the crowd went back up to Uenoyama Village, and Kenmochi again demanded contributions from the headman. When he refused they bound up four of the village men and threatened to lead them off if he did not produce either "gold and jewels" or money and *sake*. Eventually the headman signed another promise to pay the latter.

The crowds in front of Ueno Matsuzo's finally broke up on the morning of September 2, after receiving written assurance from his son that restitution would be made. They were also given four bales of rice by Saitō Chozaemon and another headman. They immediately reassembled at Kasuga Shrine, where they were urged to disperse by an unnamed prefectural official who showed up later in the day. Kenmochi Torazo challenged him to have the prefecture dispatch high officials who would hold public judgments of village headmen in front of residents; the official's counteroffer of private negotiations with Torazo and other leaders was rebuffed. The same day, the prefecture received an urgent appeal from Yatabe and his headmen for strong prefectural support against the agitators. They were not just being harassed and driven from office, they pleaded, they were being driven to personal ruin.

Kurokawa residents continued their invasions of Yatabe's compound and demands for written promises and bales of rice from various headmen. On the morning of the 5th, Kenmochi and several others left for Kanai's house. Word was passed that they were going from there to Sakata, where

Yatabe and several of his headmen had fled. In early afternoon, a large crowd set out from Kurokawa to meet up with Kenmochi and bring the officials back by force from the merchant's home in which they hid, but they were intercepted and turned away by a squad of prefectural soldiers. The next day, about 400 of them descended upon another Kurokawa village, Inomata-shinden, that had been reluctant to support them. They ordered the headman to call the villagers together, and all twenty-two households were pressured to sign a pledge of support and to make contributions of cash and *sake*. The headman was forced to distribute three bales of cooked rice to the crowd, which moved on to several other villages to extort cash, *sake*, and cooked rice from reluctant village officers. By evening they all returned to Yatabe's compound, which they continued to occupy.

On September 7, about twenty of the crowd again set out for Sakata. This time, they reached the house where Yatabe and most of the headmen were staying, but Yatabe refused to return to Kurokawa. When a squad of soldiers appeared, the crowd withdrew to another Sakata merchant's house, where they spent the night. They were again dispersed by soldiers when they showed up at Yatabe's lodging the next day (the cover term *setsuyū*, "persuasion," is the term in most documents). Drifting back to Kurokawa, they found that the crowds in Yatabe's compound were also breaking up. Then on the 9th came the prefecture's roundup.

Such was the course of events in a single village group, but it is important to remember that similar meetings and collective actions were occurring simultaneously all across Tagawa through August and early September. Another area of intense activity within Kushibiki District was Shōryūji Village Group, on the opposite, west bank of the Aka River. There, in late August, a three-day meeting was held to solicit membership pledges for the rice cooperative. It also became an occasion for sharing stories of village headman corruption—of falsely entering an expense payment to a tobacco dealer as 80 *yen* instead of 8 *yen*, of claiming expenses of

1,000 *yen* for the village group headman's official town residence, of assessing land survey fees of 1,300 *yen*, of using village group money to pay officials' field laborers, of regular gift payments from village headmen to village group headmen, and so forth. After the assembly, smaller groups invaded the houses of village headmen, interrogating and berating them (*gōdan*) in all-night sessions. They insisted on reimbursement of part of the land survey assessments and what they claimed were other overcharges; they even sought confiscation of household goods and land and banishment from the village. In early September, several of the headmen were captured and detained in a local shrine until they promised to pay 200 *yen* in restitution (W 1981:182-83, 222-25, 230-32; see also TSS 1975a:257). Such detention was not uncommon; in Tagawa Village Group, too, several headmen were held at Umebayashi Temple until they signed pledges of reimbursement and of taxation reform (W 1981:185-87, 240-47). And in Atsumi Village Group, several hundred people from twelve villages invaded the village group headman's compound; they seized his books and forced his seal on an agreement to repay over 950 *ryō* and on a letter of resignation to the prefecture (W 1981:190-94, 247-49).

Protests began in late July in Karikawa District (W 1981:205-21). Satō Hachirobei came over from Ōyodokawa Village and was active in several of the village groups, appearing before assemblies to explain the cooperative plan. He was respected for his six months in the prefectural prison and admired as a forceful and persuasive speaker (*ben ni suguretaru hito*). Several headmen reported to Matsudaira that Satō effectively prodded Karikawa villages with promises of the great benefits they would enjoy from joining the cooperative and supporting the new "Kanai Prefecture."[17] In Karikawa

[17] One report elided the two as *Kanai shōsha ken*, the Kanai Company Prefecture, W 1981:220. This and other information came to the headmen from three villagers whom they coopted into posing as interested supporters and pumping the activist, Kusaku of Soezu Village, for details and plans. They reported that Kusaku had described Kanai's house as the "new prefectural headquarters" (*shincho*).

District, too, village headmen were the principal target of harassment. The headmen in Masukawa Village Group, for example, alleged that they had been subjected to attacks by several hundred protesters, some of whom roughed them up inside while the others surrounded the outsides of their houses, shouting streams of insults. They said they had been accused of colluding with the village group headman and district tax officers to embezzle village funds. They reported that their short swords (*wakizashi*) and their sandals (*geta*), both symbols of their position, were stolen (W 1981:220).

THE ROUNDUP

Faced with this tumultuous, rebellious Tagawa countryside, Matsudaira and Suge responded much more cautiously than they had to the final Tengu protests two years earlier. For six weeks, they moved gingerly, offering only limited assistance to the village and village group officials. On occasion, they dispatched squads of soldiers, but these made no arrests, and the crowds reformed as soon as the patrols withdrew. Suge even agreed to meet with Kenmochi Torazo, although this was a gesture of caution and not conciliation: Matsudaira and Suge did refuse flatly to accept a copy of the by-laws and an accompanying petition seeking to begin operations. And all the while, they used the village group headmen to gather considerable documentation on the protests and protesters.

Matsudaira's first report to Itō Hirobumi, the new Home Minister, about what he called the "cash tax payment incident" (*kokudainō ikken*) was on August 7; a month later, on September 9, Itō gave him permission to take "emergency measures" (*rinki shobun*). Suge, the vice-administrator, admitted in a message to Itō dated September 10 that the troubles might be attributed to improprieties with tax monies by local officials. He argued, though, that these were not deliberate. They arose merely from following "old customs." More seriously, the cultivators (here he termed them *nōmin* and not *hyakushō*) had been carried to such excesses by the nefarious provocations of Honda and other insurgent ex-samurai, operating out of Kanai's house and claiming themselves to be "Kanai Prefecture." He explained to Itō that they would arrest Honda and all of the other ex-samurai provocateurs, but only the most vociferous *nōmin*. On September 15, Itō reported to Sanjō that while his ministry had been sympathetic to the Tagawa petitioners that spring, violence had now broken out, and he again gave Matsudaira and Suge permission for this unusual, but necessary, step (W 1981:60). As it turned out, the prefecture had already begun its arrests four days earlier.

Before dawn on the morning of the 11th, about one hundred soldiers surrounded the Kanai house in Tsurugaoka. When the signal was given, they broke in and arrested Honda, three other ex-samurai, and three cultivators who had stayed the night. They also confiscated trunks of official documents. At the same time, other squads were moving through the Tagawa villages, and by the end of the day over one hundred persons had been taken into custody. Many others went into hiding.

It was at just this moment that Kanai Tadanao himself was due back from Tokyo, where he had been since mid-July promoting the rice cooperative plan. Maeno Nisuke, who remained at large, acted quickly to prevent his arrest. On the 12th, Maeno very publicly called together several hundred people at Shimoyamazoe Village's Hachiman Shrine, ostensibly to welcome Kanai. While prefectural troops stood by to apprehend him there, Kanai was taken by a mountain route to Shiroyama-bayashi Village. It was there that Satō Shichibei, Watariai Jūkichi (age 27, from Takazaka), and several others met with Kanai, but they soon discovered sharp differences between Kanai's thinking and their own plans. The cultivators wanted to organize a mass attack on Sakata Prison, and at the same time, to appeal directly to the Justice Ministry in Tokyo. In particular, they wanted to inform Matsudaira Masanao at the ministry about the developments since his hearings in mid-July. They hoped that they could now convince him of the prefecture's wrongdoings.

Kanai was appalled. He had been in Tokyo throughout the August disturbances and apparently had known nothing of them. Now he strongly dissented from any such direct action; instead, he counseled petitioning Sakata Prefecture officials for release of those detained. The others ignored his timidity and began their plans to storm the Sakata Prison. They had the priest of Kamishimizu's Ryūan-ji draw up a call to march.[18] On the afternoon of the 16th, several thousands gathered at a number of sites around the plain. Matsudaira and Suge, meanwhile, had mobilized all of the Matsugaoka retainers and had dispatched them in their units across the plain and through the streets of Sakata.

One staging ground for the marchers was the forested slopes of Baba Mountain behind Kamishimizu, where about 800 persons gathered from forty-three villages.[19] In the evening, they set out across the plain, waving hand scythes, hoes, and poles, but they caught sight of a column of prefectural soldiers and decided to retreat to Baba Mountain for the night. Throughout the night, they could look down at the flickerings of large paper lanterns dotting the plain, kept burning by their home villages as signs of support. Village officers tried to persuade people to disperse, but at dawn, the crowd again set off. This time they advanced several kilometers, as far as Hirakyōden Village. There they were surrounded by prefectural soldiers in the fields just south of the settlement. A scuffle broke out in the front ranks when they refused an order to disperse and the soldiers tried to arrest one of the leaders, Itagaki Kinzō. Several of the marchers were badly injured in the ensuing fray. Itagaki and others

---

[18] It was titled an "Agreement Among Several Thousands Cultivators to Force Their Way to Sakata" (*sūsen no hyakushō Sakata e oshisageru yakujō*), although the agreement was not an accomplished fact but rather an exhortation.

[19] I have based my account on documents in W 1981:267-93. See Satō 1981:172-201 for similar actions at the other staging grounds.

were taken in hand, and the people gradually dispersed (see the guard report of the confrontation, YKS 1978:1068-70). All other groups were similarly intercepted and broken up by prefectural squads, which arrested leaders and forced the others back to their villages.

Two days later, nine of those leaders still not captured met to discuss the next move at a small, isolated shrine (Ubadō) on Mitsumori Mountain, another of the small peaks behind Kamishimizu Village.[20] The gathering included Kanai, Ōtomo, Satō Hachirobei, Kenmochi Torazo, and Satō Shichibei, and their debate produced a stunning shift in program and strategy. The plan to attack Sakata Prison was dropped, as was all talk of a tax rice cooperative and a Kanai Prefecture; none of these ideas appear in any subsequent document. Instead, they returned to earlier language and tactics: petitions carried to the national ministries in Tokyo. The Wappa Disturbances were to move into a very different third phase.

TAX REVOLT, NOT WORLD RENEWAL

Residents of the Shōnai countryside had never been aroused to such a pitch of coordinated, collective activity, and they have never since witnessed anything like those two months between the Matsudaira Masanao hearings in mid-July and the prefecture's roundup in mid-September. The remarkable intensity of the attacks on the village and village group headmen across at least two-thirds of Shōnai and over a six-week period had no precedent in earlier collective actions—the occupation of headmen's compounds and their Tsurugaoka office, seizure and scrutiny of official ledgers and records, detainment and continuous haranguing of headmen for hours and days, forced contributions of cooked rice, *sake*, and money, coerced promises of restitution, and threats of ex-

[20] It is probably mere coincidence that this mountain, also known as Morinoyama, was believed by Shōnai people to be the temporary abode of spirits in transit to an afterworld (Tsuyuki 1967).

pulsion from the village and confiscation of property. Extreme actions, though ultimately circumscribed—they stopped short of property destruction and torture. The officials suffered no injuries or deaths. But they were shown to be isolated from all other villagers, even those largeholders of similar "class," who supported the actions, not the headmen.

Some of the grievances were familiar from the Tengu League agitations: reimbursement of overcharges, elimination of all ancillary taxes, cash payments. Yet their demands had escalated and there was a further edge to their outrage. This time there were no petitions; petitions could not produce the specific answers they wanted. Kenmochi and his crowd did not plead with Yatabe and his headmen to produce their ledgers; they told him directly, orally, and they took what they did not receive. It was not distress but anger that charged their actions; it was less the sums of money involved than the abuses of the headmen. They sought restitution, apology, and accountability. They gave collective voice to standards of official conduct—or at least limits of misconduct—for which they themselves now held headmen accountable.

These August agitations were unprecedented; there was a breadth of issues, a degree of participation, and a level of intensity beyond the 1840-41 protests or even the Tengu League in 1869-70. Moreover, the cooperative plan promised a striking reordering of rice marketing arrangements. And yet there is some danger in overstating the novelty of the motivating concerns of that August month and the radicalness of the protestors. "Improper" (fusei) and "dishonorable" (fumeigi) conduct was not an unfamiliar charge to local officials, and many of the levies in question had been pressed by the Tengu League several years earlier. And as the language of the Tengu League suggested appeal to a powerful folk morality, one is tempted to interpret references to a "new prefecture" as a radical political vision complementing the Grange economics. Yet this is not really warranted by the

203

available materials. For example, references to a new Kanai Prefecture were not widespread through the districts; in fact, there was some variation in the degree to which residents implicated the prefectural leaders in their grievances. While typically the prefecture was mentioned in the alleged malfeasance, in only some areas were phrases about Kanai Prefecture bandied about. A few village groups even appealed to prefectural leaders to bring the headmen to justice. Moreover, in contrast to the detailed by-laws and pledge solicitations for the rice cooperative company, the idea of a "counter-prefecture" was never more than vague and suggestive. There were no calls for elective office and representative councils that Vlastos describes in his account of the 1869 uprisings in Fukushima (1982:171, 173-74). It was tax reform, not world reform, that agitated the Tagawa countryside in August of 1874, and it was a feeling of indignation and a set of issues that earlier protesters would have understood immediately.

EIGHT

From the Headmen's Compounds
to the Council of State

IT IS difficult, frankly, to explain convincingly why the assemblies and harassment and all talk of the rice cooperative company and Kanai Prefecture evaporated so suddenly. Perhaps the prefecture's show of force intimidated the activists. Yet should not the strong collective actions of the preceding six weeks have given the protesters enough confidence to meet this setback? Was this a pragmatic turn from direct violence to indirect legal appeals? Perhaps it was more difficult to mobilize people by mid-September because the rice harvest was beginning. But did not harvest and tax collection confront them directly with the practices they wished to reform? Had the waves of demonstrations depended so entirely on the energies of a few leaders that the mass arrests had effectively halted their momentum?

Certainly the activists who emerged after the aborted march on Sakata offered quite different counsel than Kenmochi, other village agitators, and Honda. At first, Honda's older brother Kanai Tadanao was influential, and his insistence on petitioning persuaded their fellow ex-samurai Ōtomo and those cultivators who were still at large, like Satō Hachirobei. Yet their first act disabused them of the efficacy of petitioning the prefecture, that is, of following the legal chain of pleading that Kanai had earlier advocated. Those who gathered on Mitsumori Mountain on September 19 had Ōtomo write out a request to Suge for the release of Honda and all others detained; he phrased it in a conventionally deferential "distress petition" style (W 1981:57). The next day, ten persons set out for Sakata, led by Tomigashi

Rikichi, a largeholder from Shiroyamabayashi. They were arrested by prefectural soldiers even before reaching Sakata and were never allowed to present the plea they were carrying.

So it was off to Tokyo. Singly or in small groups, using the mountain paths to elude the border guards or leaving by small boat from Kamo port, Kanai, Ōtomo, Satō Hachirobei, Maeno Nisuke, and others made their way to Tokyo by the beginning of October. There, too, they were to find disappointment and arrest. Kanai himself was the first to be apprehended, on October 10, when trying to present a distress petition to the Ministry of Justice. Four times in late October and early November, he had Kobayashi Katsukiyo make representations on his behalf at the Sain and the high court at the Ministry of Justice, but he remained in custody.[1]

Meanwhile on October 25, eight of the cultivators who had also come to the capital, including Satō Hachirobei and Satō Shichibei, presented their own distress petition. Addressed to Home Minister Itō, it pleaded that they had come to Tokyo because they were unable to get a fair hearing from their prefecture. They charged that the prefecture was not obeying Matsudaira Masanao's rulings, and asked the ministry for a "clarification" of his rulings about ancillary levies. They described their actions against local officials and their agitations to free Honda and the others. They appended a list of seventeen taxes, claiming that reimbursement (*sagemodoshi*) was due on several of them (W 1982:57-59).

---

[1] The Sain (the Chamber of the Left) was one of three branches of the central government after its 1871 reorganization. It was the legislative branch, though it had only limited powers of inquiry and initiative and its members were appointed and dismissed by the Meiji leaders. Kobayashi was a *daigennin*, a term that was replacing *kujishi* to describe the professional lobbyists, spokesmen, and barristers in Tokyo (see Satō 1981:203-204, Ch'en 1981:73). Ch'en notes that beginning in 1872 it was legal for such third parties to represent a plaintiff in court. See Ōtomo's journal (*tehikae*) covering his time in Tokyo (W 1982:36-52). Ōtomo hired another lobbyist, Taniguchi Takejirō, to help him prepare and present a total of three petitions (e.g., W 1981:67).

The ministry returned the petition, again declining to take action on the pretext that it lacked prefectural endorsement. Unlike Kanai, though, the cultivators remained free and chose to stay in Tokyo to continue petitioning.[2] But on December 10, they, and Ōtomo, were summoned to the Police Bureau, where the Bureau Chief reminded them that none of the ministries or courts had acted favorably on their petitions. He indicated that he himself would take their complaints under advisement, but in the interim, they were to return home to Shōnai and not cause any trouble. He recognized that they had little money and so would supply them with travel funds—and a police guard! Soon after, they were escorted back to Shōnai; arriving about the 25th of the month, they were immediately remanded to prefectural authorities, who kept them in detention for two months while interrogating them and taking depositions. By the end of the year, the prefecture held at least seventy-eight persons in connection with the various agitations of the year, including Honda's wife and daughter (W 1982:33-35).

MORI TŌEMON

Just when the Shōnai protests appeared extinguished, with local agitators quieted and avenues of redress in Tokyo closed, yet another person came to the fore to offer fresh leadership to the cause and to inject it with a new idiom of protest, that of the increasingly vocal "freedom and popular rights" (jiyū minken) advocates. This was Mori Tōemon, the Sakata merchant who was mentioned earlier as an occasional visitor to the Kanai house in the spring and summer of 1874 and who was now to play a dominant role as the Wappa Disturbances moved into a third phase: from the Tagawa

---

[2] See, for example, the long "distress petition" to the Police Bureau by Kenmochi Torazo, Shōji Iemon, and Kanbara Chōbei (Matsunaga 1972:343-46). The first two identified themselves as joint representatives of forty-five Tagawa villages, while Kanbara affixed his seal as representative of twenty-seven other Tagawa villages.

headmen compounds to the courtrooms and ministries of Tokyo.

Mori had been born in 1842, just before the Ōyama Disturbances, to a prosperous *sake* dealer in the heart of Sakata; the Mori house and shop sat at what is now the northwest corner of Sakata City Hall. The Karani-ya, the household's business name, was an old shop in Sakata; the household head had sat on the 36-Man Town Council since 1768.[3] The second of two sons, Mori was sent in adoption at the age of six to his maternal grandmother's household, but in 1856, both his father and his older brother died. Four years later, the grandfather of the house also died, leaving only his mother and his younger sister. In 1864, Mori returned to his natal household to become the successor head. He took a wife from Haga Shichiemon, a well-to-do house in Tōge Village at the foot of the Mt. Haguro temple complex. Mori's father had himself been adopted from the Hagas, and the current Shichiemon was to offer useful financial assistance to Mori after he had expended his own resources.

From his first years, Mori was caught up in the intellectual and political turbulence of the last Tokugawa decades. His first lessons were in the Chinese classics, which he took from Suda Bun'ei, a doctor who lived across the street from the Mori house and who had trained in radical versions of Neo-Confucian studies in Edo. Mori took up the household headship in difficult times. In 1868, the 36-Man Town Council organized a Sakata merchant militia under domain auspices. Mori saw action in the Boshin War as vice-commander of one of its squads near the Echigo-Shōnai border. The following year Sakata was occupied by Restoration forces and administered by the young Saga doctor, Nishioka. Despite his preoccupation with the Tengu protests, Nishioka devoted time to opening an academy in the town, the *Gakujutsukan*,

---

[3] The *Sanjūrokuninshū*, which operated under the domain's Sakata affairs official. Membership was limited to those households in the Central Ward (*honchō*) who were shippers or purveyors to the shipping trade (*kaisen ton'ya*).

whose course of study was a strand of Neo-Confucianism centered on restoration of the Emperor (SSS 1981:883). He recruited the young Mori as one of the instructors. Thus, in 1869, the Sakata town elite was sharply divided. While his fellow town councilman Nagahama Gorokichi was a leading agitator in the Tengu League drive and two other members, Ōseki and Neagari, were the new administration's designated rice dealers, Mori was equivocal. He ignored the popular demands for taxation reform and the merchant protests against the Tokyo direct sales policy, and seemed ready to give Nishioka and the new Meiji authorities a chance.

By 1874, though, Mori was thoroughly disillusioned by the return of the old Sakai elite. Like Kanai and Honda, he admired and encouraged Suzuki and the other petitioners in early 1874, apparently providing some financial support to those arrested. He most probably helped in drafting the by-laws of the tax rice cooperative, but he was strongly opposed to violent confrontations with officials and, like Kanai, counseled legal petitioning. He apparently divorced himself completely from the August demonstrations. At the end of the month, he warned Honda that Matsudaira and Suge would assuredly crack down with a wave of arrests, and he made plans to go to Tokyo and carry his protest through legal channels.

His close friend, Matsumoto Kiyoharu (also Seiji), has left an embellished reminiscence of their farewell meeting on the eve of Mori's departure that is redolent of martyrdom and selfless mission. For the occasion, Matsumoto had hung in the alcove a gruesome scroll of the decapitated head of Ōshio Heihachirō (Figure 14).[4] The inscription on the scroll, moreover, was thought to be done by Rai Mikisaburō, himself put to death in 1859 for Restorationist plottings. With the spirit of these two men of idealistic action filling the room,

---

[4] The image itself was rather fanciful. Ōshio had perished and his corpse was charred when he set fire to the house in which he was making his last stand against pursuing shogunate soldiers.

14. The head of Ōshio Heihachirō.

the two friends exchanged farewell cups of *sake*, sang, and solemnly pledged to sacrifice themselves for the greater good of the country (SSS 1981:884; see Kudō 1981:28). Such a sacrifice was never demanded of either, but for Mori, it was the start of a decade of constant political activism, ending only with his early death in a Yamagata inn while attending the prefectural assembly he had fought for.

On September 2, Mori set out for the capital with a servant from his house. In a letter to Matsumoto, he recounted waiting at an inn in Sendai for a boat for Tokyo, when he overheard some men talking in the distinctive Shōnai dialect. He sent his servant to make inquiries and learned that they were Sakata prefectural soldiers sent to apprehend anyone attempting to reach Tokyo to petition about the roundup that the prefecture was conducting at that very moment. Mori quietly slipped off to another inn, and reached Tokyo without further incident on the 16th.

Mori had been to Tokyo before, but he was quite unfamiliar with the new, and ever changing, government organization. He spent the first couple of weeks visiting with Shōnai acquaintances who were studying or working in Tokyo, questioning them about the various ministries, their personnel, and their modes of operation. By early October, he had also met with Kanai, Ōtomo, and the cultivator representatives, who were filtering back into Tokyo. However, for the most part he pursued a largely independent course of action. He retained a different barrister from the others, Kosui, and decided on a separate tack. He apparently felt the ministries to be unwilling or unable to initiate investigations of the prefecture, and instead drew up a "memorial" for the Sain, that highly constrained vehicle of (limited) popular participation in the government. Memorials (*kenpakusho*) were presentations of private opinion on policy questions or political issues, although there were also many that sought redress for particular grievances with deferential language quite similar to that of distress petitions (*tangansho*). It would be drawing categorical lines too neatly to identify the latter with sub-

211

jects and the former with citizens. Yet the gradual, if uneven, replacement of *tangansho* by the more direct *kenpakusho* in these early Meiji years did signify a more assertive phrasing of grievances.

Mori's first memorial, on October 9, was the more focused in content and specific in language. It exhaustively reviewed the actions of the Reform Faction ex-samurai and the aggrieved cultivators against the prefecture over the previous years in order to deflate Matsudaira's and Suge's claims that the August disturbances were merely the consequences of Honda Inri whipping up the passions of a few heady cultivators (YKS 1978:1040-43; see Satō 1981:212-14). In the second memorial, on November 27, he couched his demand for central government action against "the evils and tyrannies" (*kantoku bōrei*) of the prefecture with much broader appeals to the "right of freedom" (*jishu jiyū no ken*) that the Emperor had given to the "people" (*jinmin*). In these matters, he insisted, Kanai, Honda, and the "people of the prefecture" were the *plaintiffs* and Matsudaira and Suge were the *defendants!* What right did the latter have to lock up the former? Mori asked for a thorough investigation by the government leaders and the replacement of Matsudaira and Suge with new administrators (S 1981:214).

A New Governor and Familiar Grievances

With the barrage of petitions continuing in Tokyo, the Meiji authorities remained unpersuaded that the prefecture was taking effective measures and used the unrest as a pretext for intervention. In November of 1874, the vice-administrator Suge was forced to resign. Matsudaira was allowed to remain in office, but on December 1, Mori was summoned to the Sain where he was informed that Itō was appointing Mishima Michitsune as governor (now termed *kenrei*) over Matsudaira.[5] The 39-year-old Mishima (1835-1888) had been

[5] When Shōnai had been reconstituted as Second Sakata Prefecture, the

a Satsuma warrior-retainer who had fought against the shogunate forces in the Boshin War and moved quickly into national administration, becoming a trusted subordinate of Ōkubo (YKS 1962:358-59). He had served as vice-administrator of Tokyo Prefecture and was at the time an inspector in the Education Bureau. At Ōkubo's insistence, and like Ōhara and Bōjō before him, Mishima was installed both to restore order in the countryside and to keep watch over a suspect prefectural elite. Because this was at a moment when Shōnai's ally, Saigō Takamori, was ever more threatening to the Meiji leaders, Ōkubo and Itō were increasingly alarmed by both the rural unrest and the prefectural elite. Itō also dispatched one of his own officials, Hayashi Mohei, for an independent assessment of the prefecture's administrative practices.

Mishima arrived in Sakata in late December, bringing with him seven loyal subordinates to insert in the prefectural offices. He was soon tested to see where his sympathies lay. Mori had hurried home from Tokyo the same month, and on January 17, he presented the new governor with a petition that charged the prefecture with fifteen "offences" (zai), including allegations that:

1. not only did Matsudaira and Suge refuse to circulate Directive #222, but they arrested those who petitioned for the cash tax option;
2. they deceived the Ministry of Finance and made a profit of several hundred thousand yen by not allowing direct cash tax payments;
3. they suppressed the movement to abolish miscellaneous taxes and misrepresented Matsudaira Masanao's rulings;

---

former domain lord Sakai had been reappointed as governor (chiji). His was a largely ceremonial post (he was in fact absent from Shōnai for most of the period), and actual administration fell to Matsudaira and Suge. Now Itō was bringing Second Sakata Prefecture into line with prefectural hierarchies elsewhere by appointing a full-time governor.

4. they used an improper measuring box for inspecting tax rice;
5. after creation of Second Sakata Prefecture, they diverted public monies such as village expense funds to private uses;
6. they refused to carry out national directives that freed all prostitutes and prohibited the buying and selling of persons into prostitution;
7. they did not allow prisoners to be given food and drink, they prevented people from carrying petitions to Tokyo, and they generally violated people's rights (*minken*) (Satō 1981:215-17).

When Mishima did not respond immediately, Mori turned to Hayashi Mohei, the inspector whom Itō had sent to Shōnai. Hayashi, too, demurred, and left shortly thereafter for Tokyo and instructions from his ministry. Undaunted, Mori followed him, and in mid-February he appeared several times at the Home Ministry to pressure Hayashi and the Ministry to look in to his charges. Finally, a month later, he was recalled to the ministry, where Hayashi told him that his memorial was unacceptable. Hayashi admitted he was sympathetic to Mori's charges, but said this was not shared by his colleagues. The ministry's rejection, though, was on narrow procedural grounds: "if it were a 'distress petition' (*tangan*), it would be impossible to accept without the endorsement of the prefecture; if it were a 'memorial' (*kenpaku*), it must be submitted to the Genrōin; and if it were a 'suit' (*soshō*), it should be lodged with the Ministry of Justice" (Satō 1981:217-18).

Despite the formal rejection, Hayashi's final report to Itō questioned the profits that the prefecture had made on its tax rice sales and its requisitioning of labor and supplies for the Matsugaoka project; Hayashi urged the release of Honda and the others detained. Within a month, though, Hayashi had taken ill and died. Yet another avenue of attack was now closed to Mori, who, as we shall soon see, now turned to direct collaboration with cultivators in a sequence of both memorials and suits.

But meanwhile, with Mori off in Tokyo pressing Hayashi, the new governor Mishima had quickly assumed active direction of the prefectural administration. Throughout January, a team of interrogators was kept busy taking statements from all the jailed protestors (W 1981:76-109). In February, Mishima reviewed these statements and issued sentences (W 1981:109-11). Five of the eight ex-samurai were found innocent, while Kanai, Ōtomo, and Honda were judged to be guilty. Honda received the severest sentence: one year in prison. Twenty-five commoners were also found guilty; their sentences varied from fines of 2.25 *yen* to one year at hard labor. Shirahata and Satō Hachirobei were given thirty days at hard labor.

Mishima simultaneously began to investigate the handling of funds by forty-four village and village group headmen from the Tagawa area. In mid-February, he promulgated a reform of the rural administrative hierarchy (W 1981:128-34). All of the headmen in the prefecture (over seven hundred) were relieved of their posts and ordered to stand in election. The results must have been very encouraging to the August protesters, as very few incumbents were returned to office. In the nineteen villages of Kyōden Village Group, only five were elected; in the more than fifty villages of Shōryūji and Shima, only two were returned, and in nine others, leading activists were elected.

Optimism proved short-lived, however. By late February, it was clear that Mishima, like the governors appointed in the past, was perforce becoming a firm defender of the existing elite. Together with the election of headmen, Mori ordered a redrawing of district and village group boundaries[6] and a reorganization of village group posts that amounted to

---

[6] The former five districts of Tagawa were consolidated into four districts (*daiku*), and Akumi's three into two. Below this level, there was some amalgamation of existing village groups into a smaller number of "subdistricts" (*koku*), which I shall continue to translate as village group.

a tightening of prefectural control. Mishima drew from the former district deputy and rural magistrate stratum (100-200 *koku* retainers) for the new village group posts, and kept on the old village group headmen as their subordinates.[7] The powers of the new village headmen were diluted, and the electoral process soon discontinued. Matsudaira offered his resignation, but was allowed to remain as Mishima's subordinate.

Moreover, his investigation of the forty-four village group and village headmen proved to be a whitewash. In testimony after testimony (W 1981:112-29), the same story was repeated: local levies, they protested, were merely collected "according to custom"; New Year's gifts and occasional supplies and feasts for those district officials who had jurisdiction over them were also "customary," and in any case were only a very nominal part of village group expenses. Their explanations of the land survey assessments were also similar. Surveying and registration was mandated as the cultivators' responsibility, but "they were obviously incapable" so the obligation fell to the village headmen. They, too, found it enormously complicated, and so assembled by village group in Tsurugaoka, where they hired ex-samurai who could "read and do figures." This, they protested, took several months during the winter of 1873-74, and necessarily required living expenses in Tsurugaoka in addition to stipends for the ex-samurai. These "modest" expenses were the basis of the land survey assessments.

Mishima accepted their reasoning and calculations. In a report to Sanjō at the end of March, he excused their minor improprieties. These were merely the residue of domain period practices that survived into the 1870s because the prefectural leadership had been so "old-fashioned" (*kyūkan*). Now that he had instituted administrative reforms, he as-

---

[7] Each village group (*koku*) was to have one head (*kochō*), two administrative assistants (*yōkakari*), and one financial officer (*keisankakari*).

sured Sanjō that the prefecture was firmly set on the new Meiji pathway. He explained the 1874 disturbances with Matsudaira's familiar arguments about the traitorous Honda stirring up the gullible cultivators (W 1981:71-75).

FROM DISTRESS PETITIONS TO COURT SUITS

Mishima's reforms were hardly as reassuring to the local population as they were to Sanjō and Ōkubo, and once again, they were off to Tokyo to seek a hearing for their grievances. On April 7, five of them[8] brought an accusatory memorial against the prefecture at the Police Bureau, but it was rejected. A copy of this does not survive, and it is unclear if they had had assistance from Mori in preparing it, but they were soon to make contact with him. Ten days later, he appeared as spokesman (*daigennin*) for another of their memorials to the High Court within the Justice Ministry.[9] This was rejected because it lacked sealed proof of their claim that they indeed were the "representatives of Tagawa area villages."

While two of the five returned to Shōnai to collect such a written statement, Mori resubmitted it on May 5 as a "suit" (*soshō*) under the title, "A Suit Against the Extreme Persecutions of Prefectural Officials" (*kenshi kyokuhi assei no so*; W 1982:53-58). The suit began with eleven items, each a charge

[8] Again ranging widely in landholding circumstances: Kaneuchi Gisaburō of Bizen Village was a largeholder with 2.4 hectares in 1876. Watanabe Yojibei of Shimonagawa had only a house site to his name; and Watanabe Jirozaemon of Otsuna Village had only 0.98 hectares. I have not been able to determine the holdings of the other two, Kono Toranosuke of Tanisada Village and Saitō Yuemon of Ushiroda.

[9] The *shihō saibansho*. This was the same court to which Kanai and several cultivators had appealed the previous fall. The Minister of Justice served as chief officer of the court, which both reviewed appeals from lower courts and could instigate investigations of government officals' conduct (Ch'en 1981:54).

and a request for action. They are worth considering in detail for their adaptation of old complaints to a new format.

1. Mandatory rice borrowings (*tanebujikimai*). They explained that back in 1869, when the domain faced its 700,000 *ryō* assessment, "people" (*jinmin* is used alternately with *nōmin* throughout) were led to believe that this forced borrowing system would be eliminated and outstanding interest suspended if they contributed. In fact, it was not; even Mishima had continued to collect this interest under the guise of "enterprise capitalization funds" (*kaisan shihon*) and "elementary school funds" (*shogakkōkin*). This was patently wrong, because the former were diverted to projects for ex-samurai and school funds were already collected as an assessment on households (15 *sen* per household) and as entrance fees (12.5 *sen* per student).

2. Rural public works levies. This levy should vary annually with estimates of projects actually required for that year; instead, a constant amount was levied, with no estimates or accounting ever made public.

3. Special assessments on non-resident landholders (*irisaku yonaimai*). The original intention of this levy was to use a tax surcharge on (generally well-to-do) landholders from outside a village group to assist the poorer residents. It actually only worked to further impoverish the latter.

4. Forced rice borrowings (*tanebujikimomi*). Known popularly as "charity rice" (*sonaemai*), this had long been levied at 0.0005% of registered village yield and lent to distressed households at an annual interest of 5%. In 1868, the First Sakata Prefecture had taken over the existing stocks of 60,000 bales and declared them as a general reserve fund for years of harvest shortfalls. Then in 1873, the Second Sakata Prefecture had claimed that this grain had been stockpiled from warrior-retainer stipends. It ordered that half of the total be distributed to its ex-samurai and the other half be sold in bidding. It

218

announced that those households with outstanding loans must repay them immediately in full. (The suit did not clarify the difference between this and the first item.)

5. Wax and lacquer taxes. These were small levies payable in Akumi in cash and in Tagawa in rice. The suit argued that the Tagawa assessment in rice was unfair because its price varied from year to year. More importantly, the tax itself was unfounded, because there were very few ("one in a hundred") villages in Shōnai that had ever produced any wax or lacquer.

6. The tax rice measure box. The measuring boxes used by officials in tax collection often varied from their stated volumes. The government's new standard measure boxes should be adopted.

7. Assessments for the Matsugaoka Project. The people of the prefecture had suffered from requisitions of grain and other commodities, cash, and labor for a project that was for the private welfare of the ex-samurai.

8. Ancillary levies. The suit listed seven levies (W 1982:55) that were to have been abolished; in fact, it charged, they were still collected, but not forwarded to the Treasury Ministry. Upon investigation, any misappropriated sums should be returned to taxpayers.

9. Land survey and other local assessments. Throughout August 1874, rumors spread that village and village group headmen had diverted public tax monies for private use. Large crowds of residents had challenged the headmen, inspected their books, and confirmed these rumors. At the time, some headmen agreed to repay this money, but after the prefecture adopted emergency powers to quell the disturbances, most used this as an excuse for reneging. These agreements should be enforced.

10. Excess profits on tax rice sales. The prefecture refused people permission to tender cash taxes in 1872 and 1873 and then made about 200,000 *yen* in "profits"

(*rikin*). Although Suge had told the Home Ministry that the tax rice had been sold through designated merchants (implying that it was they who had profited), there was considerable suspicion that the prefectural officials themselves had made the sales. This excess profit should be returned.

11. The new village group officials. In his February administrative reorganization, Mishima announced that "men of knowledge" (*chishikinin*) would be appointed to village group positions regardless of samurai or commoner status. In fact, not a single commoner was appointed, and most positions were filled by former headmen and domain officials. There was much concern that this was done to control the population; the suit asked for fair appointments.

Mori followed this listing with: a long recounting of the previous Reform Faction ex-samurai protests and the 1874 August agitations; the Matsudaira Masanao hearings and the numerous petitions to prefectural and national authorities; the actions of the prefecture in suppressing these efforts; and finally the charge that Mishima, the new governor, had now come to side with and protect the old prefectural elite. The suit ended with the familiar distress plea, *kono dan tangan tatematsuri sōrō*. The five "cultivator representatives" attached a statement of endorsement, and Mori appended copies of four prefectural directives in evidence of the suit's charges (ibid.:58-62).

This suit is significant in several regards. For the cultivators, it represented a much more detailed exposition of charges than, for example, the petition of October 25, 1874; Mori apparently argued that such a detailed case was necessary. It was also the first time that they abandoned the deferential petition format that sought redress by appeal to paternal benevolence; here they have adopted the more aggressive language of the civil suit, which leveled charges as violations of specific norms of conduct. Suits did not require the endorsement of immediate superiors, and in the optimism of these first Meiji years, commoners like the Shōnai cultivators imagined that they might bring them against public officials. For Mori, the suit represented much more focus on the particular grievances of the cultivators than, for example, his petition to Mishima in January. It bears none of the more general popular rights demands that, we will see, he was then including in a separate memorial. The suit also demonstrates that both had come to implicate Mishima in the actions of the old prefectural elite and that the center of the demands was shifting to monetary restitution (*sagemodoshi*) of previous official excesses.

The suit, then, was tangible evidence of mutual accommodation and coordination between Mori and the cultivators during that spring when all were in Tokyo. It belies one possible interpretation that throughout the Wappa years the Tagawa cultivators were hapless and passive followers of a series of agitators: first baited and incited by Honda and his cooperative plan until their direct actions provoked mass arrests, then persuaded by Kanai until his tactics of petitioning national ministries proved equally abortive, and finally enticed by Mori, who recast their inchoate anger in a new rhetoric. Mori was a savvy strategist who understood that if there was any leverage in Tokyo in the spring of 1875 it was with the Genrōin and not the ministries. His leadership was essential, but his own intellectual agenda never dominated the collective actions. His fellow Tagawa activists proved equally tenacious and imaginative. Elite manipulation would be as simplistic an account of the Wappa Disturbances as of the earlier protest movements.

Again, the ministry sidestepped action. It waited three weeks before informing Mori and the cultivator representatives that the High Court within the ministry had been abolished (on May 4), that their suit had been transferred to the Fukushima Superior Court, and that they should await the (as yet unscheduled) opening of its next session. Mori protested that the judge of that court, Hayakawa, was clearly prejudiced against the plaintiffs' position; two years before,

221

it was he who had dismissed the Reform Faction ex-samurai suit against the prefecture. Mori asked that the suit be moved to any court other than Fukushima, but the ministry refused, claiming rather disingenuously that "it could not manipulate the regulations" (W 1982:116; see also Satō 1981:221).

While working with the Shōnai cultivators, Mori also continued his own crusade against the prefectural actions cast in a much broader "popular rights" idiom and seeking fundamental political reforms in Shōnai. Tokyo in 1874-75 was buzzing with enthusiastic discussions of John Stuart Mill and heated debates on personal freedom and constitutional government. Mori was an avid listener and became a more articulate constitutionalist and a more shrewd publicist. In February of 1875, various liberal political societies had joined in a Society of Patriots (*Aikokusha*; Scalapino 1962:58-59). In an effort to accommodate this opposition, a worried Ōkubo, now the dominant central leader, agreed that spring to replace the Sain with a Genrōin (a Council of Elder Statesmen) that he implied would be given wider powers. This attracted several of the liberals back into the government as Genrōin members, including Gotō Shōjirō and Kōno Togama. Yet Ōkubo proved unwilling to satisfy the jurisdictions they demanded. It was in the midst of this running battle between the liberal activists of the Genrōin and the bureaucratic conservative Ōkubo that Mori sought to press his case. He turned his attention hopefully to the new Genrōin and its leader, Gotō. On May 12, five days after bringing suit with the cultivators, Mori composed a much more sweeping memorial for Gotō. He began with ten charges against Mishima and his prefectural elite.

1. Not only had the prefecture suppressed the cash tax directive and continued to collect most ancillary levies, but many of its expenditures were also highly questionable. It should be required to make public statements of income and expenditures similar to those of the Treasury Ministry.

2. The schools in the prefecture remained "conservative and old-fashioned," and teaching was still based on the orthodox texts of the domain period. Though there had been certain reforms under Mishima, private academies flourished, samurai and commoners were still kept separated, and Ministry of Education guidelines were ignored.

3. When the cultivators forced access to the local account books, they discovered a great number of improper levies and expenditures by village and village group headmen. On their demands, some officials made restitution, while others promised to do so. After Matsudaira's September crackdown, though, these officials felt emboldened to regain their absolute powers over the cultivators, demanding return of the money they had reimbursed and ignoring the promises they had made. The recent appointments of district and village group headmen had done nothing to relieve the oppression. Almost all were drawn from former domain officials and from headmen who had just been removed. There had been little change in administrative practices. These officials should be dismissed, and "educated" people "who understand the present times" should be appointed (W 1982:63).

4. A prefectural assembly should be established. If local officials were competent, it should be possible to assemble at prefectural headquarters three or four times a year to debate policy issues with prefectural officials. This would improve communication along administrative channels and discourage any wrongdoing by prefectural officials.

5. Agricultural lands have not been resurveyed and taxes were not calculated by actual acreage and fertility. As a consequence, "the rich get richer and the poor are further impoverished" (ibid.:64). Mishima and his "evil" subordinates continued to rely on the old domain reg-

223

isters because at the time of their revision [i.e., 1866], they were able to gain personal control over some fields. An accurate survey should be carried out promptly, ownership certificates distributed, and a land tax based on acreage and fertility instituted.

6. A newspaper bureau should be established to promote learning and to permit a full debate on prefectural actions and popular interests. The fear of public scrutiny would thus deter official wrongdoing.

7. Mishima had issued an order to release all prostitutes and barmaids from their contracts, but he and his subordinates then insured that it had no practical effect. The central government promised personal liberty to all, and they should be freed immediately.

8. Prefectural officials were requisitioning people's labor without wages for the private land development project for ex-samurai at Matsugaoka.

9. Sakata Prefecture was maintaining the former domain organization of military squads and keeping them in training. These should be disbanded, and the ex-samurai made responsible for their own livelihoods.

10. Matsudaira and his clique were pursuing their private interests, ignoring and blocking directives from the central government and falsely and arbitrarily punishing those below them. Until they were all dismissed, unrest in the prefecture would continue. All of the above issues must be addressed, but the most pressing matter of all is the dismissal of the "wicked officials."

Mori went on to report allegations that Matudaira had managed to ingratiate himself with Sanjō and Iwakura and that they had protected him and prevented Mishima from accepting his resignation. He closed with a reference to the Imperial Decree of April 14 calling for a constitutional government. This had led him to hope that a joint government of the Emperor and the people could be created that would guarantee popular freedoms. Unfortunately, the people of

Sakata Prefecture remained oppressed by "wicked officials" and their "tyranny and violence" (*kasei bōren*; W 1982:62-65).

At the same time as he submitted this to Gotō, he also had it published in two Tokyo newspapers (the *Tokyo nichinichi shinbun* of May 23 and the *Yūbin hochi shinbun* of May 25 and 26; W 1982:297-98). He followed this with a second memorial to the Genrōin on June 2 to the following effect:

> The oppressive and illegal behavior of the Sakata prefectural officials has been remarkable. Its people have been sufficiently agitated to appeal to the Home and Justice Ministries, but to no avail. Then last August, there were large-scale disturbances as the people sought to expose the improper actions of their officials. The emergency powers given the prefecture have only reinforced its control. It has now arrested over 100 persons who had disputed its policies. Angered by the evils of these officials, I have requested their punishment, but the central authorities have chosen to protect them. The new governor Mishima has likewise chosen to support them and punish Kanai, Honda, and the others. Not only the people of Sakata but people everywhere are denouncing such behavior. Yet still the authorities have listened only to the claims of Mishima and Matsudaira and have not heeded "public opinion" (*kōron*). The government should immediately forgive the crimes of Kanai, Honda, et al. They should be called to the Ministry of Justice with prefectural officials for an investigation and clarification of the real nature and source of wrongdoing. (W 1982:66-67)

Mori continued to publicize his case through the newspapers; he wrote an article based on this second memorial for the *Yūbin hochi shinbun* of June 2 (W 1982:297-98) and the *Tokyo nichinichi shinbun* of June 7.[10]

---

[10] These were two leading newspapers involved in the national political debates about whether, how fast, and with what electoral restrictions the

More importantly, it was in June that the government brought prefectural governors and administrators from all over the country to Tokyo for its first Regional Officials Assembly (*chihōkan kaigi*) at Hongan-ji Temple in Asakusa. This assembly also attracted most of the leading popular rights advocates, who came to audit the proceedings. It was here that Mori first met Kōno Hironaka, the Fukushima activist who already was a nationally known figure. In his diary, Kōno described how his rooms at the inn were filled day and night during the assembly with popular rights activists and that Mori was in frequent attendance. Kōno praised Mori as a "present day Sogorō" for his efforts to protect the people of Sakata Prefecture.[11]

Mori continued to pressure the Genrōin; on June 22, while the assembly was still meeting, with Matsudaira himself in attendance, he presented a third memorial:

---

government should convene a popularly elected assembly (see Huffman 1983 on the newspapers and this 1874-75 debate). Other newspapers approached the debate more satirically. The June 14 edition of the *Asano shinbun* ran a counting rhyme from a pseudonymous reader, "the monkey-dog of the Hall of Illiteracy." Its ten verses, each in the form, "Why isn't X possible? Hasn't Y been done?" prodded the authorities on controversies of the day: treaty revision, abolition of the Education Bureau, a Tokyo prefectural assembly, a Tokyo municipal park, a Korean peace treaty, etc. Thus the first verse: *Minsen giin wa naze dekinu, Genrōin wa tatta ja nai ka* (Why isn't a popularly elected assembly possible? Hasn't a Council of State been established?). Among the ten issues of the day was the Shōnai situation; the fourth couplet was *Sakata kenshi no shobun wa naze dekinu, mei o tōshutsu shite Mori-shi ga kengen shita ja nai ka*: "Why can't the Sakata prefectural officials be punished? Hasn't Mr. Mori risked his life and offered testimony?" (W 1982:300-301). The reader has not been identified, although I doubt it was Mori himself; his witticisms tended to parody, not satire.

[11] Hattori 1974:161 contains the section from Kōno's diary that describes meeting Mori (see also Kudō 1981:30-31). Sakura Sogorō was a 17th-century village leader who was put to death by his lord after petitioning on behalf of his fellow villagers for tax relief. He became a legendary martyr in popular imagination, and even in early Meiji it was not uncommon to laud a popular activitist as a "second Sogorō" (e.g., Fukuzawa Yukichi's use of the phrase, Aoki 1981:225).

On May 12, I offered a memorial but received no response. In another memorial of June 2, I asked for an investigation of Sakata Prefecture officials, but after more than twenty days, I still do not know the government's disposition in the matter. I have come to suspect that my submissions have been shelved because there are within the cabinet some "crafty ministers" (*kasshi*), who are currying favor with the prefectural officials. It is difficult to understand how Matsudaira, accused by the people as a defendant in their suit, can now attend the Regional Officials Assembly as a *representative* of these same people! I can only conclude that this Assembly is nothing more than a patina of "culture and enlightenment"; it makes a mockery of the people. At this moment, the people of many prefectures seem inclined toward supporting the Emperor, but there are still voices of doubt and resentment. This is because the Cabinet is conducting a superficial, empty debate at the Assembly and is not addressing the real difficulties of a hard-pressed populace. Failure to correct this now will bring great troubles to the country. Even in a trifling matter concerning a single, small prefecture, if the government can satisfy the people with a fair judgment of the merits of the case and underscore the importance of a constitution, the government's standing and the significance of the Regional Officials Assembly it has called will be greatly enhanced. (W 1982:67-68)

Several days later, the cultivators Mori had worked with on the May suits finally left Tokyo for home, after giving him written power of representation.[12] There are very few clues about events in Shōnai during the spring and summer of 1875. There are no records of large protests and agitations

[12] They had been in Tokyo for several months. Hattori (1974:189) relates that they were reimbursed a total of 440 *yen* for their travel and living expenses by Tagawa area villagers, evidence that they were indeed acting for a broad population.

in the Tagawa villages while their representatives were petitioning in Tokyo, a quiescence in sharp contrast to the August 1874 disturbances. There is some evidence, though, that the prefectural officials remained nervous about the Tokyo petitioning. In May, for example, Mishima sent a delegation of subordinates around the Tagawa countryside. At selected headmen's houses and temples, they assembled people from surrounding villages. Villages that had been active in the August actions were required to send all of their residents; others were to send two or three delegates. The officials lectured the assembled sternly to adhere to all prefectural directives and warned them of the consequences of disobedience. They singled out for praise those few villages that had withheld support to the agitators and called down for special remonstration such activists as the priest of Kamishimizu's Ryūan-ji.

Back at the Genrōin, Mori's charges had fanned its heated debates with Ōkubo about the limits of its powers (YKS 1978:1075-82). Mori had been summoned to the Council on July 3 and questioned in detail by Fukuzawa Yukichi, but it was only in mid-July that the Gotō faction was able to overcome the resistance of Ōkubo, Itō, and the Home Ministry and open a formal inquiry (*suimon*) on the matter. They asked Matsudaira to provide a written defense of the prefecture's actions, and they brought Mori before them again for questioning. On August 2, he added a written coda to his oral testimony, which reiterated his earlier memorials.[13] The Genrōin reviewed the case during several September sessions. Still unsure of its limits, it dispatched one of its staff, Numa Morikazu, to Shōnai to hold open hearings.

Mori greeted the announcement of Numa's visit enthusiastically. Like Kanai Tadanao, the 32-year-old had studied at the Naganuma Military Academy, and had spent the last three months of 1869 in Sakata training the commoner mi-

---

[13] This was entitled *Sakata-ken ji no ken ni tsuki gosuimon ni taisuru shomen gokaitō* (W 1982:68-73).

litia (it is not clear if he was personally acquainted with Mori from that time). In 1872-73, he studied law in England; now he was not only a judge (*hanshi*) in the Genrōin but he also led a private study group on law and freedom of speech with Kōno Togama (Lebra 1973:63-64).

As Mori hurried back to Shōnai in October of 1875, a year of petitioning and suit filing in Tokyo drew to a close. To provide some retrospective order, we may see that year as the third and penultimate phase of the Wappa Disturbances. To be sure, such a full-scale investigation by Tokyo of much that disturbed Shōnai residents about their officials may have been imaginable to Satō Hachirobei when he brought his headman his request to pay a cash tax back in the mid-winter of 1873-74. Yet it is also true that the subsequent chain of events, with its sudden twists and turns, had been an unlikely and unpredictable one that continues to defy easy typology.

NINE

The Government Responds:
The Numa Hearings and
the Kojima Court

NUMA'S arrival was eagerly waited by Mori and the Tagawa residents, but for Mishima, his visit came at a most inopportune time, just as he was trying to conclude a land tax reform survey. No direct connections were drawn in contemporary documents between the land tax survey in Shōnai on the one hand and the Tagawa area protests and Mori's presentations on the other. It is impossible, however, to ignore their mutual significance, and to appreciate the local context for the Numa Hearings and the later Kojima Court, we must explore the process by which the survey was conducted in Shōnai.

SHŌNAI'S LAND TAX SURVEY

After several early attempts and revisions, the central authorities had promulgated a comprehensive restructuring of the land tax based on a national cadastre and a fixed cash tax on a cash assessment of acreage, graded for yield potential (Niwa 1966). By 1875, the necessary surveys were well underway in most parts of the country. In Shōnai, too, the prefecture[1] was given firm orders to accomplish its survey in

[1] On August 31 of that year, Sakata Prefecture was renamed Tsurugaoka Prefecture; two weeks later, using laborers requisitioned from the villages, the prefectural offices were moved from Sakata to the old domain school buildings in Tsurugaoka (YKS 1962:58-59, 60-61). Mishima and Matsudaira had been trying to effect this move for some time, apparently believing that

accordance with the new procedures before the end of 1875. This was to be the first complete on-site survey since Sakai Tadakatsu's cadastre in 1623. In fact, this reform stands with the 7th-century Taika reforms, Hideyoshi's late 16th-century cadastres, and the post-World War II land reform as one of the four major restructurings of landholding and taxation in Japanese history. The most important characteristic of this reform in Shōnai was that it was accomplished in two separate phases: first, a determination of registered acreage, then a calculation of the new tax burdens on that land. The former, which required much of the late summer and autumn of 1875, was done "inductively," by aggregating thousands of individual parcel measurements. But the latter, which extended over the winter and spring of 1876, was done "deductively," according to a predetermined, artifical schedule of quotas.[2]

Under the national law, the initial step was for each parcel to be measured by its registered holder, who would declare its acreage on a tag affixed to a bamboo pole on the bund of each parcel. In Shōnai, actual measurements of all parcels, the recording of an "owner" for each parcel, and exchanges of parcels to reconsolidate village boundaries[3] were accomplished largely through on-site surveying, spot checking, and negotiations among village officers.

Given the widespread underregistration in Shōnai and the unpopularity of local officials, such a survey was a highly provocative undertaking. Throughout the summer, Mishima

---

would better allow them to control the Tagawa countryside around Tsurugaoka. See YKS 1978:1070-71 on Matsudaira's reasoning to Ōkubo on the need for the move: the Sakata offices were too small, and moreover Tsurugaoka had always been the castle town and would thus impress the population and help restore order (although this was also the year that the former castle was torn down!).

[2] This account of its features is based on a contemporary memoir on the survey by a village officer in the Ōyama area: YKS 1978:190-92. I have also referred to discussions in OCS 1957:500-12 and TSS 1975a:327-50.

[3] A process termed *tobichi seiri*, very much like the *murakiri* of Hideyoshi's survey.

himself toured the countryside, ostensibly to explain the survey procedures but more accurately to discourage dissent by staging intimidating audiences. He would have all villagers assemble at the headman's house or the village shrine or temple, where he would sternly lecture them while sitting on a chair at the head of the room with several subordinates at his side and armed soldiers surrounding them (see YKS 1962:58-59, 60-61, and Satō 1981:261-63 for contemporary descriptions of these meetings). Under pressure to comply with the national deadline and determined to suppress protest, he forbade all gatherings to discuss the survey or any other matter. The results of the survey exceeded all suspicions: a doubling of total registered acreage in Shōnai, well above the mean increases for both the northeast region and the whole nation. It was one of the largest increases anywhere in the country. This was the highly explosive situation as the rice was harvested in 1875 and as Numa was arriving in Tsurugaoka.

THE NUMA HEARINGS

Numa and three other members of the Genrōin staff arrived in Shōnai on October 3, and established a hearing room at Daishō-ji Temple in Tsurugaoka, where they took testimony for about a month. Numa called in fifteen to twenty officials from the prefecture and ex-samurai from Matsugaoka, and an even greater number of village and village group headmen from throughout Tagawa. He also took depositions from many of the agitators of August 1874. Every day, each of the twenty-one Tagawa area village groups formally cooperating in the suit arranged to have six representatives in attendance. Despite the press of harvest work, many others crowded into the forecourt of the temple to observe the proceedings. The daily representatives were given small per diem allowances by their village group; at 50 *sen* per day per person, 126 persons over 60 days cost 3,780 *yen* (W 1982:120). The other major expense to the plaintiffs was having the petition and supporting materials written out again

232

for Numa; Mori was later to itemize 400 *yen* for this (4,000 sheets at 10 *sen* per sheet; W 1982:ibid.).

In early November, Numa ended his investigation. On November 7, he left for Tokyo, where he spent about six weeks drawing together the oral testimony and written evidence for a report to the Genrōin. They were weeks of mounting tension, both in Shōnai and in the capital. Even as Numa was leaving Shōnai, the central leadership was voicing concern over the independent course of the Genrōin. On the 8th, Sanjō sent a message to Gotō demanding to know the exact purpose of Numa's hearings. Gotō replied that Numa had been sent to determine the charges in Mori's presentation—to which Sanjō warned that the Genrōin was clearly overstepping its jurisdiction.

At the same moment, Mishima delivered a sharply worded protest to Ōkubo, charging indignantly that Numa had taken extensive testimony from Honda, Mori, and tens of cultivators but had not allowed the prefecture the chance to defend itself (a claim which Numa's report would show to be groundless). He reported that after Numa left, Kanai, Honda, and Ōtomo went about spreading rumors that there were to be substantial tax restitutions; now the people were stirred up once again.[4]

Indeed they were stirred up, though Mishima chose to misrepresent their concerns. First, the results of the acreage survey were being prepared, and the tax base, as we have seen, was doubling. Moreover, Numa had not had time while in Tsurugaoka to sort out the types and amounts of improper levies and expenditures for many of the villages. On the day before his departure, he ordered residents in these villages to meet with their headmen and prepare a joint written agreement on what these had been. These were to be sent to him in Tokyo. As one might expect, these meetings, which took place throughout November, were usually

---

[4] He sent a similarly worded message to Numa. These documents were not available to me, and I have relied on Satō 1981:264-68 for these two paragraphs.

less than cordial negotiations. They were more typically confrontations with the officials and confiscation of their books. For example, after seizing the village group books in Ōyama, a mass meeting of residents decided that just over 533 *yen* of a total of 967 *yen* collected as expenses toward the 1873 land tax survey had been misspent by village headmen on such items as *sake*, servants' expenses, and personal travel (Satō 1981:263).

Honda, too, was active. For example, he and six residents of Shōryūji Village detained the village headman in Tsurugaoka for six days while interrogating him about the account books and drawing up a statement for his seal. After several warnings to Sanjō and Ōkubo and protests to Numa about Honda's "agitations" and this "spreading unrest," Mishima left for Tokyo to press his case personally.

Again the principal activists adopted different strategies. Honda and several of the village men continued to mobilize rural residents to uncover official improprieties and demand restitution. Kanai lost interest and withdrew entirely—as Mori was later to write, "he turned his back on his comrades" (*dōshi o shazetsu shi . . .*); Kanai was never again active in the movement. Mori and Ōtomo, though, remained oriented toward the government proceedings in Tokyo. Under the pseudonym Ōmori Shūemon, a composite of Ōtomo Sōhei and Mori Tōemon, they wrote a sharp personal attack on Mishima. They posted it from Shōnai to the editor of the *Tokyo nichinichi shinbun*, where it appeared in the December 5 issue (YKS 1962:50-52). In it, they recounted various pleasure outings of the governor, imputing both his "indolence" and "corruption," and went on to parody the performances of prefectural and local officials before Numa as "flustered and panicked" (*rōbai*). Mori and Ōtomo themselves arrived in Tokyo two days later to press Numa.

The enraged Mishima countered by filing two libel suits with the Prosecutor's Office of the Tokyo High Court. The first was against the editor of the *Yūbin hōchi shinbun* for an earlier Ōmori article; the second was against the *Tokyo nichinichi shinbun* for the December 5 article. Never one to

234

shrink from a court battle, Mori appeared as "court spokesman" for both editors (YKS 1962:52-56). The court found against the editors, though. For violating the Libel and Slander Law, they each drew a 200 *yen* fine and one month in prison. However, this was but a sideshow to the struggle shaping over Numa's hearings.

THE NUMA REPORT

Concerning the matter of the memorial of the merchant Mori Tōemon of Tsurugaoka Prefecture, I received orders in September of this year to go to the prefecture for a careful investigation of the facts. After arriving in October, I gradually conducted detailed questioning to determine the truth or falsity of the matters and the presence or absence of evidence. The facts and evidence are clear (*jisho meiryō ni shite*): the violations by administrator Matsudaira and his subordinates of national laws and regulations are not inconsiderable (*sukunakarazu sōrō*). Accordingly, what follows is a presentation of this clear evidence to which I have added my humble opinion. (W 1982:148)

Thus began Numa's voluminous report, which he submitted to the Genrōin in five installments, from December 2 to January 15.[5] He structured it as an investigative report of nine counts against the prefectural administration. Each count was documented with evidentiary "exhibits" of oral and written testimony (*issho, nisho*, etc.: "exhibit #1," "exhibit #2," etc.). It confirms that he drew largely from Mori's first presentation to the Genrōin on May 12 in organizing his hearings. His findings, essentially a telling corroboration of Mori's charges, may be summarized as seven indictments against prefectural and local officials.

(1) *Suppression of land tax directives and manipulation of tax rice sales.* Numa agreed that prefectural officials had ignored

[5] That is, on December 2, December 8, December 17, December 27, and January 15. The complete text may be found in W 1982:148-239.

the national directives permitting cash taxes and required all taxes in rice. His calculation of its profits from selling this tax rice was limited to the 5,000 *koku* which the prefecture was to tender annually to the Treasury Ministry. This, he found, they had marketed at a price roughly twice the tax equivalency formula and yielded a profit of over 11,300 *yen*. This was then used for the Matsugaoka Project. Numa cited the testimony of Yamagishi, an official in the tax section, who admitted that his excuses to Satō Hachirobei, Suzuki Yaemon, and other Kushibiki cultivators had been fabricated. Yamagishi insisted, though, that the prefecture's tax collection procedures were "designed for the general profit of the prefecture" (*kanka ippan no rieki o hakari*; W 1982:148).

Numa went to some length to determine the complicity of village group headmen in the tax law ruse, because Matsudaira's statement to the Home Ministry in April of 1874 had placed the blame squarely on them. Numa was apparently persuaded by Yatabe of Kurokawa Village Group that he never received the cash tax directives until March of 1874, when the son of the adjacent village group headman brought it around with instructions from a prefectural tax official to enter it in his 1872 official notebook—"I so entered it," he admitted (W 1982:150). Matsudaira and Suge asked the village group headmen for other backdated documents later that year when Matsudaira Masanao conducted his investigation. Numa concluded that at least by 1874, all levels of officials were implicated. Their actions were in clear violation of national law, and he urged that the ill-gained profits be returned to taxpayers. He also found that the prefecture had ignored government regulations on new tax deadlines to accommodate adoption of the Western calendar; as we saw above, it continued to insist on full payment by the end of the calendar year, now a month or so earlier than before. Numa charged that it dealt extremely harshly with those who missed the deadline, confiscating and auctioning off houses and property.

(2) *Self-serving disposition of public lands.* Testimony revealed several instances in which prefectural officials had manipu-

lated land certificates for certain public lands so that they or their friends or associates could assume ownership. These included sections of public forest land and the land created when the extensive castle moat was filled in. These, Numa recommended, should be returned to the public domain.

(3) *Use of public funds and corveé for private ex-samurai projects.* Numa charged that Matsudaira and Suge had mistakenly considered private projects like Matsugaoka to be their public duty; they had neglected their real responsibilities while diverting public resources and official time to these projects. He included the testimony of Ikeda Rai, who had been the district deputy for Kushibiki District, within which was Matsugaoka. Ikeda admitted that half of his time was spent supervising at Matsugaoka (W 1982:164-65). Yatabe testified that he was ordered to "volunteer" villagers and later sent Numa a written itemization of 8,857 worker-days of Kurokawa residents at Matsugaoka (W 1982:160-61). Numa found Matsudaira's representations to be at considerable variance with the facts, and recommended that cultivators should be reimbursed for their requisitioned labor and materials.

(4) *Diversion of local tax monies by headmen for private purposes.* Numa agreed with Mori that village and village group headmen had levied taxes that they then used for private purposes and personal entertainment, and that this had been at the root of the August agitations. Moreover, he found that the prefecture, instead of investigating this misconduct and ordering restitution, had protected the headmen and defended them in reports to national ministries.

Again Yatabe provided some telling details, especially about the assessments for the aborted 1873 land survey. Yatabe attributed the high assessments to the difficulties of working under changing prefectural directives. He described renting a temple in Tsurugaoka at the beginning of October 1873, where he began to work with his headmen on the survey books. Several weeks later he and other village group headmen from Kushibiki District were called in by Ikeda Rai, who by then had been reposted as the tax officer for the area. He informed them that an actual survey should be avoided; rather, they were to assume a 50% tax rate on all parcels and so inflate the tax burdens. He dismissed their protests that the cultivators already knew that such a survey was in progress and threatened that they would no longer be welcomed at Matsugaoka, where they apparently had some investments. Later they were called back and told to scale down the tax burdens they had just recorded upwards. All of this, Yatabe argued, proved very expensive in per diem costs (ibid.:159-60).

Two headmen from the Saigō Village Group around Ōyama testified that they and their village group headman had put up at another Tsurugaoka temple to work on the land books. Sakata Prefecture, however, imposed its own deadline of full payment. They admitted that they often patronized a restaurant in the neighborhood (whose proprietor was none other than Kamo-ya Bunji), where they enjoyed *geisha* entertainment; when they did not go out, they had food and *sake* delivered to the temple. They protested, though, that such living expenses amounted to only 90 *yen* of a total assessment of 670 *yen* (ibid.:170).

Numa was unwilling to accept these and other statements on face value, and he had village group headmen, village headmen, and representatives of residents go over local account books and agree upon those expenditures that had been "improper" (*fusei tsukaiharai no bun*). These negotiations—if that is an accurate term for what must have been contentious confrontations—presented a rather different picture of Saigō Village Group finances. The land survey assessments and 1872 village group expenses totaled 1,162.3463 *yen*, of which it was "agreed" that 413.6093 *yen* had been improperly spent. The statement listed thirty-one separate items—five restaurants, eight brothels, four rotating credit groups, and other expenditures for *sake*, food, prostitutes, and "miscellaneous gifts" (ibid.:170-71). These statements from each village group in Tagawa composed the entire second installment of the Numa Report (ibid.:170-93)—

page after page of similar itemizations, almost all of which revealed "improper expenditures" of 30-40%.

(5) *Falsification of domain fief rolls.* Numa charged that the prefecture had deceived the Treasury Ministry by manipulating the domain fief rolls that it was required to submit in 1872. Using aliases and false names, thirty-five people had been dropped from the rolls, while thirty-five new names had been added. Numa was not able to determine just why these falsifications were done, although he surmised that it was to punish those samurai outside the Matsudaira-Suge faction and pad the fiefs of their supporters. (Curiously, though, none of the Reform Faction leaders were among those dropped.)

(6) *Refusal to disband military squads.* Numa corroborated Mori's claim that the prefecture had ignored directives and maintained its former retainers in their military units, armed and in constant practice. As in other matters, it had lied to central authorities about this.

(7) *Arbitrary prison terms and punishments.* Numa meant by this charge that the prefecture continued to apply older domain period procedures and standards of justice, especially with its former warrior-retainers. A particularly incriminating case was that of Arichi Tomoemon, a foot soldier in the Sakai retainer band, who had been sentenced to life imprisonment in September of 1872; this was reduced to ten years in April of 1874. From Arichi, Numa heard the following story (W 1982:201-202; see also Satō 1981:244-45). In late 1870, his squad was sent to Tokyo for assignment to the Tokyo municipal government. The squad leader ordered his men to pack lightly, assuring them that they would be provided with duty uniforms and expense money from the domain mansion in the capital. In fact, the expense money was woefully inadequate and they had to provide their own uniforms; they only had funds to have their own clothes recut or to buy secondhand garments, but their commanders insisted that the assignment was important and that their uniforms be fresh, good-quality cotton. At one point the squad

even composed a joint letter of resignation in frustration. He complained that the patrol duty was long, with only two or three breaks in a month. He admitted that several times he and others had sneaked away to Yoshiwara brothels, but this had been at no endangerment to the squad. They returned to Shōnai ten months later, with commendations from the Tokyo authorities and their domain elders. But a month later, Arichi was summarily sentenced to life imprisonment.

His squad leader had a plausible defense. He testified to Numa that Arichi and two others had disobeyed orders and left their assignments to go off whoring in Yoshiwara. They had taken squad funds, which they were forced to repay after the squad's return to Shōnai. But most embarrassing had been the Yoshiwara brothel people showing up at the guard headquarters seeking payment for Arichi's outstanding debts. With such public knowledge of Arichi's behavior, his commander had to report the matter to Matsudaira; to insure discipline among his troops, he was forced to seek disciplinary action. Actually, Arichi's conduct warranted the death penalty, he pointed out; instead, he and Matsudaira together agreed on reduction to life imprisonment.

Numa concluded that Arichi's treatment had been harsh and arbitrary and that it was not an isolated case; there were, he found, tens of former warrior-retainers who had suffered imprisonment, confinement, forced retirement, and reduction of fiefs. He cited the testimony of Furukawa Rokutarō, who recounted that in August of 1872, his father was returning home from a pilgrimage to Mt. Haguro, when he lost his way, fell into the Aka River, and later died of injuries suffered in the fall. When Rokutarō submitted the usual documents of household succession, Matsudaira reduced his fief grant from 43 to 33 koku, arguing that his father had died in a manner "unbefitting" a samurai (fukakugo)—presumably in a drunken stupor. Numa noted in his report, however, that this was an anachronistic domain custom; with the domains abolished, the new national law did not allow such arbitrary punishments (W 1982:205-206).

Although Numa structured his report somewhat differently, the above seven counts concisely summarize his findings. He marshaled voluminous evidence to substantiate these indictments. Though Numa was not an entirely impartial investigator, his report constitutes the most exhaustive material on prefectural activities that has survived. It overwhelmingly sustains many of the charges that Mori and the Tagawa residents had been raising against the prefecture for two years.

And yet scattered through the report are several cases that give us pause, that hint at the immense difficulties of sifting among conflicting claims. One such dispute concerned the cultivators of Shimokonaka Village in Ōyama Village Group. In 1871, they had developed a section of their *yachi* wetlands into paddy fields. Their headman, Tomigashi Jiroemon, testified that at the end of the following year, he was ordered by the village group headman, Satō Yasumasa, to have the cultivators tender a rice contribution (*kennōmai*) from these new parcels to the domain lord, Sakai. The villagers refused, protesting that as yet their yields were minimal. Satō was adamant, though, and the cultivators reluctantly came up with fourteen bales in 1872 and again in 1873, unable to avoid what they saw as Satō's order. Now, Tomigashi told Numa, he was very regretful for having forced the order on the residents. Satō then testified that he had talked with the Saigō Village Group headmen in 1872 about the appropriateness of rice gifts to their lord from Shimokonaka and other villages in the two areas which had received kind domain consideration in recent paddy land developments. He had broached this with Tomigashi, and was later told that the residents were "not unwilling," so he petitioned his superiors that they be allowed to offer such a voluntary contribution (*sunshi*). The third person to testify, a domain retainer assigned to the Sakai household, said that he had received a petition from the village group headmen to that effect and had accepted the rice in the firm belief that the offer had in fact originated willingly with the villagers

241

(*komae* was his term, the "little people," a condescending term long in use; W 1982:222-26; see also Satō 1981:250-51).

Another local conflict that was exposed by the Numa Hearings concerned about three hectares of land along the Aka River in Kurokawa Village. Back in 1861, several residents had received permission to develop this into paddy land, but had given up when they realized that either its soil condition was too poor or water access too problematic. Yet they remained the registered landholders and paid its levies. Then in 1870, they responded to a request from Yatabe, the village group headman, and gave permission for the domain to use it for a time (*tōbun okariage*) as an experimental mulberry plot. Their problems began in 1874, when they asked that the land be returned to them. When prefectural officials denied their numerous requests—and they rejected the prefecture's offer to buy the land outright—they protested to Numa that the prefecture had in fact appropriated the land. Yet a district official testified that the prefecture had had no idea that the area was privately registered. He turned it over to three ex-samurai with orders to plant mulberry bushes with their own funds. It was only several years later that he learned the area was privately registered. When his offer that the prefecture buy it for 200 *yen* was rejected, he found himself in a difficult position, caught between the Kurokawa residents and the three mulberry growers, who stood to lose their investment (W 1982:207-15; see also Satō 1981:247-48).

Other cases confront us with the issue of just what had been the nature of prefectural wrongdoing. Arichi, for example, may have been singled out unfairly and punished quite excessively, but his commander had felt fully justified, given the public embarrassment to his leadership, the squad, and the "domain" in the Tokyo limelight. Perhaps, too, Matsudaira was genuinely appalled at Furukawa's rather ignominious drunken tumble into the Aka River. Let us accept that the officials were not entirely duplicitous in their reasoning. What is more relevant—and most striking—is the gulf between their standards of judgment and those of Numa,

242

Mori, and the Tagawa cultivators. The defendants protested that they were following customary procedures, that they were working for the general welfare, that they were caught in changing circumstances. In contrast, Numa repeatedly emphasized their "violations of existing national laws and directives" (*kokka kitei no hōrei kisoku*). Mori on his part stressed their "wickedness" and "tyranny" and denials of freedoms and rights.[6] The rural activists attacked their "improper" (*fusei*) and "dishonorable" (*fumeigi*) behavior as public officials.

All three were expressing an indignation at the private use of public resources—land, people's corvée, taxes. What they shared was a clear distinction between public and private, between *ko* and *shi*—a distinction they drew upon as a novel standard of accountability. They formulated the distinction differently, but to each it was the foundation of complaint against a local elite whose conception of political activity blurred public duty and private interest. Sakata Prefecture was indicted for its unwillingness, its inability, to accept that distinction. The insistence on accountability in this local dispute was as much an attempt to *limit* official actions, to clarify prerogatives of public authority, as it was to broaden public responsibility.

The May 5 suit to the Genrōin, the Numa Hearings, and the subsequent report represent the high point of 19th-century Shōnai protest. This judgment is not intended as a gratuitous compliment, nor does it depend on some ethnocentric measure of progress and political maturation. It is simply that these moments stand as the fullest collective expression and farthest official recognition of a principle of political conduct that challenged existing ideals of benevolent paternalism and emerging ideals of bureaucratic state guidance: that there be explicit standards of official conduct, that the people share

---

[6] His previous memorials and hearings testimony spoke of *kantoku* ("wickedness"), *kasei bōren* ("tyranny and violence"), and *ōren kasei* ("misappropriations and tyranny").

directly in their formulation and enforcement, and that there be recompense for those public actions in violation of such standards. It was this clear and concerted insistence on accountable official conduct that set apart the Mori/Tagawa suit and testimonies at the Numa Hearings from the 1841 petitions, the Ōyama defense at Shiono, and even the Tengu League demands.

Ultimately, though, the government's responsiveness to the suit did not match the forcefulness of Numa's language. His report may have been far-reaching in its condemnation of the local political elite, but he revealed fewer sympathies with the plaintiffs' reasoning. He pointedly ignored Mori's "popular rights" demands for schools and a progressive educational policy, a prefectural assembly, a newspaper bureau, and release of all prostitutes and bar girls from their contracts. Indeed, except for a suggested award of 11,300 *yen* in count (1), Numa stopped short of recommending any corrective or punitive action. He made no mention of restitution for other tax improprieties, appointment of new local officials, publication of prefectural accounts, abolition of ancillary levies, or removal of Mishima and Matsudaira. His most consistent theme was violation of national laws, a perspective that would eventually infiltrate and condition even the Shōnai plaintiffs' thinking.

Numa's circumspection may be attributed at least in part to the the Genrōin's embattled position. Slowly its prerogatives were eroding. When Kōno Togama introduced the full Numa Report during Genrōin proceedings on January 27, he noted that if this had occurred before recent revisions in the Genrōin charter, they could have called prefectural officials for interrogation, but that was now beyond their powers. Still the report clearly documented prefectural improprieties, and he proposed forwarding it to the government for "reference" with an attached "opinion" (*ikensho*) of prefectural wrongdoing. This was debated and agreed upon in a session several days later[7]

[7] In the debate, on February 3, Yamaguchi Naomichi challenged Kōno

Surprisingly, the government leaders responded. In late February, based on the Numa Report findings, Sanjō ordered the Ministry of Justice to take action—it was to accept and resolve the suit that Mori and the five cultivators had brought before the ministry the year before. To keep it out of the Tokyo limelight, the ministry decided on March 2 to dispatch one of its middle-level judges, Kojima Iken (alternately, Kojima Koreyoshi), to hear the case in Tsurugaoka. Mori and Ōtomo, who had remained in Tokyo since November to monitor the debates, quickly returned to Shōnai.

As we look back through the hazy filters of surviving documents at the actions of the various principals, Sanjō's decision may appear as unexpected as the sudden end to plans for the rice cooperative. Perhaps he, more than Ōkubo, saw the need to maintain a viable Genrōin. More likely, both were prompted by the report to move against a local elite that had persistently circumvented their centralizing policies. Numa had cast his findings in terms they could readily appreciate: prefectural deviance from central initiatives. This was the time to act; by accepting the Genrōin report, they preempted its further debate and Tokyo publicity. This was further contained by assigning ministry subordinates to hold an on-site court hearing. They were to prove as accurate in their judgment as they had been four years earlier, when they agreed to Shōnai's administrative reconstitution.

THE KOJIMA COURT

Kojima's arrival in mid-April, with a retinue of Justice Ministry subordinates, stirred much resentment and consternation among top prefectural officials. Under orders, they provided Kojima with a former Sakai mansion on the edge of town for use as a temporary courtroom. His first act was to summon Mori and the five cultivators who had brought suit

---

for even raising the matter. In their afternoon session, the twelve members attending discussed whether to send it as a "report to the throne" (*jōsō*) or simply as a "notification" (*tsūchō*), eventually agreeing to the former (W 1982:239-46).

before the ministry back in May of 1875. He told them that while the suit had been officially returned to them at the time, a copy had been retained in the ministry files and he was now ordered to open a special inquiry into its merits. However, because more than a year had elapsed, he wanted them to revise their document. He realized that it would take too much time to collect another formal statement of representation from all Tagawa villages, so he agreed to accept it with only a couple of names. The fifteen-clause suit, entitled "A suit seeking restitution of improper levies and expenditures and seeking reform of the oppressive measures of Tsurugaoka Prefecture"[8] was submitted on May 2. Mori signed as one plaintiff and Honda and Ōtomo signed as court spokesmen (*daigennin*) of four commoner representatives. This format further demonstrates the separate though coordinated course of action that Mori had followed from the outset. The suit named several middle-level prefectural officials as formal defendants. Without preface, it was a listing of fifteen charges. Each was a request for restitution (. . . *no bun sagemodoshi o yōkyū suru koto*), followed by a brief statement of reasoning:

1. Request #1: Refund of all profits made by the prefecture on sales of 1872 and 1873 tax rice.

    Reasoning: The prefecture suppressed the national directives on cash taxes, enforced payment in rice, denied and jailed all petitioners, and made profits exceeding 100,000 *yen* by selling this rice. In all these actions, it "prevented the freedoms of the cultivators" (*nōmin no jiyū o samatagerare*).

2. Request #2: Return of all interest charges on mandatory seed and food rice borrowings in 1873-75 (estimated at 53,066 *yen*).

---

[8] *Tsurugaoka-ken assei o aratame narabi fusei kashutsu no kinkoku shokan o jūkyū suru no so.* The text appears in W 1982:68-73; the defendants' response is on pp. 73-75, and the collected testimony and submitted documents are on pp. 75-100.

Reasoning: The prefecture ignored the national directive #81 of March 1873, which wrote off much of
these loans. Instead, it continued collection, diverting the money to the Matsugaoka Project (for
which it also used forced labor) and to its "school
fund" (despite the fact there were separate school
fees).

3. Request #3: Abolition of the prefecture's "welfare rice
reserves" and return of all interest charges made
since 1872 on loans from these reserves.

Reasoning: These reserves were originally collected as
surcharges on non-resident landholdings; the original aim had been to surcharge lands with low tax
burdens in order to help indigent resident cultivators. They were not used for this purpose.

4. Request #4: Return of all interest charges made since
1872 on loans from a surcharge (similar to count
#3) on undertaxed lands.

Reasoning: similar to count #3. (This appears to be
the identical levy as #3, and probably is simply a
different term used in certain areas of Shōnai.)

5. Request #5: Return of 1873-75 assessments for stipends of land tax collectors and inspectors (estimated at 3,790 yen).

Reasoning: These tax collectors and inspectors were
now prefectural officials, and their salaries should
come out of the prefecture's general administrative
budget, not from village group levies.

6. Request #6: Return of all ancillary levies for repairs,
rice losses, and watchmen at the three prefectural
granaries (Tsurugaoka, Kamo, and Sakata) for the
years 1872-75 (estimated at 4,703 bales).

Reasoning: Since cultivators should have been permitted to tender cash taxes since 1872, it was unreason-
able (fujōri no suji) that the expenses of the prefecture's granaries should be separately assessed its
taxpayers.

7. Request #7: Reimbursement for two domain period ancillary levies (the levy in lieu of porterage in the domain lord's procession to Edo and the levy for allowances for domain retainers' servants).

Reasoning: Both of these should have been abolished with the establishment of the prefectures, but in Shōnai they were continued.

8. Request #8: Reimbursement for 1873-74 levies in Kushibiki District for transporting tax rice to Sakata.

Reasoning: These should have been abolished after the government's directive #231 in 1872.

9. Request #9: Request for an investigation of appropriations toward construction and repairs to village group headmen's houses and a review of tax exemptions.

Reasoning: House construction, repairs, and land taxes on compounds of village group headmen had always been assessed annually as a village group levy. These were particularly heavy in recent years due to fires and major repairs. The plaintiffs were asking that they be declared the public property of each village group.

10. Request #10: Return of rice reserves (*kakoimomi*).

Reasoning: These reserves were stockpiled by the former domain over several hundred years through annual assessments of 0.0005% on registered yields; they were lent back to cultivators at 7% interest. Matsudaira received permission from the central government to appropriate these stocks as government property, and his handling of them was highly improper. He assessed warehousing costs as regular tax levies, but declared that the reserves had been generated from samurai fiefs and stipends, and auctioned them off.

11. Request #11: Return of rice reserve charges (*fujiki kashimomi daimai*).

Reasoning: This was originally another distress bor-

248

rowing fund, but for a long time, only an annual interest charge had been levied. As with item #2 above, these should have been cancelled in 1872, pursuant to directive #81; thus, the plaintiffs argued, restitution should be made for interest paid in 1873–74.

12. Request #12: Reimbursement for the special national levy (*kokuyaku*) in 1875.

   Reasoning: This levy had been an ancillary domain tax since 1809, charged annually to help it meet the more occasional sums [of the same term] that the shogunate levied on the domains. This was continued in the Meiji era, but there had been much doubt about the correct amounts in the previous few years. The amounts and procedures should be carefully investigated.

13. Request #13: Restitution for all misappropriated village and village group expenses.

   Reasoning: During the August 1874 actions against local officials, numerous examples of their improper expenditures came to light. Many of the officials gave written promises of reimbursement, and some actually made payments. However, most then used the emergency powers given the prefecture to ignore these written promises and take back their money. The prefecture even protected this behavior, and its administrative reorganization only strengthened the powers of the village group headmen. The plaintiffs asked for negotiations with the officials to determine proper and improper items and the amounts to be returned.

14. Request #14: Reimbursement with interest for all labor and materials requisitioned from cultivators for the ex-samurai agricultural projects in Tagawa.

   Reasoning: The prefecture had been wrong to divert public funds and to requisition the people's labor

249

and supplies for what were actually private development projects.

15. Request #15: Careful inspection of prefectural tax and
expenditure ledgers.

Reasoning: As demonstrated by the above charges,
there had been many questionable aspects to taxes
in this prefecture. Moreover, the government's directive #53 in April of 1874 urged officials to exercise particular sensitivity in taxation matters.
Thus, the plaintiffs urged, account books for the last
several years should be subject to close auditing.

The plaintiffs concluded: "we would like to have a fair and
open decision rendered on these items that we bring in
suit."[9]

Almost exactly a year had passed since Mori and the five
cultivator representatives had tried to submit their joint suit
to the ministry in Tokyo, and there were few changes in
language and substance. Mori's calls for sweeping societal
reforms were still given no place in a suit that remained focused on the prefecture's fiscal improprieties: its improper
levies, manipulations of tax funds and rice stocks, embezzlement, and falsified expenditures. There was one difference,
however, which suggested that Mori and the Tagawa cultivators had given close reading to Numa's report: their presentation to Kojima was now much more explicitly legalis-
tic. This time they couched every argument as a prefectural
violation of a national law or ministry directive. The copious
supporting documents they added were largely copies of all
relevant laws, directives, and prefectural memoranda. They
sought judgment on these grounds—and they sought justice
in the particular form of monetary restitution.

Kojima took even more time than Numa, summoning
tens of local and prefectural officials, merchants, and protesters in his five weeks of hearings. Most of them had already
testified during the Numa Hearings. This time neither Ma-

---

[9] *migi no jōken kōmei seidai no osaiban nashikudasaretaku shusso tatematsuri sōrō
nari.*

tsudaira nor Suge could avoid testifying, though there is no evidence of a personal appearance by Mishima. As before, residents of each village group sent six delegates every day to audit the proceedings; although the busy spring rice season was beginning, many more came on their own accord. Again the twenty-one Tagawa village groups which formally backed the suit shared the considerable expenses of document preparation (6,000 sheets this time) and daily allowances for the representatives (W 1982:119-20). All in all, in the twenty months from the first petitions in Tokyo in the fall of 1874 to these final days at Kojima's court, Mori and the Tagawa village groups had spent at least 9,000 *yen* in travel to the capital, living expenses in Tokyo and Tsurugaoka, legal assistance, and document transcription (W 1982:117-20).

In the course of his investigation, Kojima ordered four of the fifteen counts (#3, 4, 7, and 12) to be dropped from the suit, "on mutual agreement of the defendants and plaintiffs." Igawa (1972:67) has suggested that Honma Mitsuyoshi personally intervened to persuade Mishima to abolish preemptively the tax surcharges on absentee landholdings (count #4). The intent, Igawa speculated, was to weaken the plaintiff coalition by appeasing the large landholders and so undermining their continued support for the suit. His reasoning is not entirely persuasive; in abolishing the levy retroactive to the previous year, Mishima was in effect offering reimbursement for the past year's amount. In any case, it would be the first and only overt Honma appearance in the Wappa Disturbances, in pointed contrast to previous cases. This is the more interesting question, and I would suggest several reasons for their non-involvement. Tagawa had been the area for most protest actions since 1874, while Honma holdings were concentrated in Akumi. Further, the Honmas by now had little to gain from either the prefectural policies or the cultivators' cooperative rice sales plan. And finally, Honma Mitsuyoshi had retired from the main house headship in October of 1875, plunging the Honmas into a bitter intramural succession fight (Satō 1976:205-206, 208-11). The Honmas—

and Mitsuyoshi—were to reemerge in Shōnai public affairs only in the late 1870s.

It was June 16 when Kojima closed the court and returned to Tokyo. To the plaintiffs' dismay, he left without rendering any decision, declaring that for several of the charges he would have to question and consult with people in the Treasury and Home ministries.[10]

THE RESULTS OF THE LAND TAX SURVEY

Meanwhile, throughout the winter and spring of 1876, Mishima was struggling to complete the land tax reform calculations. We have seen that the survey in the autumn had almost exactly doubled Shōnai's registered acreage. Normatively, the next step would have been to check cultivators' declarations of their mean yields for each parcel; using these, cash land values would be calculated with average autumn rice prices. Had this been done, taxes would have increased as dramatically as acreage, and Mishima and Matsudaira would have faced an explosive situation indeed.

Instead, however, they began manipulating. A basic principle behind the national reform was to secure roughly the same land tax revenue totals as before the reform. This was used also by Mishima to establish a prefectural goal. This total, divided by a standard percentage (3%, the new "tax rate"), yielded the total necessary land value (tax base). This was then used to fix rough quotas for Akumi and Tagawa and their districts. The surveyed acreage totals were used to calculate the mean "target yield" (shūkaku mokuhyō) that would produce such a quota for Akumi and Tagawa and, within them, for each district.

The next step was to rank villages within the districts according to diagnostic criteria such as soil type, drainage conditions, and water supply (see TSS 1975a:243-46 and Tawara

---

[10] He did, however, find several Tsurugaoka rice merchants and prefectural officials guilty of manipulations of the rice price and other officials guilty of falsifications of the domain fief registers. Technically these were verdicts on items in Numa's findings, not the fifteen-clause suit.

1972:45-46 for ranking of West Tagawa villages). On that basis, individual villages were assigned a mean "yield"; it was, finally, up to the villages to establish their own internal ranking schedule to distribute their total among their many parcels, reaching some adjustment, perhaps, with the actual yields that had been declared by the landholders.

This charade was easily recognized by the cultivators as early as the summer of 1876, but it engendered little opposition for a very simple reason: in Shōnai, the target quotas (the taxable land values expressed in cash per district) were set quite low. This was done by the simple expedient of using an artificially low cash conversion rate; compared with the mean tax rice conversion price in 1872-73 of 4.39 *yen* per *koku*, yields for the purposes of the tax revision were to be calculated at 3.10 *yen* per *koku*, about 25% lower. This is even more remarkable when we realize that the 1872-73 conversion rate was itself below the market prices that year (that was, after all, what started the 1874-76 disturbances!). As a result, and despite the 85% increase in registered paddy land acreage, total tax revenues for paddy land parcels declined 12.7% (calculated at a constant rice price). At a comparative calculation against mean annual tax rice prices, the revenue drop was a steep 25%, unusually large even for the northeastern region.[11] Particularly dramatic were the declines in tax burdens in those villages most active in the August 1874 actions—in Ōyododawa, the decline was 20%; in Kamishimizu, 35%, in Bizen, 37%; in Nishiitaya, 34%; in Takazaka, 33%; in Shimonagawa, 17% (TSS 1975a:367).

THE END OF THE PREFECTURE

It was not mere coincidence that as the final land tax calculations were announced, Tsurugaoka (Second Sakata) Prefecture was folded into Yamagata Prefecture. As we have seen,

[11] See Table 14 in Tawara 1972:45. These figures are for all land outside of the settled areas of Tsurugaoka and Sakata. That the drop in Shōnai's former shogunate lands was only 6.2% while that in Sakai lands was 14.9% is evidence that the tax burden was leveled out.

the Meiji leaders appointed Mishima to bring the entrenched local elite under closer scrutiny, but Mishima was often drawn to defending these prefectural interests, both against the central ministries and the Shōnai population. Matsudaira and his fellow officials were able to play on this to preserve their political position and further their economic programs. However, these commercial initiatives of the Sakai elite and their efforts to keep the retainer band together as a political and economic force were finally thwarted. Their administrative vehicle, the prefecture, was abolished in August of 1876. It was amalgamated with Okitama and Yamagata into a new Yamagata Prefecture, and Mishima moved to Yamagata City as its governor. Many of the old prefectural officials were dismissed, although a few remained as county heads (*gunchō*) or village group headmen.

The domestication of this somewhat unruly prefecture was symbolized on September 19, when a party of high Meiji officials, including the Prime Minister, Sanjō Sanetomi, Yamagata Aritomo, and Itō Hirobumi, arrived in Tsurugaoka for a tour of the Chōyō School, the newly opened elementary school and showpiece of "Culture and Enlightenment" in Shōnai. With Mishima, Matsudaira, and other notables on hand, Honma Mitsuyoshi presented a special set of triple gold cups as a gift for the Emperor.

THE KOJIMA DECISION

Meanwhile, back in Tokyo, Kojima had drawn up a lengthy written summary and a draft judgment by early August. His superiors passed this up to their minister, Iwakura, with a request for immediate action (W 1982:247-90 see also Satō 1981:277-83). A final decision, however, was not to be announced for almost two years.

The initial delay was caused by an autumn uprising in Kagoshima in southern Kyūshū by followers of Saigō Takamori. Somewhat reluctantly, Saigō himself came to lead this major rebellion against the Meiji government, the first real

254

test of its police forces. The fighting continued through 1877, and largely absorbed the attention of the central leaders. It also raised their long-standing fears about the old Sakai retainers' loyalties to Saigō. Would they come to Saigō's embattled cause? Mishima took no chances. In April of 1877, he had two hundred-man brigades of government troops sent from Sendai to patrol the streets of Tsurugaoka and dampen any thoughts of support for Saigō by the ex-samurai at Matsugaoka. Matsudaira and Suge were, in fact, beseeched by Saigō's men to render assistance, but demurred. Suge remained in retirement at his home on the edge of Tsurugaoka, studying Western classics and Chinese poetry. Matsudaira wrote Sanjō to assure him that he would not move against the government. Mishima, it seems, had succeeded in drawing the Sakai retainers away from the Saigō faction and into the Ōkubo fold.

In January of 1877, Honda and a number of cultivators went to Tokyo to press for Kojima's decision (W 1982:100). Parenthetically, this was Honda's last involvement in the cause. While in Tokyo, he joined the National Police Bureau, and was sent off, appropriately enough, against the rebellious Saigō forces! A decision was still not forthcoming after the rebellion in Kyūshū had been put down. Both Ōtomo, in November of 1877, and Mori, in the spring of 1878, lobbied the ministry. It was not until June 3, 1878, that the decision was finally released, and it proved to be, essentially, a summary of Kojima's draft twenty months earlier (text: W 1982:290-96).

It represented at best a partial victory for the plaintiffs. They were awarded reimbursements in demands #2, 5, and 6 that totaled 63,652 *yen*, but their demands #1, 8, 10, 11, and 14 were rejected. With reference to demand #1, Kojima's draft concluded a lengthy collation of evidence against the prefecture's taxation procedures with a list of five ways in which the officials had "oppressed the people" (*jinmin o assei suru*) and reaped a profit of 11,300 *yen*; this was a corroboration of Numa's findings. Kojima, however, denied reimbursement in charge #1 on the rather tenuous grounds that these illegal procedures had not actually *increased* the cultivators' land tax burdens. That is, the prefecture's profits did not come from increasing tax rates but from manipulations after collecting taxes. Indeed, if market conditions had been adverse and the rice price had fallen, the cultivators would have been protected from a loss. The profit was illegal, but Kojima ruled that it did not belong to those who had paid the taxes.

Kojima tread a middle ground in the matter of the Matsugaoka Project, too. He agreed that the project had been started on government land and then sold nominally to twelve individuals for development, and that the use of prefectural officials to oversee a project of potential benefit to large numbers of samurai was appropriate. However, he opined, these officials, in their natural desire to hasten land development, *did* overstep their authority in requisitioning villagers' labor and supplies through the village group headmen with what appeared to be official directives. And yet, backpedaling, Kojima concluded that at the time these villagers freely offered their labor and materials as a "favor" (*onkei*), with no expectation of wages; thus, their subsequent requests for restitution had no standing.

Kojima did find for the plaintiffs in count #2, agreeing that the prefecture had continued, illegally, to collect interest on its forced rice loans and had diverted these monies to the Matsugaoka Project. This represented the bulk of the total award, over 53,000 *yen*.[12] He also agreed with the reasoning of the plaintiffs in counts #5 and #6, adding another 10,600

[12] It is important to note, though, that by 1878, the Matsugaoka project was on the verge of collapse and something of a white elephant to the prefecture. Even before the decision, Matsugaoka leaders decided they would give back the land to the government and so petitioned Mishima. Mishima immediately consulted with Ōkubo, who praised the Matsugaoka project and arranged for the central government to contribute 3,000 *yen*. The Justice Ministry now protected the individual ex-samurai by ordering Yamagata Prefecture to assume reimbursement of this money.

yen to the award. He denied them their request #8 on the grounds that Ōtomo agreed with Yatabe and other Kushibiki officials that repayment had already been made. Finally, he denied the plaintiffs in counts #10 and #11, again finding that the prefecture had ignored government directives and manipulated the reserve stocks but concluding that this did not constitute improper conduct toward the people of the prefecture.

We do not know just how people in Shōnai first reacted to the decision, but Mori, at least, was quite satisfied. The liberal intellectuals and political organizers of the Movement for Freedom and Popular Rights had become even more numerous and vocal since 1875, and the decision was prominently featured in several national newspapers. The *Osaka nippō* lauded it editorially as a great victory for popular rights; it praised Mori as "the famous popular rights advocate," the second Sakura Sōgorō (W 1982:303-305). It observed that only eleven years before, Mori would have met the same martyr's fate as the first Sōgorō, but the growth of popular rights and Mori's perseverance at the Genrōin and the ministries insured that he would live to celebrate the victory. In this and other articles, then, there was little or no mention of the rural agitations; the focus remained on what Mori had done for the people.

Indeed, for the moment Mori *was* prominent, though he has since slipped into obscurity. One of the leading thinkers in this popular rights movement, Ueki Emori, featured four activists on the engraved cover of his 1879 pamphlet, *Minken jiyū ron* (A Treatise on Popular Rights and Freedom)—Fukuzawa Yukichi, Itagaki Taisuke, Kiuchi Sōgorō, and Mori Tōemon (Figure 15). Yet it is equally noteworthy that there is nothing in the pamphlet text (Ienaga 1974:15-47) to indicate Ueki's familiarity or concern with the Wappa Disturbances themselves or with any of the other local incidents of the day. It was instead, like much of his writing, a mix of abstract theory and impassioned polemic, highly influential to his comrades in the movement, but of doubtful appeal to

257

15. Mori Tōemon featured on the cover of Ueki Emori's
1879 pamphlet, *Jiyū minken ron* [Treatise on Freedom and
Popular Rights]. Clockwise from upper right:
Itagaki Taisuke, Kiuchi Sogorō, Mori Tōemon, Fukuzawa
Yukichi.

(equally committed) protesters like Kenmochi Torazo and Shirahata Goemon. Even the "Country Song of Popular Rights" which Ueki appended to the pamphlet (translated and discussed by Bowen 1980:206-208) was a general and florid paean to "the rights of freedom," "wisdom," and "scholarship." One can imagine the *daikoku mai* counting rhyme animating the Tsurugaoka celebrations in the summer of 1841, but despite the thirdhand reference to its popularity in the countryside (ibid.:206), it is hard to believe that Ueki's "Country Song" (or his own counting rhyme; Ienaga 1960:170-73) could have been heard on the lips of the Tagawa cultivators.

Mori, of course, had been indispensable in sustaining the momentum of the Shōnai protests and securing a government ruling. It is equally clear that his conception of what was at stake was rather different from that of his fellow plaintiffs. But this does not pose an inscrutable paradox; it was a common characteristic of Shōnai protests. We need only distinguish his energy, his political astuteness, and his modest personal wealth, all of which were essential, from his own political motivations and aspirations. It is understandable but unconvincing for the liberal newspapers to appropriate the Kojima decision as a victory for the Movement for Popular Rights and Freedom.

Indeed, despite the substantial monetary award and the trumpetings of the liberal press, there is reason to consider the central government as the ultimate victor. In Kojima's carefully worded compromise, the partial restitution offered the plaintiffs was a warning to prefectural officials who might disobey national directives and harbor pretensions of private economic initiative. A week after the decision, Matsudaira was sentenced to 235 days in prison for his administrative malfeasance. At the same time, it did not offer enough to the plaintiffs to undermine prefectural authority; Mishima remained unscathed by the wording of the decision. Ironically, though not unexpectedly, Kojima's reasoning carefully followed the legal strategy of the suit. He imposed a fine distinction between prefectural actions vis-à-vis the central government—ignoring and flaunting national directives—and its improprieties and malfeasance vis-à-vis the Shōnai people. Each count was resolved in terms of the former principle. Writing a decision for the centralist bureaucrats, Ōkubo and Itō, it was a a natural rationale, but it bears observing that it was a constitutional logic, not a populist logic. Matsudaira and his staff were held accountable to the state, not to the people.

TEN

Aftermath

FROM LATE 1878 through 1879, the plaintiffs' award was to be allocated by village unit in proportion to land tax valuation. Mori and other leaders were given a share of the award by most people as "gratitude money" to cover the costs they had incurred. As we will see, Mori was later to itemize over 4,500 *yen* in personal funds expended. One of the few to refuse to contribute was the main Honma house. As the largest landholder in Shōnai it had received over 1,150 *yen* of the award. Mori promptly took the Honmas to court for their unwillingness to contribute 400 *yen* of that award toward his expenses. The Honmas responded that they had never asked Mori to undertake this class action suit and that the reimbursement of money was due to "official benevolence" (*kan no jinkei*, W 1982:122-24). Their argument carried the Sakata Circuit Court.

Mori, though, was a tenacious litigator. Undeterred, he returned to court duels with Mishima. Now the governor of the consolidated Yamagata Prefecture, Mishima had conceived a passionate commitment to construction of roads and other public works; indeed, he was as widely known then as the "roads governor" (*dōrō kenrei*) as he was later known in Fukushima as the "devil governor" (*oni kenrei*). His plan was to use the award for prefectural public works, and he ordered the Akumi and Tagawa County heads (*gunchō*) to pressure village officers to "contribute back" the village shares to his fund. In Akumi, fifty-two village headmen threatened the county head with their resignations in protest. Given the deep vein of antagonism against these officials by residents,

261

one can appreciate their unwillingness to serve once again as the "front men" for controversial government levies.

In Tagawa, Mori took up the cause of his wife's father, Haga Shichiemon, a large landholder in Tōge Village. Haga had been called before Kimura Junzō, the district head (and soon to be Tagawa County head). Ill at the time, Haga sent his son, who listened silently while Kimura strongly encouraged him to donate the Haga share of the award. Kimura argued that Haga had not asked the plaintiffs to represent him, but had merely benefited from their efforts. Haga himself went to Kimura two days later to decline politely, thinking privately that if his share was to be contributed anywhere, he would prefer it to go to the Tōge Village School Fund or to reserves for distressed cultivators. Kimura, however, was insistent. He intimated that almost everyone in the district was willing to contribute, that Haga was a lone holdout, that he might find "social intercourse" (*shakai kōsai*) to be a bit difficult in the future if he continued to refuse. Haga later explained to Mori that he was too ill to resist and signed the pledge that Kimura had ready for him. Mori immediately petitioned the prefecture as Haga's representative. He asked that the pledge be returned, charging that if even such prosperous people as Haga were cowered by prefectural pressure, soon *all* people in Shōnai would be forced to submit (YKS 1962:58).

We do not know how Mori's protest was resolved, but Mishima was able to avoid returning about two-thirds of the total award. This he diverted to a "school capitalization fund" (*gakkō kin*) and a general "contributing fund" (*kennō kin*), both of which were supplemented by further "gifts" from leading Shōnai merchants. He then announced his intention to use most of this money to construct a bridge near Sakata over the Mogami River, which would be the first bridge connection between Tagawa and Akumi. Mori again took exception to this disposition of the money. In a long petition to Mishima, he listed eight reasons why it was outrageous to build the Mogami bridge; his essential objection

262

was that it would be of primary benefit to town commercial interests, while the court award was for the cultivators. He admitted that it was difficult to divide the award among and within villages; those with minimal holdings wouldn't get enough for a day's *sake*. But rather than a bridge, Mori proposed that the prefecture invest the award in government bonds (which would benefit the country) and use the interest as a reserve fund for poor harvest years in Shōnai. Given the performance of government bonds in the 1880s, Mori proved a more effective political activist than financial seer; given the trading and rice transport needs of the cultivators, the bridge was certainly the better alternative for rural residents.[1]

A FINAL COURT DECISION

There was one count in the Kojima suit that remained undecided—the charge (#13) of gross misuse of village and village group expense levies. Kojima held that the prefecture was not responsible for such actions of local officials and that the plaintiffs must seek damages directly from the village and village group headmen in the Sakata Circuit Court.[2] Officials in some areas had already made restitution. When Mori brought suit with Watanabe Jiroemon and two others as plaintiffs, they sought 15,000 *yen* as representatives of people in fifty-five villages of fourteen Tagawa village groups (W 1982:124-42). In 1880, this court ruled in favor of the plaintiffs and awarded them the full amount. A subsequent

---

[1] Even here, though, Mishima managed to leave a residue of rumor and controversy. One of his subordinates later claimed that the funds actually went toward building a new road along the Mogami to connect Shōnai with the interior Shinjō Basin (YKS 1962:475-76; see ibid.:265-66).

[2] This was the local hearing room for the Sendai Superior Court. Superior courts had been established in 1875 in each region of the country. In northeastern Japan, it was first located in Fukushima and later moved to Sendai. Its three judges went on periodic circuits of the prefectures in their jurisdiction to hear cases (Ch'en 1981:55-56).

appeal by more than fifty of the headmen was rejected by the full Superior Court and payments began in March of that year.

This conclusion to the Kojima demands is revealing in several respects. The spread of plaintiffs across Tagawa and, within villages, across all levels of landholding again reminds us of the broad base of indignation that the issue of local corruption generated (see Tables 12 and 13). That this was six years after the August 1874 agitations demonstrates its continued potency. The plaintiffs' supporting materials again included impressive analyses of the village headmen's books and careful calculations of improper levies. The headmen's appeal to the court called on "custom" (*kanshū*)—that is, the customary nature of local expenses (the gifts to superiors on ceremonial occasions, food and drink at officials' meetings, travel expenses, and so on). The court dismissed this with the same reasoning Numa had used: even if one went back into the distant past and found a legitimate origin for these practices, "customs must change through the force of time" (*kanshū wa ikioi ni yorite tenkan subeki mono nari*), and since the formation of the prefectures, "old abuses" (*rōshū*) had been gradually eradicated (W 1982:127-28).

At the same time, disbursement of the Sakata Court award also signaled an end to cooperation among the Wappa agitators. Both Kanai and Honda had drifted away several years before, but when Honda heard that Mori was receiving most of the "gratitude money" from the cultivators, he joined with Ōtomo in a court suit against Mori that demanded a "fairer" division among them. Honda and Ōtomo saw the money as a gesture of gratitude for the assistance they had rendered; Honda in particular must have felt he had been more actively involved than Mori.

Mori interpreted the money as reimbursement for expenses incurred. In a pre-trial paper (SSS 1981:775-80), he complained that it was he who had borne the burden of petitioning in the years after the September 1874 arrests. He wrote that he had received 15 *yen* a month for expenses while

TABLE 12
Distribution of Registered Landholdings in Twelve Villages
Involved in the Kojima Suit

Village	Number of Households	0-1 ha.	1-3 ha.	3-5 ha.	over 5 ha.
Katakai	24	20	3	1	0
Kōya	9	7	0	2	0
Nishiiwamoto	16	11	5	0	0
Inari	19	12	5	2	0
Ōyodokawa	38	20	10	6	2
Kamishimizu	75	34	34	4	3
Hirakyōden	29	14	12	2	1
Kurokawa-kamigumi	70	27	40	2	1
Tsubade	25	9	14	1	1
Bizen	17	12	3	2	0
Shimonagawa	71	52	17	1	1
Ōtsuna	47	34	12	1	0
Total	440	252 (57%)	155 (35%)	24 (6%)	9 (2%)

SOURCE: Satō 1963:51, 69.

TABLE 13
Distribution of Landholdings in Takazaka Village, 1876

Registered Land-holdings	No. of Households	No. of Households Participating in 1875 Suit	Wappa Leaders
0 - 0.5 ha.	40 ⎱ 64%	24 ⎱ 63%	3
0.5 - 1.0 ha.	23 ⎰	16 ⎰	
1.0 - 2.0 ha.	26 ⎱ 29%	18 ⎱ 71%	2
2.0 - 3.0 ha.	2 ⎰	2 ⎰	1
3.0 - 5.0 ha.	6 ⎱ 7%	4 ⎱ 71%	
over 5.0 ha.	1 ⎰	1 ⎰	

SOURCE: Satō 1963:53.

in Tokyo from "like-minded Tagawa cultivators" (*Tagawa gun yūshi nōmin*), but that all else had been at his own expense. He had tried to run his family *sake* business while in Tokyo, but finally had to liquidate it in December 1876. Much of his personal fortune had gone into his petitioning activities. In contrast, he alleged, the Kanai brothers and Ōtomo had been given several thousand *yen* prior to September 1874. They, too, received 15 *yen* per month when in Tokyo *and* their households had been given additional sums in their absence. Also in preparation for the suit, Mori drew up in defense a list of all the 30-odd petitions and presentations he had made (W 1982:114-17) and a detailed report of all of his expenses from September 1874 to June 1876 (ibid.:117-21). He arrived at a total of roughly 4,500 *yen*, falling into four general categories.

1. Travel expenses to and from Tokyo. He calculated covering the 129 *ri* trip in 17 days at 1.50 *yen* per day. Thus each one-way trip was 25.50 *yen*.
2. Living expenses in Edo and in Tsurugaoka during the Numa and Kojima proceedings. The former were 75 *sen* per day and the latter, 50 *sen* per day.
3. Costs of having thousands of pages of documents transcribed and drawn up for submission.
4. Funds to a number of the Tagawa leaders for travel and living expenses.

Mori's arguments and records did not persuade the Sakata Circuit Court. It sided with Honda and Ōtomo, and awarded them 1,159 *yen* in late 1881. Ever the litigant, Mori appealed to the full Superior Court, lost again, but continued to resist paying them for several years (texts: ibid.:143-47).

Distribution of the 1880 award led to similar divisions among rural Wappa leaders. In Takazaka Village, for example, Takayama Kuzaemon was alleged to have absconded with 150 *yen* after deceiving three of his fellow activists and the villagers with whom the four had entered into a loan agreement.[3] The three then turned on the Takazaka villagers

---

[3] TSS 1975a:269-70. The documents left to us do not clarify this case.

in a legal suit that dragged out through much of the 1800s and ended inconclusively.

Honda was later killed in 1886 while on duty—ironically, as the Police Bureau Chief of Fukushima Prefecture, where Mishima had gone as governor. Mishima himself was to breed popular unrest but garner official sanction through his entire career. While still governor of Yamagata, he was appointed governor of Fukushima in January of 1882; he served in both posts until July, when he devoted full time to Fukushima. One can pick up his activities in Bowen's account of the Fukushima Incident of 1882, which Mishima precipitated with his highhanded road projects and disregard of the assertive prefectural assembly, whose chairman was none other than Kōno Hironaka (Bowen 1980:8-31). From Fukushima, he moved to Tochigi, the prefecture to the south, doubling as governor of both from late October 1883. In Tochigi the next year, he was faced with a fanatical group whose plot to assassinate government leaders aborted, and who retreated to Mt. Kaba, where they issued a call to popular uprising. This went unheeded, but Mishima ordered in hundreds of police and imperial troops to track them down (ibid.:31-49). Mishima was soon after moved to Tokyo, where he was named head of the Public Works Bureau in the Home Ministry and then Inspector General of the Police Agency. The government awarded him a viscount title, but he died at the age of fifty-three in 1888.

Mori and Political Parties in Shōnai

Of all the leaders of the Wappa protests, only Mori maintained a prominent political profile in Shōnai. He remained in contact with popular rights leaders throughout Japan. In 1879, he was one of the founding principals in Shōnai's first

Takayama Kuzaemon had apparently joined with Mori in the latter's suit against Honda and Ōtomo. Takayama himself itemized some 4,500 *yen*, which appear to have been personal funds that he advanced to the movement. Thus, there may have been more to this Takazaka case than the charges of defrauding.

political society, the *Jinseisha* or Effort and Character Society
(SSS 1981:882). Centered in Sakata and attracting many of
the town's educated residents, the society organized lecture
series and petition drives to publicize, educate, and generate
local support for the reform issues of the day—a National
Assembly, press freedoms, and so on. Private rotating credit
associations (*mujinkō* or *shinbokukō*) were something of a fad
across the country at the time, and Mori formed one as part
of the Jinseisha. Increasing membership in the society thus
generated capital, and in 1881, this occasioned a rift in the
Jinseisha. A self-styled conservative faction broke off as the
Akumi Nōdankai to emphasize promotion of local industry.
The remaining membership reorganized into a "progressive"
Akumi Kyōkai; Mori persuaded it to use its funds to open
Shōnai's first newspaper, the *Ryōu shinbun*. In early 1883, the
newspaper was shut down by the prefecture; the Akumi
Kyōkai soon after reorganized into the Shōnai Freedom
Party (Jiyūtō), with Mori as one of its three directors. It was
associated with Itagaki's national Freedom Party and continued to pressure for liberal political reform. Throughout the
early 1880s, these Sakata political groups engaged the prefecture in a running battle, typically on issues of elections and
usually directed against the Akumi County head, who was
in effect the prefectural administrator of Akumi. Sakata may-
oral elections were particularly contentious. At least three
(one of which was won by Mori) were invalidated by the
county head on a variety of pretexts; he was met with suits
and recall demands.

Equally fervent political societies sprang up in the early
1880s in Tsuruoka, as Tsurugaoka had recently been renamed, although these were more purely debating and discussion circles. The by-laws of one began with a lofty statement of purpose: to advance knowledge, to ensure freedom,
and to stimulate industry. In practice, this meant sponsoring
lectures and trade exhibits. Another promised to dedicate itself to learning and research. It and several others opened free
public newspaper reading rooms (TSS 1975a:411-14).

Not surprisingly, neither the Sakata nor the Tsuruoka political societies were able to attract large segments of the
countryside to their causes. One reason for this—and evidence of issues that *did* move rural residents—surfaced during the visit in late 1881 of a national ministry official on
tour to take the pulse of "popular feelings." Two months
before, the emperor had passed through Shōnai on his tour
of northeastern Japan, his route in and out of Tsuruoka lined
by flag-waving schoolchildren. Now, the official touring in
the imperial wake was given a different perspective of local
education.

On November 29, representatives of fifty-five Akumi villages met with him to present "a memorial of popular sentiment" (*minjō jōshinsho*). Their concern was Akumi school
assessments, and their anger was directed at the way taxes
and benefits were divided between town and countryside.
Akumi County, they testified, was divided into four blocks;
the west block included Sakata and twenty-nine surrounding
rural villages. Sakata had tax rolls of 3,000 households and a
land tax base of only 140,000 *yen*; the twenty-nine villages
had only 1,400 households, but a land tax base of 770,000
yen. Because school assessments were calculated from land
tax, the burdens of the rural households were fifteen times
that of town households. Moreover, the school in Sakata,
Takusei gakkō, was a "spectacular three-story skyscraper"
(*sansō no kōrin, unkan ni sobie*) while many villages could not
even afford a building and had to rent space in a private
house or hold classes in their temple. "We fear we have become slaves (*dōrei*) to the townspeople," they told the official. Their appeals of distress (*tangan*) to the county head
went unheeded, and they asked the visiting official to relieve
the oppression of the local officials (YKS 1978:1129-33).
Mori personally appeared as spokesman for several of the
village representatives, but his political society's membership
was largely drawn from Sakata, and the tax and funding dis-
criminations that villagers felt so acutely must have damp-

ened their fervor for the more general political reform battles.

There were regions of Japan in the 1880s where alliances of convenience or like-mindedness were forged between the Movement for Freedom and Popular Rights and rural protesters, but this apex of political rights advocacy in the country caused little stir in Shōnai. When neighboring Fukushima erupted in 1882, it drew from Shōnai only a letter and gift of support from the anonymous *Akumi gun no suke*, the "Defender of Akumi." It bore the address of Mori's newspaper (SSS 1981:890). In 1885, Mori died of a stomach ulcer in a Yamagata inn while representing Akumi in the prefectural assembly. He was forty-four years old. By then, other Sakata popular rights advocates had been arrested by the prefecture and sentenced to labor in Hokkaidō development projects. Political rights advocacy came to an end in Shōnai as the region, with the entire country, came to feel the full effects of the Matsukata Deflation.

THE LAND TAX REFORM AND THE MATSUKATA DEFLATION

The most immediate result of the Land Tax Reform of the mid-1870s had been the broad reductions in the mean per-unit tax rates. We have seen that the timing and pattern of the reductions link them directly to the Tagawa demonstrations of 1874 and subsequent petitioning and suits in Tokyo. However, there were other eventual consequences of less universal benefit. One matter that had not been immediately resolved in the surveys was disposition of parcels that had been abandoned by the registered holder. This had been occurring for at least a hundred years, and in some villages, such abandoned parcels amounted to over half the village acreage. Cultivation and tax responsibilities were then assigned by headmen to remaining households, but in many villages, these households were not automatically accorded legal title in the 1874-75 survey. In fact, Tawara (1972) has argued on the basis of his research in Hayashizaki Village, between Tsuruoka and Ōyama, that these parcels were not assigned until the end of the decade. When they were, several leading households were able to intervene to claim many of them. The result in Hayashizaki and, Tawara surmised, in the many other Shōnai villages with such parcels, was a concentration of holdings.

It is hard to know how far to generalize from his projections, but it is clear that concentration was soon aggravated by the impact of the recessionary Matsukata program on the new fixed land tax. By the end of the 1870s, the national government faced a serious fiscal crisis of its own doing. To meet its expenses in quelling Saigō's uprising in 1877, it had issued large quantities of non-convertible paper currency, which fueled inflation and added to the spiraling foreign debt. In 1881 Matsukata Masayoshi replaced Ōkuma Shigenobu as finance minister and immediately began implementing a series of deflationary, tight-money retrenchments.[4] Liable now for a fixed cash land tax, cultivators found themselves whipsawed by the national economy. Rice growers had prospered with commodity price inflation, but when rice on the Tokyo central market plunged from 14.10 *yen* per *koku* in 1881 to 4.60 *yen* in 1884, the fixed tax obligations and the short money supply forced many smallholders to mortgage their paddy lands. About 43% of Tagawa land was tenanted in the early 1880s, a proportion that remained fairly constant into the early 20th century.

One example of rural distress was another school dispute, this time in 1883 in Harima-kyōden Village, midway be-

---

[4] Matsukata (1835-1924) had been a key figure in designing the Land Tax Reform. His reform program after elevation to Finance Minister had some of the trappings and even substance of the "three great reforms" of the Tokugawa shogunate (Yoshimune's Kyōho Reforms, Sadanobu's Kansei Reforms, and Tadakuni's Tenpō Reforms). However harsh in the short term, Matsukata's measures were more successful in the longer term than those of his predecessors, and he himself enjoyed a longer term. He was to serve as Finance Minister until 1901, except for two very brief stints as Prime Minister.

tween Tsuruoka and Ōyama. Attendance at the village elementary school had fallen rapidly with the hard times, from 65% in 1881 to 53% in 1882 and then 38% in 1883. The same year, several of the settlements in the school district began a boycott drive to keep all children out and close the school. Their concern was money—the rising school budget and supplementary funds assessed by household, by land tax, and as attendance fees. Only after much negotiation was the school kept open, but the incident was a small reminder of the considerable dislocations of those years (TSS 1975a:418-19).

Suge Redux

Matsukata's induced recession also hit hard at the old Sakai retainer band. In 1878, the Meiji leaders had finally ended fief stipends for the ex-samurai in settlement for government bonds. Many had used these as capitalization for commercial ventures; in Shōnai, the organization of banks was a particular favorite. Most of these then collapsed in the early 1880s, lengthening the application lines in Tsuruoka for ex-retainers to sign up for pioneering schemes in Hokkaidō (TSS 1975a:423). Many left; Tsuruoka shrank from about 5,000 households in the late 1870s to about 3,000 households in the mid-1880s (ibid.:469). But that was to prove the low point in town fortunes. Matsukata's policies came at a high price, but they were effective in restoring currency values, reducing interest rates, and controlling inflation. Under these new conditions, a rivalry emerged in Shōnai: not between Sakata and Tsuruoka or between town and country, but rather between an assortment of vaguely liberal merchants and rural entrepreneurs in political and commercial competition with a resurgent and unbowed "domain retainers faction" (gokarokuha), led by the redoubtable Suge.

Sakai Tadazumi and his brother Tadamichi were largely absent from Shōnai in the 1870s; in fact, they spent the latter part of the decade studying in Germany. On their return,

272

they and their small accompanying group of ex-retainers were ignored by the national government, which had brought many of the other former domain elite into the government. They were instead invited to return to Shōnai by Suge Sanehide, who had retired from his vice-administrator position at the height of the Wappa Disturbances, but who remained a spiritual leader for those ex-retainers who struggled on at Matsugaoka and in certain neighborhoods in Tsuruoka. With "our lord" (*otonosama*) now back home, Suge moved more directly to revive the old Sakai warrior ethic of loyalty and commitment. The new school system offered little of the moral education of the former domain school, so Suge instituted small, mandatory study circles (*oyoriai*), which met several times a week at a hall in the Sakai residential compound. These were age cohorts of ex-retainers, who recited and heard lectures on the "Nine Chinese Classics" (*shisho gokyō*) for an hour or so in the evening. In 1890, on the occasion of the raising of the statue to Saigō Takamori in Tokyo's Ueno Park, Suge composed a volume of "Last Lessons of the Venerable Nanshū [i.e., Saigō]" (*Nanshūō Ikun*), which immediately became a supplemental text in the study groups.[5] Suge also organized another set of small groups known as "Diligent Application Groups" (*Sessa takuma no kai*), which functioned as mutual criticism circles (Koyama 1958:736-37). Some have also alleged that he tacitly consented to less organized youth gangs, which menaced

---

[5] In about 1920, after Suge's death, a third volume was added to the curriculum, the "Last Teachings of the Master Suge" (*Gagyū sensei ikyō*). The following lesson suggests that his later teachings were little changed from his days as domain elder and prefectural official. "No matter how fairly one treats tenants, most of them are extremely greedy things and can only talk of their own personal hardships. Whenever this happens, you should brace yourself and quietly listen to what the tenant has to say before kindly and politely explaining the reasons [for your actions or decisions]. If he continues to insist on his personal greed, you should firmly remove him from his tenancy. Even if you cannot find someone else to take over the land, it is better to let it run to wild grasses [than relent]" (Koyama 1958:741). See Koyama 1958:734-37 for a later (1938) account of the study groups.

townspeople, invaded the newspaper reading rooms, and disrupted the speeches and meetings of the political societies.

Suge's effort to reconstitute a Sakai subculture in the town would have been but a quaint anachronism had he also not shrewdly realized the need for a secure financial and political base in the region. The domain retainer elite was again engaged in capitalist ventures for decidedly uncapitalist aims. And once again, the main Honma house, and especially the retired head Mitsuyoshi, provided critical assistance. Mitsuyoshi helped Sakai to establish the Sakata Rice Exchange in 1886, which was then administered by Suge and other senior ex-retainers. The exchange did not have attached rice warehouses, so it relied on the old domain granaries along the Araita riverbank in Sakata. These had passed through several owners in the 1870s before the Honmas purchased them. Later in the 1890s, the rice exchange and the Honmas collaborated in building an enormous warehouse complex to replace Araita, the Sankyō Granaries (Koyama 1958). By the early 20th century, Sankyō dominated the rice marketing in Shōnai. The ex-retainer faction had also managed in 1886 to gain control of one of the larger banks in Tsuruoka, and with a revived silk export market, even the moribund mulberry and silkworm project at Matsugaoka enjoyed a revival.

In each of these ventures, the "domain retainer faction" faced competition from other merchants in Tsuruoka and surrounding areas, loosely designated as the "townspeople's faction." They controlled another set of banks and formed a rival Tsuruoka Rice Exchange and attached Tsuruoka Granaries. Indeed, industrial manufacture did not really begin in Shōnai until the mid-1890s, when these rival commercial interests imported machinery and techniques from Kyoto and Fukui for automated silk thread factories. With the Shōnai Habutae Factory in 1894 and the local invention of a new spinning machine, automated filature became the dominant local industry. Between 1902 and 1912, twenty-three filature companies were started in the Tsuruoka area and production increased sixfold (TSS 1975a:469-76).

In the late 1880s and 1890s, local electoral fights for national and prefectural representatives and for town council were often waged along these factional lines of antagonism (TSS 1975a:427-501). The idiom of interests was the political language of the two major national political parties, the Progressive Party (*Kaishintō*) of Ōkuma Shigenobu, under whose banner were found candidates of the retainer faction and of conservative Akumi landlords, and the Freedom Party (*Jiyūtō*) of Itagaki Taisuke. By the turn of the century, however, the local faction labels conformed poorly to actual alignments.

In 1902, for example, there were two contentious issues before the Tsuruoka Town Council: household tax assessments for the wealthiest townspeople, which earlier councils had been raising, and a government-mandated elementary school expansion that would require a consolidated school district with surrounding rural areas, and was strongly opposed by the major town taxpayers (a reversal from the Akumi school dispute twenty years earlier). In the 1901 elections for half the council seats, Suge had packed the candidacy lists and mobilized his faction for door-to-door canvassing and, apparently, intimidation of rival candidates (TSS 1975a:497). His people's victory enabled the selection of his choice for the new mayor, Hayashi Mōsei, a teacher who had engineered a purge of "progressive" administrators and instructors at the Tsuruoka Middle School (ibid.:496-97). In 1902, Hayashi and the new council pressed successfully for a postponement of the school plan and voted substantial reductions in tax assessments to the town's largest taxpayers, Kazama Kōemon, a leader of the townspeople's faction, and Sakai Tadazumi (ibid.:500-501). Political interests again divided town and villages, and the town's business elite from its commercial middle class.

This brief account does violence to the intricacies of political in-fighting and the details of banking and filature operations in the last two decades of the 19th century, but it does highlight the political distance traversed in the century. One

275

hundred years before the 1902 council meetings, the decision-making circle of domain officials and designated merchants had been divided by a factional power struggle between the domain elder Shirai Yadayū and Honma Mitsuoka. Both offered competing plans to restore the official domain accounts to fiscal solvency through more stringent regulation of tribute exactions. The issues and language of local elite politics had been radically altered, and even if the local population was excluded from both the 1800 deliberations and the 1902 council meeting, their collective agitations at vulnerable moments had been essential in that transformation.

AGRARIAN CAPITALISM

Shōnai's economic resurgence in the 1890s had three dimensions, which together represented the transition to a local capitalist economy. We have seen how financial and marketing arrangements and how the filature-led local industry were spurred by a favorable national economy and rivalry among area business cliques. The third element of the capitalist transition in Shōnai was the reorganization of tenancy relations and massive private investments in agricultural infrastructure, especially irrigation-drainage networks, in the period 1890-1920. What is most remarkable is that neither the shift in exchange relations nor the changes in manufacturing and agrarian production triggered any united and sustained opposition.

Shōnai's "rice revolution" around the turn of the century was linked in several respects to consequences of the Land Tax Reform. Final assignments of parcels in the late 1870s and even more seriously the induced recession of the early 1880s had driven many smallholders to a mortgage tenancy, but had allowed some largeholders to increase their holdings further. Yet the Land Tax Reform had also largely equalized tax rates across the plain; the resurveying and regrading of parcels had narrowed the tax advantages of lands opened

276

after the 17th-century cadastre, which were the bulk of most large holdings. With little or no land tax obligations to the domain, the registered holders could tolerate the water-logged soils and unstable yields of such paddy fields. Now with fixed and higher tax duties, the holders of such parcels were less able to ignore their liabilities.

There were three sets of measures that were to transform rice work and the paddy landscape. The first was a region-wide adoption of the so-called Meiji Methods (*Meiji nōhō*), a package of cultivation methods that included new seed selection techniques, better nursery bed construction, linear trans-planting, and, foremost, an autumn tilling after harvest and a spring tilling with a horse-drawn plough.[6] These practices were also known as the Fukuoka Methods for the area of southwest Japan that popularized them in the early Meiji pe-riod and that refined the particular ploughshare and narrow ploughsole design. To Shōnai cultivators, they were simply the "drained field/horse plough" (*kanden bakō*) program. Shōnai's worst problem was the waterlogged soil over much of the flat central plain; the autumn post-harvest tilling was intended to aerate the soil and promote field drying. This stiffened the soil, which was less amenable to spring hoeing and required instead a spring ploughing.

The *kanden bakō* techniques spread rapidly across the plain in the 1890s, vigorously promoted by local landowner soci-eties which sponsored inspection trips to Fukuoka, hired Fu-kuoka cultivators to teach ploughing, and underwrote equip-ment loans to tenants. By 1908, 94% of Shōnai's fields were dry-tilled by plough. There was some stabilization of yields and improvement in market reputation by the turn of the

[6] On rice cultivation practices in the mid-1880s before the Meiji Nōhō, see the 1885 report in YKS 1978:483-93. See Jinno 1977, Ōba 1977, and Uno 1978:523-60 for three excellent studies of the adoption of the Meiji Methods in a single Akumi village, Toyohara. Draft animals had long been used to "wet till" fields after they had been manually "dry tilled" with the *kuwa* hoe and flooded with water. The new methods now used horses or oxen for dry field ploughing.

century,[7] but the switch to these Meiji Methods was not without further implications. The deeper plough depth required increased quantities of fertilizer, but the rice varieties more responsive to increased fertilizer proved less resistant to certain common diseases. Greater quantities of water were now needed at transplanting, straining the capacities of the irrigation-drainage networks. And plough handling proved cumbersome and inefficient in the variably and irregularly shaped paddy parcels.

These and other factors predisposed the landowner societies of Akumi and Tagawa (the latter now divided into East and West Tagawa Counties) toward support for large-scale "arable land adjustment projects" (*kōchi seiri jigyō*) in the first two decades of the 20th century. Financed largely by assessments to the registered owners (with only minimal government subsidies), coordinated by the landowner societies and irrigation associations, and carried out by the off-season labor of villagers, these projects totally reshaped the paddy fields. In village after village across the plain, with backbreaking labor by hoe and shovel and straw basket, existing bunds were leveled and water channels filled in. Field areas were then recarved into blocks of uniform, rectangular 0.1 hectare parcels (Figure 16). Bunds were reformed and water channels redug so that each parcel was directly accessible by path and was fronted by a water delivery channel and backed by a drainage ditch.

The first paddy adjustment pilot project was in 1900 in East Tagawa, and included portions of the Nakagawa Yachi, where protestors had gathered sixty years before. Again, there were important variations in the course of the many subsequent projects over the next twenty years,[8] but together they had several consequences for an increasingly capitalist Shōnai agriculture. The 1874–75 Land Tax Reform survey

[7] See the table of Shōnai yields, 1889–1923, in Satō 1958:144 and the graph of yields in Harima-kyōden Village, 1877–1955, in TSS 1975b:366–67.

[8] Among the sources are Baba 1964, Satō 1958, TSS 1975b:352–55, and Isobe 1977, 1978:728–39.

16. After the Meiji Agricultural Methods: spring tilling with horse-drawn plough in rectangular fields.

had uncovered most but not all of the underregistration that provided a margin for the parcel holder against tax demands and for the tenant against rent levels. The erasure of existing field boundaries now eliminated any remaining excess. The rectangularization also reduced the total number of parcels, and thus the acreage required for the perimeter bunds; the result was an increase in actual rice acreage (divided among the landowners in proportion to previous holdings) but a loss for cultivators who grew catch-crops of beans and other vegetables along the bunds during the growing year. Land leveling and improvements in irrigation and drainage allowed marginal lands to be brought into rice cultivation, and the plain was even more extensively rice monocropped as a result (see Table 14). Finally, the projects promoted a shift in tenancy agreements from a volumetric grain measure of rents and land values to an acreage measure. Previously, rent standards (in effect, the rent maximum before the customary

TABLE 14

Acreage and Tenancy Rents before and after Land Adjustment
Projects, Sakai-shinden Village, Akumi County

	1908		1911	
	acreage (ha.)	tenant rent (koku)	acreage	tenant rent
Rice parcels				
(by grade:) top	48.1	1.1	114.0	1.20
middle	112.5	1.0	67.5	1.07
lower	12.8	0.9	8.5	0.97
Non-rice parcels	7.7	0.5 (rice)	6.1	0.5 (rice)
Totals	181.1		196.1	

NOTE: It was between 1908 and 1911 that the projects and subsequent land
allocation and grading were conducted.
SOURCE: Shirai 1961:97.

reductions) were expressed in bales of expected yield; a parcel for which rent was one bale was known as a "one-bale
parcel" (ippyōba) and its price as "one-bale parcel x yen."
With uniform 0.1 rectangles, acreage could serve as a meaningful measure. Isobe (1977) and others argue that it also
became a visible, uniform standard for evaluating relative
abilities of households—a prod to adopting new techniques
and a yardstick for tenants' performance. Finally, the assignment of parcels after a project was an opportunity for landowners to consolidate their holdings and for landlords to re-
write previous tenancy agreements and to remove
troublesome tenants.

Indeed, the reorganization of tenancy arrangements facilitated by the projects may be seen as the third component in
the rise of agrarian capitalism in Shōnai. Again, the Honmas—and in particular, Mitsuyoshi—had assumed the initiative. By the 1890s, 3,000 of Shōnai's 27,000 cultivator
households held at least a parcel of Honma paddy land in

tenancy. Throughout the decade, Mitsuyoshi designed a series of policies to rationalize house operations. He required written tenancy agreements that stipulated cultivation methods, delivery conditions, and forfeiture procedures, and he tightened the three-tiered hierarchy of tenant overseers (Kamagata 1956:215-16, Hosogai 1959). In 1889, he established a four-hectare "Honma Farm," to which tenants were brought for demonstrations of horse ploughing and other new techniques. Honma-controlled banks advanced loans to tenants to purchase the needed ploughshares and fertilizers. The largest landlord in Shōnai (indeed, in all of Japan) was exceptional, but only in scale and detail. By the turn of the century most large landholders exhibited a new concern toward rice production and agrarian infrastructure investment.

THIS NASCENT industrial and agrarian capitalism, a denser administrative matrix, and renewed lines of vertical political authority were at once the aftermath of 19th-century developments and Shōnai's prelude to the 20th century. Curiously, they brought not the much heralded "differentiation of a (previously uniform and solidary) peasantry," but rather more of a homogenization and rigidification of a previously variable and volatile agrarian population. Tenancy conditions were now more uniform and exacting, the administrative hierarchy more streamlined, rice marketing more concentrated, and the nation-state more strident in its calls on its citizen-children.

But even more noteworthy, Shōnai's transition to the 20th century engendered little organized opposition. Nothing in the popular rights movement and Matsukata Deflation of the 1880s, the formation of rival commercial cliques that locked up regional investment capital and rice marketing in the 1890s, or the capitalist manufacturing and agriculture of the early 1900s spawned anything like the broad popular protests of the first Meiji decade. To be sure, there were frequent local incidents of all sorts, such as the Harima-kyōden Village school dispute of the early 1880s, but we may conclude with mention of the only two brief moments of broader resistance. The first was in the spring of 1898, following a disastrous autumn harvest that was being compared to the worst of the 1830s. Convinced that traders on the local rice exchanges were artifically manipulating prices to keep them high, and resentful of strict quality grading at the Sankyō Granaries, a mob of several hundred sacked the Sakata Rice Exchange. The action was dubbed the Pine-sandal Disturbances (*Matsugeta sōdō*) because many of the protesters wore the crude pine sandals made in the mountain villages surrounding the plain. In a perfect display of deference and defiance, they had shown enough consideration to remove their sandals at the exchange entrance, leaving an enormous mound of footwear as they went in to accost the nervous dealers. There seem to have been few other organized actions despite clear evidence of hardship. The Harima-kyōden Harvest Book, for example, noted a mean yield of 0.7 *koku* per 0.1 hectare in the village for 1897, less than half that of most years of that decade. In Tsuruoka, 1,539 households were served with notices of tax delinquency for 1898, and 556 households were threatened with property attachment (TSS 1975a:487). No doubt these dislocations were cushioned and frustration blunted by efforts of municipal relief committees to subsidize low-cost rice sales. The amounts were not impressive (in Tsuruoka they totaled 1,500 *koku* for the year; ibid.), but the campaign was well publicized.

More serious frustration coalesced around the paddy adjustment projects after 1900—directed against the enforced participation, the low wages paid the village labor, the division of project costs between landlord and tenant, abrogations of tenancies, and so on (see Isobe's 1977 and 1978 studies of Toyohara and Satō 1958). Most of these remained isolated disputes and negotiations, except for an organized resistance in the Hirata District of Akumi that began in 1913. At the end of that year, about 1,000 tenants (some of whom owned their own land as well) were called together by a local owner-tenant, Watanabe Heijirō, at one of the larger temples to discuss common grievances. The result of the assembly was a Noble Deeds Group (*Gikyodan*) under Watanabe, to agitate for improvements in tenant agreements. They eventually drew up a five-point distress petition (*tangansho*) for presentation to the Akumi Landlord Association. In it, they called for:

1. a return to pre-project volumetric calculations of rent;
2. elimination of a new security deposit required when assuming a tenancy;
3. retraction of surcharges on inferior rice grades (rent was due in Sankyō Granary grade 2 rice, but grade 3 and grade 4 rice was much more typical; the difference was charged the tenant);
4. an end to the miscellaneous surcharge of 1-2% (its term, *shitajiki*, was the same as one of the disputed 19th-century ancillary levies);
5. and a nominal payment of 10 *sen* per bale for the tenant to transport the rent rice (Kanno 1978:435-36; Satō 1958:159-60).

The *Gikyodan* was brusquely rebuffed, and Watanabe and several others spent much of 1914 trying to rouse Akumi tenants and to negotiate privately with the landlords. In 1915, he petitioned the governor to rule on the five demands (text in Satō 1958:160), but the latter declined. Progress in negotiations came only after a Sakata merchant assumed control of large holdings in Hirata District and provoked much dissension with attempted tenancy changes. A boycott of rent rice ensued, the police chief in Sakata became concerned that unrest would spread, and he and prefectural officials eventually forced a series of bargaining sessions between the landlord and the tenant group. In 1916, an accord was reached in which the landlord capitulated on all five demands. The Gikyodan then used this as a successful model for individual negotiations with other Akumi landlords. The group disbanded several years later, its objectives satisfied.[9]

[9] I am here following Kanno's (1978:436-37) interpretation, which I find more persuasive than Satō's (1958:160-61).

ELEVEN

Concluding Reflections

FROM SAKAI Tadakatsu's arrival in Shōnai in 1623 until the present day, this rice plain has experienced four moments of sustained, collective protest. All were in the 19th century and occurred in two periods—in the early 1840s, at the beginning of the end of the Tokugawa shogunate, and in the late 1860s and early 1870s, the end of the beginning of the Meiji nation-state, if we might so characterize that shakedown decade.

In late 1840, it was fear of new surveys and higher tribute payments that impelled cultivators to join local rural officials and town merchants in challenging the direct shogunate transfer order. Honma and other large landholding merchants provided financial subsidies and orchestrated many of the assemblies and petition attempts. Domain elders, too, eventually swung around to support the drive. Under the rhetorical banner of the munificent acts of the lord Sakai, this broad-based movement was able to exploit the fault lines dividing the tributary elite and score a rare success in reversing the shogunal order.

Two years later, a parallel issue stirred similar anxieties and actions. Jurisdictional transfer of lands around Ōyama raised fears of new levies, in an atmosphere of commercial rivalries between Ōyama and Tsurugaoka townspeople and between Ōyama and rural *sake* brewers. Petitions and blockades organized by some of the *sake* brewing elite of Ōyama gained wide cultivator participation, as they again tried to play shogunate against domain. The protests came close to violence, but they were not sustained. The participants divided against themselves while the elite maintained a united front.

284

Twenty-five years later, as a Restoration army occupied and partitioned Shōnai, the Tengu League actions across the Akumi districts sought repeal of most ancillary levies and reform of local administration. Again, town merchants and rural cultivators were arrayed against village officers, designated merchants, and prefectural officials. They won at least partial concessions from the confused, imported prefectural officials, who lacked the necessary force and the confidence in their own local headmen to deal decisively with the protests.

The fourth set of disturbances was even broader in participation and more extensive in its goals. Initial requests to make tribute payments in cash became plans for a marketing cooperative for the entire plain; grievances then shifted to the malfeasance of local headmen and restitution for prefectural wrongdoings. Tagawans' response to mass arrests was to press their case even more resolutely at Tokyo ministries and courts until they were given "fair and open" hearings by Numa and Kojima.

I had first expected to find clear differences between the two protests of the 1840s and those thirty years later, given the exacerbation of political and economic tensions in the country during those decades, the wider currency of capitalist logic, and the political reorganization into the Meiji state. In fact, the similarities prove equally compelling. Even the protesters of the mid-1870s sought redress for new if egregious variations of familiar injustices: arbitrary ancillary levies, suspicious village expenses, closed land registers and village records, and rigged conversions of a land tax in kind. The Wappa Disturbances were tax protests, as were the earlier movements: mass mobilizations to prevent or minimize existing or anticipated exactions of a political elite that were felt to be onerous and excessive. In each case, their indignation was acute, their language sharp, their target focused. Rhetorical conventions changed, but the 1841 petitions carried to Edo, the 1844 defense at the Shiono hearings, the Tengu League's eighteen-count demands in 1869, and the suits brought by the cultivators to Tokyo in 1875 all shared a tone and substance.

We must be cautioned, though, against dismissing them as "merely" tax revolts: as rear-guard defenses of a status quo, as apolitical brushfires, as narrowly self-interested. Their deference was to an idealized order, not an existing distribution of power; they used values as threats, to caution and chasten elites. And at every point the stakes were high. Challenging a prerogative or questioning a directive were perturbations that shook a village group headman's confidence, a prefectural governor's tenure, and a shogunate minister's reforms. The movements leave indelible images: the thousands of cultivators who massed in correct cosmological patterns in Nakayama Yachi to block Sakai's procession to Edo; the human blockade around the Ōyama shogunate office; the Tengu bands attempting to storm the Sakata Prison in 1869; the impassioned testimony of the fish peddlar Shirahata and the merchant Mori before Judge Kojima, unbowed by the glares of prefectural officials. For those involved, success or failure irrevocably altered their daily lives and fortunes: blocking the impoverished Kawagoe domain lord from taking over Shōnai, losing property and position for the Ōyama brewers and villagers punished at Obanazawa, serving notice to the local officials and gaining large concessions in the land tax reform of 1874-75. They bandied about no great "selfless" political principles, but their choices did not always conform to a "selfish" economic logic. They could be as self-sacrificing as self-serving, and only exposed the clumsiness of such analytical dichotomies.

In actions and actors, the four movements had further parallels. To be sure, the Tagawa activists demonstrated a particular knowledge of the specifics of official wrongdoing and of avenues of appeal. They were confident of their leverage between local, prefectural, and national arenas; they were quick to protest arrests, and had little compunction about pressing direct appeals to the highest officials. Leaders often acted as "representatives" (sōdai)—but they spoke for "like-minded people" rather than as officially designated representatives of village units. Their procedural acumen, lines of organization, and ability to exploit the differences they perceived within the political elites were all impressive, but not unprecedented. In each of these periods there was a mix of private pleading to superiors and formal, unauthorized petitioning above their heads, peaceful assemblies and more forceful and occasionally violent confrontations. These tactics were often strategically combined and occasionally fortuitously juxtaposed, but rarely did they comprise a simple sequence from the lawful and deferential to the violent and defiant.

These complicated scenarios were carried off by a composite cast, a broad spectrum of participants—samurai, merchants, large landholders, smallholders, and the landless. Certainly in all four cases, momentum was carried by a small core of leaders: the local officials and town merchants in 1840-41, the Ōyama *sake* brewers in 1843, Sakata merchants like Nagahama in 1869, and Kanai, Honda, Mori, and several large and small landholders in the 1870s. Their practical advice, financial aid, and logistical support were invaluable, but in each case, too, we have seen much mutual conditioning and accommodation between leaders and supporters.

Of equal significance, none of the four movements revealed or precipitated enduring solidarities of community, party, or class. The Tengu imagery, Shigetane's lectures on Hirata Atsutane's thought, and the new cooperativism of the *kokudai kaisha* not withstanding, there were no successful appeals to communitarian ideologies behind any of the mobilizations. At least by the measure of landholding, Shōnai Plain was sharply stratified, but there was no apparent class basis or bias to participation or leadership. In a 1963 article, Satō Shigerō attempted to read the Wappa "Uprising" as the efforts of "petty bourgeois smallholders" to check the paddy accumulations of large landlords. Igawa (1972) has proposed a developmental sequence from the 1840s protests, which he considered to be "all cultivator" (*zen nōmin*) struggles against the feudal overlords, to the two early Meiji movements, which were led by the "semi-proletarian" small tenants and day laborers against the agrarian capitalist largeholders. Both tried to squeeze fluid stratification into a procrustean typology of "small village landlords" (*nōson kojinushi*), "wealthy cultivators" (*gōnō*), "smallholders" (*shōnōmin*), and "semi-proletarians" (*han puro*). Both have further assumed rather than demonstrated a consciousness of class interests within these categories. Nothing in the preceding chapters can support such formulations. Satō has recently advanced a new interpretation of the Wappa Disturbances (1981) as a harbinger of the Movement for Freedom and Popular Rights, but this too is a narrow mold. Mori Tōemon, it is true, was an effective, irrepressible political rights activist who was crucial in redirecting the Wappa protests from petitioning to court suits, but his conception of the struggle was not widely shared, and his later political society attracted few supporters from the protesters. Behind none of these four movements was there a solidary peasantry or an aggrieved proletariat or an enlightened minority, but a structurally diverse rural population that harbored common resentments and suspicions toward political authority.

Parallels and similarities among Shōnai's four cases are remarkable, yet two issues seem to set the Wappa protesters apart from previous actions: market access and official accountability. What had earlier been drives to minimize exactions in a commercialized tributary polity were now a more clearly elucidated desire for unimpeded access to rice marketing—and for no small measure of retribution from a regional political elite whose restrictions and policies frustrated such access. These restrictions and policies, we have seen, were not the dying reflexes of a feudal dinosaur. Suge and Matsudaira's policies were something new, a more aggressive effort to assume an actively commercial role in the regional markets, to control the local economy; for this reason they were more threatening than earlier policies of domain times. Yet the prefecture was politically vulnerable in

288

its hostile relations with the new Meiji state. By striking at this political vulnerability, the Wappa agitators were able to thwart the prefecture's economic initiatives.

I have argued that Ōkubo's appointee Mishima was sent in as governor of the Second Sakata Prefecture to rein in this unruly local elite, but that he soon came to share its attitude toward the populace. However, despite this common interest in working with Matsudaira and Suge, Mishima's vision was of a very different Meiji Japan—and one that was equally mistrusted by most Shōnai residents. His passion for "modern" public works, his pride in opening the two huge Western-style schools in Sakata and Tsurugaoka (over alternate proposals for a larger number of more modest schools), his promotion of a (poorly understood) Western-style agriculture to replace the "old-fashioned, backward ways"—these were the program of an impatient, self-assured modernizer, single-mindedly committed to a new Japan as wealthy nation and strong state.

Again, it would be wrong to read his disputes with Shōnai residents, especially the Tagawa cultivators and dissident ex-retainers, as the clash of a larger vision and narrower, local priorities. Many in Shōnai shared a vision of a different future and were enthusiastic for new structures (the rice cooperative, open books regularly audited, equitable schooling). But they did reveal in their memorials and suits and testimony a particular concern for making authority accountable, for more clearly defining the limits of official prerogatives. They were less worried about the criteria of selection than the standards of performance, and they preferred local understandings of propriety and reasonableness to Mori's abstract formulas of universal rights. It was this groping toward a new, more explicit measure of public conduct that set the Wappa Disturbances apart from the earlier movements.

The immediate compromises by Mishima in the land survey and by the Meiji government with the Kojima award did not work to the lasting advantage of most Shōnai cultivators.

In the latter instance, they won the money but lost the principle. Kojima's decision asserted the primacy of national law over prefectural practice, not a locality's claims on its officials. The Land Tax Reform brought immediate relief but also created the conditions for a homogenizing agrarian capitalism under which some were to prosper and others to suffer, but against which few were to join in sustained resistance. The irony of collective protest in Shōnai was that it was characteristic of a 19th century of great structural diversity and fluctuation rather than an early 20th century of uniformity and rigidity.

Shōnai ultimately confounds though it does not refute our broad historiographic paradigms. That its 19th-century experiences of collective protest were narrowly focused and out of phase with peaks of rebellion elsewhere in the 1830s, 1860s, and 1880s might be construed as signs of a relative regional prosperity that carried Shōnai contentedly into the modern era. This study suggests that that would be a mistaken interpretation. Whatever the real growth in aggregate economic output for the area, it was not individual prosperity but individual vulnerability to the "floating world" of rice production and commercial exchange that compromised enduring social solidarities.

It would be equally mistaken to relegate areas like Shōnai to the margins of a history of mid- and late-century crisis that pits widespread proletarian struggle or extensive political agitations against an increasingly centralized, bureaucratic state that snuffed out these radical challenges. If Shōnai provides us with less dramatic episodes than, for instance, Nambu Domain in 1853, Edo in 1866, Nagaoka in 1870, and Chichibu in 1885, its patterns were probably more common. I suspect that similar contextual studies of other 19th-century countrysides will yield similar portraits of collective action. Protest seldom fuses the disparate interests that draw people together into a transcending consciousness. Protest that transforms social structures and fundamentally alters cultural meanings is rarer still. The struggle for a new Japan was

decided in areas like Shōnai, where people were largely unmoved by the radical intellectual discourse of the times but
equally unpersuaded by the blandishments of their rulers,
where they chose to fight their own limited engagements
with nervous and divided authorities.

In light of the barbarous adventures to be launched in the
1930s in name of the Japanese people and a second "Restoration" (Najita 1974:128-37), we may applaud that they did
not go meekly into the new era. But for the very same reasons, we may also lament that the Tengu gangs and the rice
cooperative visionaries did not force more fundamental reform with more extreme action. But they would have been
as unmoved by our praise or opprobrium as they were by
Shigetane's lectures and Mori's exhortations and Mishima's
admonishments. They, as most of us in our own lives,
grounded their actions in the contingencies of their daily
lives and judged their reach by the exigencies of their everyday interactions.

APPENDIX

Early Spring Rice Prices and Domain Mean Tax Levels, 1697–1862

Year	domain rice price	Edo rice price	Osaka rice price	domain principal land tax rate (mean)
	(early spring price in *ryō* per 1 *koku*)			
1697	0.67	1.04	na	43.6%
1698	0.71	1.20	na	45.6%
1699	0.87	0.87	na	46.7%
1700	0.77	1.24	na	45.5%
1701	0.87	1.37	na	45.2%
1702	1.00	1.29	na	37.5%
1703	0.71	1.19	na	45.2%
1704	0.77	1.13	na	45.8%
1705	0.83	1.01	na	41.8%
1706	0.77	1.10	na	46.3%
1707	1.00	1.14	na	45.0%
1708	0.80	1.06	na	47.3%
1709	0.67	1.01	na	46.6%
1710	0.71	0.94	na	44.8%
1711	0.63	1.14	na	45.9%
1712	0.74	1.51	na	45.4%
1713	1.04	1.57	na	47.1%
1714	1.65	2.24	na	47.1%
1715	1.08	1.74	na	47.8%
1716	1.43	2.09	na	41.1%
1717	1.25	2.15	1.55	46.7%
1718	1.14	1.81	1.07	44.4%
1719	0.56	0.91	0.91	46.4%
1720	0.63	1.15	1.41	37.2%
1721	0.83	1.41	1.31	45.6%
1722	0.60	0.86	0.71	46.8%

1723	0.49	0.73	0.70	41.6%
1724	0.36	0.73	0.84	44.7%
1725	0.42	0.87	0.96	41.7%
1726	0.52	0.80	0.94	46.6%
1727	0.47	0.73	0.66	47.0%
1728	0.47	0.71	0.66	45.3%
1729	0.38	0.65	0.49	45.3%
1730	0.35	0.61	0.53	45.0%
1731	0.39	0.82	0.75	43.4%
1732	0.80	1.04	1.47	46.6%
1733	0.60	0.81	0.78	44.2%
1734	0.42	0.69	0.69	45.5%
1735	0.46	0.73	0.66	47.3%
1736	0.65	0.84	0.78	44.7%
1737	0.65	1.01	1.01	46.3%
1738	1.20	1.56	1.60	45.2%
1739	0.75	1.19	1.17	47.3%
1740	0.92	1.34	1.38	45.3%
1741	0.74	1.16	1.10	46.2%
1742	0.67	1.21	0.98	46.2%
1743	0.68	0.95	1.12	46.2%
1744	0.64	0.87	0.94	46.1%
1745	0.76	1.08	1.17	46.2%
1746	0.72	1.19	1.07	45.8%
1747	0.78	1.16	1.03	42.6%
1748	0.74	1.18	1.02	43.3%
1749	0.68	1.21	1.04	44.6%
1750	0.61	1.04	1.02	46.1%
1751	0.59	0.99	0.92	46.1%
1752	0.51	0.73	0.71	46.4%
1753	0.49	0.74	0.67	44.0%
1754	0.48	1.03	0.91	41.9%
1755	1.11	1.31	1.40	37.6%
1756	0.72	1.21	1.12	46.6%
1757	0.62	1.23	0.94	44.4%
1758	0.50	1.16	1.08	46.6%
1759	0.50	0.89	0.84	46.2%
1760	0.53	0.84	0.79	46.5%
1761	0.46	0.99	0.71	44.9%
1762	0.52	1.11	1.00	45.0%
1763	0.61	1.11	0.92	36.9%
1764	0.49	1.00	0.96	46.6%
1765	0.84	1.14	1.01	32.9%
1766	0.61	1.25	0.95	47.2%

APPENDIX

Year	domain rice price	Edo rice price	Osaka rice price	domain principal land tax rate (mean)
		(early spring price in *ryō* per 1 *koku*)		
1767	0.77	1.14	1.09	35.7%
1768	0.74	1.14	1.16	46.4%
1769	0.67	1.05	1.07	44.4%
1770	0.65	1.11	1.01	44.0%
1771	0.59	1.09	0.95	42.6%
1772	0.48	1.05	0.83	45.0%
1773	0.45	0.83	0.80	38.2%
1774	0.52	0.91	0.85	45.6%
1775	0.58	1.07	0.85	45.3%
1776	0.64	1.12	0.93	39.9%
1777	0.63	1.08	0.89	43.8%
1778	0.54	1.02	0.89	44.9%
1779	0.49	0.93	0.71	45.5%
1780	0.53	0.91	0.73	39.7%
1781	0.65	1.01	0.89	44.5%
1782	0.79	1.14	1.22	45.7%
1783	1.09	1.35	1.53	38.3%
1784	0.81	1.09	1.17	47.6%
1785	0.91	1.12	0.94	40.8%
1786	1.03	1.43	1.75	38.4%
1787	0.83	1.23	1.35	47.6%
1788	0.81	1.08	1.14	44.4%
1789	0.78	0.96	0.96	42.2%
1790	0.58	0.97	0.91	47.6%
1791	0.83	1.28	1.22	44.1%
1792	0.83	1.21	1.27	46.9%
1793	0.67	1.15	1.00	47.1%
1794	0.60	1.00	0.98	45.2%
1795	0.98	1.11	1.23	36.3%
1796	0.77	1.04	1.17	46.9%
1797	0.73	1.05	1.00	47.5%
1798	0.81	1.01	0.91	39.1%
1799	0.63	1.09	1.05	45.3%
1800	0.83	1.23	1.11	41.5%
1801	0.71	1.11	1.07	47.5%
1802	0.75	1.08	0.94	47.4%
1803	0.67	0.91	0.83	44.3%

1804	0.66	0.86	0.86	40.5%
1805	0.53	0.89	0.90	47.3%
1806	0.52	0.93	0.89	47.4%
1807	0.73	1.02	1.06	43.7%
1808	0.84	1.23	1.20	44.0%
1809	0.60	0.98	0.96	47.5%
1810	0.62	0.88	0.88	47.0%
1811	0.61	0.86	0.92	44.3%
1812	0.52	0.87	0.82	47.3%
1813	0.75	0.93	1.01	41.7%
1814	0.67	0.98	1.02	46.7%
1815	0.64	0.96	0.92	44.7%
1816	0.77	1.09	1.02	41.7%
1817	0.69	1.04	0.90	43.1%
1818	0.55	0.89	0.79	47.0%
1819	0.56	0.86	0.79	46.4%
1820	0.53	0.89	0.93	47.4%
1821	0.65	1.09	0.93	45.2%
1822	0.61	1.02	0.93	46.6%
1823	0.59	0.97	0.98	46.7%
1824	0.69	1.01	0.95	44.8%
1825	0.83	1.12	1.16	43.6%
1826	0.65	1.00	0.89	47.4%
1827	0.70	0.88	0.86	44.0%
1828	0.95	1.16	1.29	43.3%
1829	0.69	1.15	1.08	47.4%
1830	1.18	1.17	1.31	40.2%
1831	0.83	1.14	1.13	47.4%
1832	1.18	1.11	1.19	41.4%
1833	1.54	1.56	1.83	37.0%
1834	0.83	1.43	1.12	47.4%
1835	1.18	1.53	1.32	32.6%
1836	2.10	3.03	2.31	39.5%
1837	1.24	2.00	1.47	47.0%
1838	1.78	2.03	1.82	35.2%
1839	1.05	1.20	1.02	32.4%
1840	0.72	1.17	0.96	47.2%
1841	0.80	1.17	1.19	34.7%
1842	0.60	1.11	1.03	47.3%
1843	0.58	1.11	1.16	47.3%
1844	0.82	1.49	1.15	39.3%
1845	1.11	1.43	1.37	46.0%
1846	0.76	1.77	1.26	46.0%
1847	0.97	1.26	1.27	45.2%

Year	domain rice price	Edo rice price	Osaka rice price	domain principal land tax rate (mean)
	(early spring price in *ryō* per 1 *koku*)			
1848	0.80	1.17	1.37	47.2%
1849	0.94	1.60	1.58	45.0%
1850	1.27	1.66	2.22	38.2%
1851	0.93	1.26	1.22	47.1%
1852	1.27	1.49	1.32	38.5%
1853	1.37	1.86	1.58	47.1%
1854	1.15	2.06	1.19	40.2%
1855	0.77	1.86	1.00	47.1%
1856	0.77	1.91	1.11	42.4%
1857	1.00	1.69	1.49	42.9%
1858	1.06	1.89	1.83	46.9%
1859	1.30	1.77	1.58	41.8%
1860	0.94	1.40	1.99	44.2%
1861	1.09	2.11	1.91	47.6%
1862	1.58	2.09	2.19	47.6%
1863	na	na	na	47.6%
1864	na	na	na	47.5%
1865	na	na	na	47.6%
1866	na	na	na	45.0%

SOURCES: rice prices: Iwasaki 1981:460-65
   domain mean tax rates: Tsuruoka kyōdo shiryōkan

CHARACTER LIST

THIS character list is limited to those local and unusual terms and phrases not found in general dictionaries and to the verses cited in the text.

chibikichō 地引帳
chiharai 地払い
chiken torishirabe 地券取調べ
daigennin 代言人
Daikoku mai 大黒舞
fumeigi 不名義
fusei 不正
Gagyū sensei ikyō 巨牛先生遺教
Gikyodan 義挙団
gōdan 強談
goeijō gokitō 御永城御祈禱
gokarokuha 御家禄派
gonsanji 権参事
hyakushō no kikan 百姓の亀鑑
hyakushō tari to iedomo nikun tsukaezu 雖為百姓不仕二君
hyōta zukuri 俵田作り
irisaku yonaimai 入作与内米
Jinseisha 尽性社
kaidai itchi banmin jishu no ken 海内一致万民自主ノ権
kaimai 廻米
kairyōha 改良派
kanden bakō 乾田馬耕
kantoku bōrei 姦慝暴戾
karen chūkyū 苛斂誅求
kenpakusho 建白書
kokake 小商

kokudai kaisha 石代会社

kokudainō 石代納

konkyū yonaimai 困窮与内米

kujishi 公事師

kyokuchoku 曲直

manninkō 万人講

nanidozo inari daimyōjin 何卒居成大明神

nankyū hyakushō 難窮百姓

oieryū お家流

ōren kasei 横斂苛政

Ōu no zokkai 奥羽の賊魁

saikakukin 才覚金

sakutokumai 作得米

sanpō ryōchigae 三方領地替

seiichii inari daimyōchi 正一位いなり大みやう地

Sessa takuma no kai 切磋琢磨会

setsuyū 説諭

shinchōgumi 新徴組

shōmon shōko 証文証拠

suimon 垂問

sunshikin 寸志金

tanebujikimai 種夫

tangansho 歎願書

teatemai 手当米

tenbi chibi renjū 天火地火連中

tengu tō 天狗党

tenkan 添翰

Tsurugaoka ken assei o aratame narabi fusei kashutsu no kinkoku shokan o
jūkyū suru no so 鶴岡県圧制ヲ革メ并不正課出ノ金穀償還ヲ請求
スルノ訴

Verses

(a) page 98

Kawagoe mo	川越も
watari tomarite	渡り止りて
sata nagare	沙汰ながれ

(b) page 99

mizu no yaku	水の役
mito toriage	水戸取揚
nagaretara	流れたら
naga no hinobe no	長の日延の
haru wa kinuran	春は来ぬらん

(c) page 100

ichi ni ima made ita kuni o	一に今まで居た國を
ni ni niwaka ni tokorokae e	二に俄に所替へ
san ni Sakai no jūyaku wa	三に酒井の重役は
yottsu yoroshiku hakarite	四つよろしく計りて
itsutsu izure no hyōgi ni mo	五ついづれの評議にも
muttsu muri na koto nareba	六つ無理な事なれば
nanatsu Nagaoka hikiwatashi wa	七つ長岡引越は
yattsu yamu to no gosata nari	八つやむとの御沙汰なり
kokonotsu kōgi mo kimarite	九つ公儀も極りて
tō ni tōkoku osuwari osuwari	十に当國お居りお居り
masu masu Sakai no Daikokumai wa	ますます酒井の大黒舞は
misai na misai na	みさいなみさいな

REFERENCES

Unpublished Materials and Published Document Collections

Abe Korechika
1869-70 unpaginated entries for 1869-70, *Ki* [Notebooks], 1833-1889. Unpublished manuscript in Tsuruoka-shi kyōdo shiryōkan.

Amarume-chō kyōiku iinkai (comps.)
1979 "Satō Kiyosaburō nikki" [Diary of Satō Kiyosaburō], *Amarume-chō shi shiryō* 1:165-95.

anonymous
1841 *Yume no ukihashi* [The Floating Bridge of Dreams]. Original scroll preserved at Chidō hakubutsukan, Tsuruoka; 20th-century copy of the 87 inscribed drawings at Tsuruoka-shi kyōdo shiryōkan, Tsuruoka.

1867 *Manji san yori kome heikin men* [Mean principal land tax rates from 1660]. Pamphlet K169, Tsuruoka-shi kyōdo shiryōkan, Tsuruoka.

Igawa Kazuyoshi (comp.)
1970 "Tengu sōdō" [The Tengu Disturbances], in *Nihon shomin seikatsu shiryō shūsei* [A Collection of Documents on Japanese Popular Life], 13:527-55. Tokyo: San'ichi shobō.

Matsunaga Goichi (ed.)
1972 "Osorenagara katitsuke o motte tangan tatematsuri sōrō" [An 1874 petition from Kenmochi Torazo et al.], in *Kinsei minshū no kiroku* [People's Records of the Tokugawa Period], volume 1 (*Nōmin* [Cultivators]), pp. 343-46. Tokyo: Shinjinbutsu ōrai sha.

Naitō Morikazu
1841 *Kappo no tama*. 56 folios. Manuscript in Tsuruoka-shi kyōdo shiryōkan, Tsuruoka.

Ōkurashō (comp.)
1962 *Meiji zenki zaisei keizai shiryō shūsei* [A Collection of Documents on Early Meiji Finance and Economy], volume 2. Tokyo: Meiji bunken shiryō hakkōkai.

Ono Takeo
1964   "Tenpō kaikyo roku" [A Record of the Brilliant Achievements of the Tenpō Era], in Ono Takeo, *Tokugawa jidai hyakushō ikki sōdan*, volume 1, pp. 37-142. First published in 1927 and originally compiled by Saitō Kiyoshi in 1921. Tokyo: Toe shoin.

Sakata-shi shi hensan iinkai
1971   *Sakata-shi shi, shiryōhen* [The History of Sakata City, Documents], volume 5 (*Honma-ke monjo* [Honma House Papers]). Sakata: Sakata-shi yakusho.

1977   *Sakata-shi shi, shiryōhen* [The History of Sakata City, Documents], volume 7 (*Seikatsu bunkahen* [Culture and Life]). Sakata: Sakata-shi yakusho.

1981   *Sakata-shi shi, shiryōhen* [The History of Sakata City, Documents], volume 8 (*Shakaihen* [Society]). Sakata: Sakata-shi yakusho.

Tsuruoka-shi shi hensan iinkai
1981   *Wappa sōdō shiryō* [Documents of the Wappa Disturbances], volume 1. Tsuruoka: Tsuruoka-shi yakusho.

1982   *Wappa sōdō shiryō* [Documents of the Wappa Disturbances], volume 2. Tsuruoka: Tsuruoka-shi yakusho.

Yamagata-ken shi hensan iinkai
1962   *Yamagata-ken shi, shiryōhen* [The History of Yamagata Prefecture, Documents], volume 2 (*Mishima monjo* [Mishima Papers]). Yamagata: Yamagata-ken cho.

1975   *Yamagata-ken shi, shiryōhen* [The History of Yamagata Prefecture, Documents], volume 12 (*Ōhara monjo/Notsuke monjo* [Ōhara Papers/Notsuke Papers]). Yamagata: Yamagata-ken cho.

1978   *Yamagata-ken shi, shiryōhen* [The History of Yamagata Prefecture, Documents, volume 19 (*Kingendai shiryō* 1 [Modern Period Documents 1]). Yamagata: Yamagata-ken cho.

1980   *Yamagata-ken shi, shiryōhen* [The History of Yamagata Prefecture, Documents], volume 17 (*Shōnai han* [Shōnai Domain]). Yamagata: Yamagata-ken cho.

Yuza-chō shi hensan iinkai
1978   *Bunrin ki* [The Journal of Bunrin]. *Yuza-chō shiryōshū* [A Collection of Yuza Town Documents], volume 3. Yuza: Yuza-chō yakuba.

REFERENCES

SECONDARY LITERATURE

Akiyama Takashi, Kitami Toshio, Maemura Matsuo, and Wakao Shunpei (eds.)
1979   *Zuroku nōmin seikatsu shi jiten* [An Illustrated Encyclopedia of the History of Rural Life]. Tokyo: Kashiwa shobo.

Aoki Kōji
1966   *Hyakushō ikki no nenjiteki kenkyū* [A Chronological Study of Peasant Uprisings]. Tokyo: Shinsei sha.

1967   *Meiji nōmin sōji no nenjiteki kenkyū* [A Chronological Study of Meiji Farmer Disturbances]. Tokyo: Shinsei sha.

1971   *Hyakushō ikki sōgō nenpyō* [A Comprehensive Chronology of Peasant Uprisings]. Tokyo: San'ichi shobo.

Aoki Michio
1972   "Keio ninen Ushū Murayama chihō no yonaoshi ikki" [Millenarian Uprisings in Murayama Region, 1866], in Sasaki Junnosuke (ed.), *Murakata sōdō to yonaoshi* [Rural Disturbances and Millenarian Uprisings], volume 1, pp. 162-210. Tokyo: Aoki shoten.

1981   "Kinsei minshū no seikatsu to teikō" [Resistance and Popular Life in Early Modern Japan], in Aoki Michio et al. (eds.), *Ikki* [Uprisings], 4:167-226. Tokyo: Tokyo daigaku shuppankai.

Baba Akira
1964   "Tochi kairyō jigyō o chūshin to suru Shōnai no enkaku" [A History of Shōnai Based on Land Improvement Projects], in *Tochi kairyō jigyō chōkan sōgō kōka chōsa: Mogamigawa chiku* [A Survey of the Long-term Comprehensive Effectiveness of Land Improvement Projects: Mogami River District], volume 5. Sendai: Nōrinshō Tōhoku nōseikyoku.

Beasley, W. G.
1972   *The Meiji Restoration.* Stanford: Stanford University Press.

Bellah, Robert
1957   *Tokugawa Religion: The Values of Pre-industrial Japan.* Glencoe: Free Press.

1978   "Baigan and Sorai: Continuities and Discontinuities in Eighteenth-Century Japanese Thought," in Tetsuo Najita and Irwin Scheiner (eds.), *Japanese Thought in the To-kugawa Period, 1600-1868*, pp. 137-52. Chicago: University of Chicago Press.

Bendix, Reinhard
1978   *Kings or People: Power and the Mandate to Rule.* Berkeley: University of California Press.

Blacker, Carmen
1975   *The Catalpa Bow.* London: Allen & Unwin.

Bolitho, Harold
1974   *Treasures Among Men: The Fudai Daimyo in Tokugawa Japan.* New Haven: Yale University Press.

1979   "The Echigo War, 1868," *Monumenta Nipponica* 34(3):260-77.

Borton, Hugh
1938   "Peasant Uprisings of Japan in the Tokugawa Period," *Transactions of the Asiatic Society of Japan*, 2nd series, 16:1-219.

Bowen, Roger W.
1980   *Rebellion and Democracy in Meiji Japan: A Study of Commoners in the Popular Rights Movement.* Berkeley: University of California Press.

Brow, James
1981   "Some Problems in the Analysis of Agrarian Classes in South Asia," *Peasant Studies* 9(1):26-39.

Burton, W. Donald
1978   "Peasant Struggle in Japan, 1590-1760," *Journal of Peasant Studies* 5(2):135-71.

Cancian, Frank
1974   "Economic Man and Economic Development," in John J. Poggie and Robert N. Lynch (eds.), *Rethinking Modernization: Anthropological Perspectives*, pp. 141-56. Westport, CT: Greenwood Press.

Chambliss, William Jones
1965   *Chiaraijima Village: Land Tenure, Taxation, and Local Trade, 1818-1884.* Association for Asian Studies Monographs and Papers #19. Tucson: University of Arizona Press.

Ch'en, Paul Heng-chao
1981   *The Formation of the Early Meiji Legal Order.* Oxford: Oxford University Press.

REFERENCES

Craig, Albert
1961   Chōshū in Meiji Japan. Cambridge: Harvard University
        Press.

Crawcour, E. Sydney
1965   "The Tokugawa Heritage," in William W. Lockwood
        (ed.), The State and Economic Enterprise in Japan, pp. 17-
        44. Princeton: Princeton University Press.

Davis, Winston
1984   "Pilgrimage and World Renewal: A Study of Religion
        and Social Values in Tokugawa Japan, Part II," History
        of Religions 23(3):197-221.

Dore, Ronald
1965   Education in Tokugawa Japan. London: Routledge and
        Kegan Paul.

Enomoto Sōji
1975   "Shōnai han" [Shōnai Domain], in Kodama Kōta and
        Kitajima Masamoto (eds.), Shinpen monogatari hanshi [A
        New Edition of Tales of Domain History], 1:213-50.
        Tokyo: Shijinbutsu yukiki sha.

Fukaya Katsumi
1981   "Bakuhansei shakai to ikki" [Uprisings and Society un-
        der the Tokugawa Polity], in Aoki Michio et al. (eds.),
        Ikki [Uprisings] 1:99-160. Tokyo: Tokyo daigaku shup-
        pankai.

Genovese, Eugene
1969   The World the Slaveholders Made: Two Essays in Interpre-
        tation. New York: Pantheon.

Gluck, Carol
1978   "The People in History: Recent Trends in Japanese His-
        toriography," Journal of Asian Studies 38(1):25-50.

Greenough, Paul R.
1983   "Indulgence and Abundance as Asian Peasant Values: A
        Bengali Case in Point," Journal of Asian Studies 42(4):831-
        50.

Hanley, Susan B.
1983   "A High Standard of Living in Nineteenth-Century Ja-
        pan: Fact or Fantasy?" Journal of Economic History
        43(1):183-92.

Hanley, Susan B., and Kozo Yamamura
1977   Economic and Demographic Change in Preindustrial Japan,
        1600-1868. Princeton: Princeton University Press.

Harootunian, H. D.
1970   *Toward Restoration: The Growth of Political Consciousness in Tokugawa Japan.* Berkeley: University of California Press.

1974   Review of W. G. Beasley, *The Meiji Restoration. The Journal of Asian Studies* 33(4):661-72.

1978   "The Consciousness of Archaic Form in the New Realism of Kokugaku," in Tetsuo Najita and Irwin Scheiner (eds.), *Japanese Thought in the Tokugawa Period, 1600-1868,* pp. 63-105. Chicago: University of Chicago Press.

Hattori Shiso
1974   "Jiyū minken to hōken guso: wappa jiken gaisetsu" [Feudal Tribute and Freedom and Popular Rights: An Outline of the Wappa Incidents], in *Hattori Shiso zenshū* [The Collected Works of Hattori Shiso], 11:149-208. Tokyo: Fukumura shuppan k.k.

Hauser, William
1974   *Economic Institutional Change in Tokugawa Japan: Ōsaka and the Kinai Cotton Trade.* Cambridge: Cambridge University Press.

Hayashi Hideo (ed.)
1980   *Zuroku Nihon bunka no rekishi* [An Illustrated History of Japanese Culture], volume 10. Tokyo: Shogakkan.

Hayashi Motoi
1971   *Zoku hyakushō ikki no dentō* [Traditions of Peasant Uprisings, Continued], Tokyo: Shinkyo sha.

Hayashiya Tatsusaburō
1977   "Kyoto in the Muromachi Age," in John W. Hall and Toyoda Takeshi (eds.), *Japan in the Muromachi Age,* pp. 15-36. Berkeley: University of California Press.

Henderson, Dan Fenno
1965   *Conciliation and Japanese Law: Tokugawa and Modern,* volume 1. Seattle: University of Washington Press.

1975   *Village "Contracts" in Tokugawa Japan.* Seattle: University of Washington Press.

Hibbett, Howard
1959   *The Floating World in Japanese Fiction.* Oxford: Oxford University Press.

Hosogai Daijirō
1959   "Senchōbu jinushi—Honma-ke no jinushi keizai kōzō" [A Thousand *Chōbu* Landlord—The Structure of the

Landlord Economy of the Honma House], *Tochi seido shigaku* 1(3):33-70.

Huffman, James L.
1983 "The Popular Rights Debate: Political or Ideological?" in Harry Wray and Hilary Conroy (eds.), *Japan Examined: Perspectives on Modern Japanese History*, pp. 98-103. Honolulu: University Press of Hawaii.

Ienaga Saburō
1955 *Kakumei shisō no senkusha: Ueki Emori no hito to shisō* [A Pioneer of Revolutionary Thought: Ueki Emori, the Man and His Ideas]. Tokyo: Iwanami shoten.

1960 *Ueki Emori kenkyū* [A Study of Ueki Emori]. Tokyo: Iwanami shoten.

1974 *Ueki Emori senshū* [Selected Works of Ueki Emori]. Tokyo: Iwanami shoten.

Igarashi Bunzō
1977 "Sakata no minzoku geinō" [Folk Performing Arts of Sakata], SSS 1977:776-82.

Igawa Kazuyoshi
1966 "Shōnai han ni okeru kinsei gōki no mizuchō aratame" [The Late Tokugawa Revision of Land Tax Registers in Shōnai Domain], *Rekishi no kenkyū* 12:1-20.

1967 "Inasaku tansaku chitai no nōmin bunkai to sono gen'in" [The Differentiation of the Peasantry in a Rice Monoculture Area and Its Causes], in *Yamagata kōko to rekishi* [Archeology and History of Yamagata], pp. 265-83. Yamagata: Yamakyō shigakkai.

1969 "Tengu sōdō to Sakata ken" [Sakata Prefecture and the Tengu Disturbances], *Rekishi* 37:13-27.

1972 "Ushū Shōnai chihō ni okeru nōmin tōsō" [Agrarian Struggles in the Shōnai Region of Ushū], in Sasaki Junnosuke (ed.), *Murakata sōdō to yonaoshi* [Rural Disturbances and Millenarian Uprisings], volume 1, pp. 45-72. Tokyo: Aoki shoten.

1973 "Bakumatsu ishinki ni okeru inasaku tansaku chitai no tochi shoyū to nōgyō keiei" [Agrarian Economy and Landholding in a Rice Monoculture Region in Late Tokugawa and Early Meiji], in Kudō Sadao kyōju kanreki kinenkai (ed.), *Mogamigawa ryūiki no rekishi to bunka* [History and Culture in the Mogami River Basin], pp. 295-324. Yamagata: Yamagata shigaku kenkyūkai.

Igawa Kazuyoshi and Satō Shigerō
1969   "Meiji ishin to nōmin tōsō: Tengu sōdō kara Wappa ikki
        e" [Agrarian Struggle and the Meiji Restoration: From
        the Tengu Disturbances to the Wappa Uprisings], *Reki-
        shigaku kenkyū* 352:9-20.

Ihara Saikaku
1959   *The Japanese Family Storehouse, or The Millionaires' Gospel
        Revisited.* Translation by G. W. Sargent. Cambridge:
        Cambridge University Press.

Irokawa Daikichi
1975   "The Survival Struggle of the Japanese Community,"
        The Japan Interpreter 9(4):466-92.

Isobe Toshihiko
1977   "Kōchi seiri o kikaku to suru tochi hensei no tenkai"
        [The Development of Land Consolidation as Catalyzed
        by the Arable Land Adjustment Projects], in Toyohara
        kenkyūkai (ed.), *Zenji nisshi*, pp. 191-227.

1978   " 'Toyohara tochi' hensei no kentō" [An Investigation
        of the Formation of Toyohara Lands], in Toyohara
        kenkyūkai (ed.), *Toyohara-mura*, pp. 695-769.

Iwasaki Masaru
1981   *Kinsei Nihon bukkashi no kenkyū—kinsei beika no kōzō to
        hendō* [A Study of Commodity Prices in Early Modern
        Japan: Structure and Fluctuations of Rice Prices]. Tokyo:
        Ohara shinseisha.

Jinno Tadayoshi
1977   "Kandenka to Meiji nōhō no keisei" [The Shift to
        Drained Fields and the Formation of the Meiji Methods],
        in Toyohara kenkyūkai (ed.), *Zinji nisshi*, pp. 465-515.

Johnson, Linda L.
1983   "Patronage and Privilege: The Politics of Provincial
        Capitalism in Tokugawa Japan." Ph.D. dissertation,
        Stanford University.

Kamagata Isao
1956   *Tohoku nōson fudōki* [A Gazetteer of Farming Villages of
        Northeastern Japan]. Tokyo: Tōyō keizai shinpōsha.

Kanno Masashi
1978   *Kindai Nihon ni okeru nōmin shihai no shiteki kōzō* [The
        Historical Structure of Rural Control in Modern Japan].
        Tokyo: Ochanomizu shobo.

Kashiwagura Ryōkichi
1961 "Kaidai" [Commentary], in Honma-ke shozo shiryō
hensan iinkai (eds.), *Honma-ke monjo* [Honma House Pa-
pers], volume 1, pp. 1-59. Yamagata: Yamagata-ken.

Kelly, William W.
1982a *Water Control in Tokugawa Japan: Irrigation Organization
in a Japanese River Basin, 1600-1870.* East Asia Papers
Series #31. Ithaca: Cornell University China-Japan Program.

1982b *Irrigation Management in Japan: A Critical Review of Japanese Social Science Literature.* East Asia Papers Series #30.
Ithaca: Cornell University China-Japan Program.

Kokushō Iwao
1959 "Dewa-kuni kōryō Ōyama hyakushō ikki" [The Ōyama
Peasant Uprising in the Shogunate Territories of Dewa],
in Kokushō, *Hyakushō ikki no kenkyū, zokuhen* [Addi-
tional Studies of Peasant Uprisings], pp. 119-30 (original
article, 1932). Tokyo: Minerva shobo.

Koyama Magojirō
1958 "Daijinushi to Shōnai mai no ryūtsū: Sankyo sōkō no
tenmatsu" [Large Landlords and the Shōnai Rice Trade:
A Detailed Account of the Sankyo Granary], in Nihon
nōgyō hattatsushi chōsaki (eds.), *Shuyō chitai nōgyō seisanryoku keisei shi, jokan* [History of the Formation of Agricultural Productivity in Principal Regions], 1:719-88.
Tokyo: Nōrinsho nōgyō sōgō kenkyūsho.

Kriedte, Peter, Hans Medick, and Jurgen Shumbohm
1981 *Industrialization Before Industrialization: Rural Industry in
the Genesis of Capitalism.* Cambridge: Cambridge University Press.

Kudō Sadao
1971 "Kaidai" [Bibliographic Commentary], SSS 1971:6-35.

1981 "Kaidai" [Bibliographic Commentary], SSS 1981:4-42.

Kuroda Denjirō
1939 *Shōnai tenpu ikki no kaihō* [A Revised Account of the
Shōnai Domain Transfer Uprising]. Yamagata: Yamagata nōmin keizai kenkyūkai.

Lebra, Joyce C.
1973 *Ōkuma Shigenobu: Statesman of Modern Japan.* Canberra:
Australian National University.

Lindert, Peter H., and Jeffrey Williamson
1983   "English Workers' Living Standards During the Industrial Revolution: A New Look," *Economic History Review*, 2nd series, 36(1):1-25.

Matsumoto Ryōichi
1977   "Sakata no shūgendō" [The Mountain Ascetics' Sect in Sakata], SSS 1977:646-50.

Medick, Hans
1976   "The Proto-industrial Family Economy: The Structural Function of Household and Family During the Transition from Peasant Society to Industrial Capitalism," *Social History* 3:291-315.

Mikawa-chō shi hensan iinkai (eds.)
1974   *Mikawa-chō shi* [The History of Mikawa Town]. Mikawa: Mikawa-chō yakuba.

Minami Kazuo
1967   "Edo no kujiyado" [Suit-inns of Edo], *Kokugakuin zasshi* 68(1):68-79, 68(2):69-83.

Morris, Ivan
1975   *The Nobility of Failure*. New York: Alfred A. Knopf.

Nagai Masatarō (comp./annotator)
1973   *Dewa hyakushō ikki roku* [A Record of Dewa Peasant Uprisings]. Tokyo: Kokusho hakkōkai.

Naganuma Gensaku
1983   *Nakagawa shi* [A History of the Nakagawa Canal Network]. Tsuruoka: Nakagawa tochi kairyōku.

Najita, Tetsuo
1970   "Ōshio Heihachirō (1793-1837)," in Albert M. Craig and Donald H. Shively (eds.), *Personality in Japanese History*, pp. 155-79. Berkeley: University of California Press.

1974   *Japan: The Intellectual Foundations of Modern Japanese Politics*. Chicago: University of Chicago Press.

1975   "Intellectual Change in Early Eighteenth-Century Tokugawa Confucianism," *Journal of Asian Studies* 34(4):931-44.

1982   "Introduction: A Synchronous Approach to the Study of Conflict in Modern Japanese History," in Najita and Koschmann (eds.), *Conflict in Modern Japanese History*, pp. 3-21.

Najita, Tetsuo, and J. Victor Koschmann (eds.)
1982   *Conflict in Modern Japanese History: The Neglected Tradition.* Princeton: Princeton University Press.

Nakayama Einosuke (ed.)
1974   *Edo Meiji kawaraban senshū* [A Selection of Tokugawa and Meiji Period Folk Prints]. Tokyo: Kashiwa shobo.

Nishikawa Shunsaku
1981   "Protoindustrialization in the Domain of Chōshū in the Eighteenth and Nineteenth Centuries," *Keio Economic Studies* 18(2):13-26.

Niwa Kunio
1966   "The Reform of the Land Tax and the Government Programme for the Encouragement of Industry," *The Developing Economies* 4(4):447-71.

Oakes, James
1982   *The Ruling Race: A History of American Slaveholders.* New York: Alfred A. Knopf.

Ōba Masaoto
1977   "Meiji nōhō no dōnyū katei: taiō sagyō yōgo no henka o tegakari ni" [The Process of Introducing the Meiji Methods: Clues from Changes in Corresponding Agricultural Work Vocabulary], in Toyohara kenkyūkai (ed.), *Zenji nisshi,* pp. 47-70.

Ooms, Herman
1975   *Charismatic Bureaucrat: A Political Biography of Matsudaira Sadanobu, 1758-1829.* Chicago: University of Chicago Press.

Ouwehand, Cornelis
1964   *Namazu-e and Their Themes: An Interpretative Approach to Some Aspects of Japanese Folk Religion.* Leiden: E.J. Brill.

Ōyama-chō shi hensan iinkai
1957   *Ōyama-chō shi* [The History of Ōyama Town]. Ōyama: Ōyama-chō yakuba.

Oyokawa Shirō, Kashiwagura Ryōkichi, and Yamazaki Yoshio
1953   *Yamagata-ken nōchi kaikaku shi* [A History of the Land Reform in Yamagata Prefecture]. Yamagata: Shakei kenkyūkai.

Popkin, Samuel
1979   *The Rational Peasant: The Political Economy of Rural So-*

ciety in Vietnam. Berkeley: University of California Press.

Rappaport, Roy A.
1979   *Ecology, Meaning, and Religion*. Richmond, CA: North Atlantic Books.

Robertson, Jennifer
1979   "Rooting the Pine: Shingaku Methods of Organization," *Monumenta Nipponica* 34(3):311-32.

Saitō Osamu
1983   "Population and the Peasant Family in Proto-industrial Japan," *Journal of Family History* 8(1):30-54.

Saitō Shōichi
1982   "Shōnai han no Tenpō kikin to han no taiō" [The Tenpō Famines in Shōnai Domain and Domain Measures], *Rekishi* 58:45-64.

Sakurai Tokutarō
1979   "Kesshū no genten: minzokugaku kara tsuiseki shita shochiiki kyōdōtai kōsei no paradaimu" [The Foundation of Regimentation: A Folklore Paradigm of Local Community Formation], in Tsurumi Kazuko and Ichii Saburō (eds.), *Shisō no bōken: shakai to henka no atarashii paradaimu* [The Hazards of Thought: New Paradigms of Society and Change]. Tokyo: Chikuma shobō.

Satō Jisuke
n.d.   (annotator) "Shirahata Goemon ichidai ki" [A Record of the First Shirahata Goemon], *Hakuboku* 15:41-52.

1975   *Wappa ikki: Tōhoku nōmin no ishinki* [The Wappa Uprising: The Restoration Period for Farmers in Northeastern Japan]. Tokyo: Sanseidō.

Satō Saburō
1975   *Shōnai han Sakai-ke* [The Sakai House of Shōnai Domain]. Tokyo: Chūō shoin.

1976   *Sakata no Honma-ke* [The Honma House of Sakata]. Tokyo: Chūō shoin.

Satō Shigemi
1958   "Shōnai chihō ni okeru nōgyō seisanryoku tenkai no keiki: kōchi seiri to sono eikyō" [The Catalyst for the Rise in Agricultural Productivity in Shōnai: Paddy Land Adjustment and Its Effects], in Nihon nōgyō hattatsushi

312

chōsakai (eds.), *Shuyō chitai nōgyō seisanryoku keisei shi, jokan* [History of the Formation of Agricultural Productivity in Principal Regions], volume 1, pp. 129-66. Tokyo: Nōrinshō nōgyō sōgō kenkyūsho.

Satō Shigerō
1963a   "Inasaku shōhin seisan chitai ni okeru chiso kaisei" [The Land Tax Reform in a Commercial Rice Area], *Rekishi no kenkyū* 10:78-117.

1963b   "Wappa ikki no nōgyō kōzō" [The Agrarian Structure of the Wappa Uprising], *Rekishi hyōron* 156:42-57, 158:68-79.

1965   "Kinsei gōki ni okeru inasaku tansaku no jinushi keiei" [Farm Economy of Rice Monoculture Landlords in the Late Tokugawa], *Shigaku zasshi* 74(4):433-57.

1980   *Bakumatsu ishin no seiji kōzō* [The Political Structure of the Late Tokugawa and Early Meiji]. Tokyo: Azekura shobō.

1981   *Wappa sōdō to jiyūminken* [The Wappa Disturbances and Freedom and Popular Rights]. Tokyo: Azekura shobō.

Satō Tōichi
1967   "Shōnai chihō no nōson monjo kaidoku no tame no shiryō jakkan" [Several Examples for an Interpretation of Village Documents of the Shōnai Region], in *Yamagata-ken no kōko to rekishi* [Archeology and History of Yamagata Prefecture], pp. 284-93. Yamagata: Yamakyō shigakkai.

Satō Tōzō
1983   *Satō Tōzō-ke keifu* [A Generational Profile of the Satō Tōzō House]. Mikawa-chō: privately published.

Scalapino, Robert A.
1962   *Democracy and the Party Movement in Prewar Japan: The Failure of the First Attempt.* Berkeley: University of California Press.

Scheiner, Irwin
1973   "The Mindful Peasant: Sketches for a Study of Rebellion," *Journal of Asian Studies* 32(4):379-91.

1978   "Benevolent Lords and Honorable Peasants: Rebellion and Peasant Consciousness in Tokugawa Japan," in Tetsuo Najita and Irwin Scheiner (eds.), *Japanese Thought in the Tokugawa Period, 1600-1868*, pp. 39-62. Berkeley: University of California Press.

1982 Review of Roger Bowen, *Rebellion and Democracy in Meiji Japan. Journal of Japanese Studies* 8(1):179-86.

Scott, James C.
1976 *The Moral Economy of the Peasant: Rebellion and Subsistence in Southeast Asia.* New Haven: Yale University Press.

Shirai Yoshihiko
1961 "Kōchi seiri kenkyū no ichi kadai—Meijiki Yamagata-ken Akumi-gun kōchi seiri no chōsa to kanren shite" [A Topic in the Study of Arable Land Adjustment: Relating to a Survey of Meiji Period Arable Land Adjustment in Akumi County, Yamagata Prefecture], *Suiri kagaku kenkyū* 5(1):84-100.

Sippel, Patricia
1977 "Popular Protest in Early Modern Japan: The Bushū Outburst," *Harvard Journal of Asiatic Studies* 37(2):273-322.

Sheldon, Charles D.
1958 *The Rise of the Merchant Class in Tokugawa Japan, 1600-1868: An Introductory Survey.* Locust Valley, NY: J. J. Augustin.

1975 "The Politics of the Civil War of 1868," in William G. Beasley (ed.), *Modern Japan: Aspects of History, Literature, and Society*, pp. 27-51. Berkeley: University of California Press.

Smith, Robert J., Jr.
1960 "Pre-industrial Urbanism in Japan: A Consideration of Multiple Traditions in a Feudal Society," *Economic Development and Cultural Change* 9(1, part 2):241-57.

1972 "Small Families, Small Households, and Residential Instability: Town and City in Pre-modern Japan," in Peter Laslett and Richard Wall (eds.), *Household and Family in Past Time*, pp. 429-72. Cambridge: Cambridge University Press.

Smith, Thomas C.
1959 *Agrarian Origins of Modern Japan.* Stanford: Stanford University Press.

1973 "Pre-modern Economic Growth: Japan and the West," *Past and Present* 60:127-60.

1977   *Nakahara: Population and Family Farming in a Japanese Village, 1717-1830.* Stanford: Stanford University Press.

Soranaka Isao
1978   "The Kansei Reforms: Success or Failure?" *Monumenta Nipponica* 33(2):152-64.

Takeda Tsutomu
1978   "Kome kedashi gyō no eigyō keitai to seikaku" [Characteristics and Forms of Operations of Rural Rice Bulkers], in Toyohara kenkyūkai (ed.), *Toyohara-mura*, pp. 157-90.

Takigawa Matajirō
1959   *Kujiyado no kenkyū* [A Study of Suit-inns]. *Kiyō* #8 [Bulletin #8]. Tokyo: Waseda daigaku hikakuhō kenkyūsho.

Tawara Otoyori
1972   "Shōnai hitotsu nōson ni okeru chiso kaisei to sono zenshiteki jōken" [The Land Tax Reform in a Shōnai Village and Its Historical Preconditions], *Sonraku shakai kenkyū* 8:3-64.

Thompson, Edward P.
1968   *The Making of the English Working Class.* Harmondsworth: Penguin Books.

1971   "The Moral Economy of the English Crowd in the Eighteenth Century," *Past and Present* 50:76-136.

1977   "Folklore, Anthropology, and Social History," *Indian Historical Review* 3(2):247-66.

1978   "Eighteenth-century English Society: Class Struggle without Class?" *Social History* 3(2):133-65.

Tilly, Charles
1979   "Did the Cake of Custom Break?" in John M. Merriman (ed.), *Consciousness and Class Experience in 19th Century Europe.* New York: Holmes & Meier.

1983   "Flows of Capital and Forms of Industry in Europe, 1500-1900," *Theory and Society* 12(2):123-42.

Togawa Anshō
1973   *Nihon no minzoku* [Folklore of Japan], volume 6 [*Yamagata*]. Tokyo: Daiichi hoki shuppankai.

Totman, Conrad
1967   *Politics in the Tokugawa Bakufu, 1600-1843.* Cambridge: Harvard University Press.

1980   *The Collapse of the Tokugawa Bakufu, 1862-1868.* Hono-
        lulu: University of Hawaii Press.

Toyohara kenkyūkai (ed.)
1977   *Zenji nisshi: Yamagata-ken Shōnai heiya ni okeru ichinōmin
        no nisshi, Meiji 26—Showa 9* [The Diary of Zenji: The
        Diary of a Farmer of Shōnai Plain, Yamagata Prefecture,
        1893-1934]. Tokyo: Tokyo daigaku shuppankai.

1978   *Toyohara-mura: hito to tochi no rekishi* [Toyohara Village:
        A History of Its Land and People]. *Kenkyū sōsho* #98
        [Research series #98]. Tokyo: Nōrinshō nōgyō sōgō
        kenkyūsho.

Tsuchiya Takao and Kannō Michio (eds.)
1968   *Meiji shonen nōmin sōjō roku* [Records of Agrarian Dis-
        turbances in the Early Meiji Period]. Originally pub-
        lished 1933. Tokyo: Keisō shobō.

Tsuda Hideo
1975   *Tenpō kaikaku* [The Tenpō Reforms]. *Nihon no rekishi,*
        volume 22. Tokyo: Shogakkan.

Tsuruoka-shi kyōdo shiryōkan
n.d.   *Dewa Shōnai nigun ezu* [An Illustrated Map of the Two
        Counties of Shōnai], facsimile of 1861 map.

Tsuruoka-shi shi hensan iinkai
1974   *Tsuruoka-shi shi* [TSS, The History of Tsuruoka City],
        volume 1. Tsuruoka: Tsuruoka-shi yakusho.

1975a   *Tsuruoka-shi shi* [TSS, The History of Tsuruoka City],
        volume 2. Tsuruoka: Tsuruoka-shi yakusho.

1975b   *Tsuruoka-shi shi* [TSS, The History of Tsuruoka City],
        volume 3. Tsuruoka: Tsuruoka-shi yakusho.

Tsuyuki Tamae
1967   "Morinoyama kuyō" [Memorial Services on Mt. Mo-
        rino]. *Nihon minzokugaku kaiho* 49:30-33.

Uno Tadayoshi
1978   " 'Toyohara bugarichō' no bunseki" [An Analysis of the
        Toyohara Village Harvest Books], in Toyohara ken-
        kyūkai (ed.), *Toyohara-mura,* pp. 517-602.

Varley, H. Paul
1967   *The Ōnin War.* New York: Columbia University Press.

Varner, Richard E.
1977   "The Organized Peasant: The *wakamonogumi* in the Edo
        Period," *Monumenta Nipponica* 32(3):459-83.

Vlastos, Stephen
1982 "*Yonaoshi* in Aizu," in Najita and Koschmann (eds.), *Conflict in Modern Japanese History*, pp. 164-75.

Walter, John, and Keith Wrightson
1976 "Dearth and the Social Order in Early Modern England," *Past and Present* 71:22-42.

Waters, Neil L.
1983 *Japan's Local Pragmatists: The Transition from Bakumatsu to Meiji in the Kawasaki Region*. Cambridge: Harvard University Press for Council on East Asian Studies.

Wilson, George
1982 "Pursuing the Millennium in the Meiji Restoration," in Najita and Koschmann (eds.), *Conflict in Modern Japanese History*, pp. 176-94.

1983 "Plots and Motives in Japan's Meiji Restoration," *Comparative Studies in Society and History* 25(3):407-27.

Wolf, Eric R.
1983 *Europe and the People Without History*. Berkeley: University of California Press.

Yamamura, Kozo
1979 "Pre-industrial Landholding Patterns in Japan and England," in Albert Craig (ed.), *Japan: A Comparative View*, pp. 276-323. Princeton: Princeton University Press.

Yoshino Hiroko
1980 "In'yō gogyō ni yoru Nihon minzoku no kōzōteki haaku" [English title: "Exploring Japanese Folklore Structures through the Concept of Ancient Chinese Cosmic Dual Forces and Five Natural Elements"], *Minzokugaku kenkyū* 45(2):134-59.

INDEX

Abumi-ya, 35, 37
accountability, 8, 243-44, 250, 259-60, 289
agriculture: arable land adjustment projects, 278-280; by-employment, 62-63; commercialization, 58-60, 64; harvest shortfalls, 66-70; rice prices, 292-96; rice yields, 43-44, 278n. *See also* Meiji Methods
Amarume Village Group, 105, 111-12, 124, 149-50
Aoki Kōji, 10-12, 124

Bendix, Reinhard, 8
benevolent paternalism, 21, 46, 76, 79n, 103-104
Bolitho, Harold, 6, 77, 96
Borton, Hugh, 77, 84, 102n
Boshin War, 126-28, 136, 141, 208
Bowen, Roger W., 20, 21-24, 259, 267

capitalism: agrarian, 63, 276-81, 288, 290; definition, 7; in 19th-century Japan, 8, 10; in Shōnai, 38, 274
Chambliss, William Jones, 6, 7
commercialization, 23-24, 38, 64; rice prices, 292-96; rice trade, 35
community, 13, 45-46, 287
court spokesman (*daigennin*), 206, 217, 246
court suits, 214, 217, 220-21; Tagawa suits against prefecture, 217-21, 246-51

daikoku dance, 99-101, 299

Directive #222, 165, 173, 185-86, 213
distress petitions (*tangansho*), 73-76, 81-83, 211-12, 214, 220, 269, 283
domain retainers faction, 272, 274-75

fusei (fraudulent, improper), 171, 203, 238, 243
Futakuchi Village, 49, 117n, 118, 131

Genrōin, 214, 221, 222-27, 233, 244-45
Gotō Shōjurō, 182, 222

Hanley, Susan B., 15-18, 22n, 24n, 43, 49
Harootunian, Harry D., 18-19, 21, 24n
Honda Inri, 160, 175, 187, 200, 207, 215, 217, 221, 234, 246, 255, 264, 267
Honma house, 62; contributions and loans to Sakai, 38-39; rise of, 37-38
Honma Mitsuaki, 79, 84
Honma Mitsuoka, 38, 40, 57-60, 276
Honma Mitsuyoshi, 102, 127, 131-35, 137, 145-47, 151, 161n, 166n, 251-52, 254, 274, 280-81

Irokawa Daikichi, 13-14

Kamo-ya Bunji, 83-84, 101, 238
Kanai Tadanao, 160-61, 181, 200-202, 205-206, 215, 221, 234

319

Kansei Reforms, 57, 271n
Kenmochi Torazo, 191-97, 199, 202, 207n
Kojima Iken: court hearings in Shōnai, 230, 245-52; decision, 254-60
Kōno Hironaka, 226, 267
Kurokawa Village Group: 1874 actions, 191-97; land dispute in, 242

land survey: attempted survey (1872-74), 163-65, 219, 237-39; revision of registers (1867), 125-26; Tadakatsu cadastre (1623), 30, 231
Land Tax Reform (1875-76), 4, 230-32, 252-53, 276-77, 286, 290
landholding: landlords, 40-41; pawning, 45, 57; smallholders, 44-45; tenancy, 47-48, 280-83

mass assemblies: Akumi, 86, 139-41, 282-83; Amarume, 142; banners, 90-93; Kurokawa, 192-97; Nakayama Yachi, 87-94; Nezumigaseki, 136-37; Ōyama, 123, 234; Tagawa, 189-91, 197-99
Matsudaira Chikahiro, 122-23, 137, 152, 165, 183, 199-200, 224, 226-27, 236, 259
Matsudaira Masanao, 178n, 184-87, 200-201, 236
Matsudaira Nariyasu (Kawagoe), 78-79, 96
Matsugaoka Project, 157-63, 219, 224, 236-37, 247, 255, 274
Matsukata Deflation, 270-72, 281
Meiji Methods, 277-78
Meiji Restoration, 9, 15, 19
memorials (kenpakusho), 211-12, 214, 222-27, 269-70
Mishima Michitsune, 212-14, 215-17, 223-24, 225, 228, 233-35, 253-54, 256n, 261-63, 267, 289
Mizuno Tadakuni, 96, 98, 106
Mori Tōemon, 188; articles to newspapers, 225, 234-35; background, 207-209; court suits against prefecture, 217-22, 263-64; death, 270; at Kojima Court, 245-50; and Kojima decision, 255-59, 263-64; memorials to Genrōin, 222-27; and Numa Report, 243-44; petitioning Mishima, 213-14, 262-63; and political parties, 267-69; suit against Honda, 264-66; suit against Honma, 261; in Tokyo (1874-75), 209-212, 214
Movement for Freedom and Popular Rights, 22, 257-59, 268, 270, 288

Najita, Tetsuo, 19-20, 24n
nation-state, 8
Neo-Confucianism, 18, 21, 59, 208, 209
Noble Deeds Group, 282-83
Numa Morikazu: background, 228-29; hearings in Shōnai, 230, 232-34, 250; report to Genrōin, 235-45, 255

Ōkubo Shigenobu, 182-84, 213, 228, 233, 256n, 260, 289
Ōkuma Shigenobu, 134-36, 153-54, 156, 161n, 182-83, 275
Ōshio Heihachirō, 21, 67, 209-210
Ōyama, 134; agitations for tax reductions, 123; dispute in Shimonaka Village, 241-42; Ōyama Disturbances, 111-19, 284, 287; sake brewers, 107-110, 116-18, 284, 287
Ōyodokawa Village: 1872-73 tax ledgers, 167-71, 184. See also Satō Hachirobei

peasant uprisings, 10-11, 17
petitioning: in Akumi, 139-42, 155-
56; conventions, 73-76; in Edo,
54-55, 81-85, 94, 111-12;
Nuinosuke, 74-75; at Shiono
trials, 114; in Tagawa, 173-78,
213; in Tokyo, 130-31, 161, 181-
82, 206
pilgrimages, 90-91, 95-96, 102
Pine-sandal Disturbances, 282
Popkin, Samuel, 17, 23

Reform Faction, 160-61

Saigō Takamori, 153, 161, 182,
213, 254-55
Sakai Domain: administrative
structure, 30-33; debt
cancellation, 59, 70-71; Edo
patrols, 122-23; 1811 budget, 61;
fiscal problems, 41-43, 57-61;
population, 33-34; tax base, 42;
tax rates, 46, 292-96; tax
reductions, 46, 67-69, 104, 123-
24, 128-29; taxes and levies, 34,
125-26
Sakai Tadaaki, 78-79, 106
Sakai Tadakata, 77-78, 94, 106
Sakai Tadakatsu, 26-27, 54-56
Sakai Tadazumi, 122, 128, 129,
153, 272-73, 275
Sakata Civil Affairs Office, 131-32
Sakata Prefecture, 135-36, 144-45;
Bōjō Toshiaki, 150-52; Ōhara
Shigemi, 144, 150; Tokyo rice
sales plan, 146-48, 151
Sakura Sogorō, 226, 257
Sakurabayashi Village, 48-55
Satō Hachirobei, 176-78, 183, 198,
202, 205, 206, 215, 229
Scheiner, Irwin, 20-24, 45-46, 103-
104
Scott, James C., 23
Second Sakata Prefecture

(Tsurugaoka Prefecture): 1875
administrative reorganization,
215-17; 1872-73 economic
program, 156-67; end of, 253-54;
formation, 152-54; headquarters
move to Tsurugaoka, 230n
Shirahata Goemon, 177-78, 215
Shirai Yadayū, 59-60, 276
Shōnai Plain: agricultural
development, 34-35; early
history, 26; maps, 27-29;
physiography, 26
Sippel, Patricia, 124-25
Suge Sanehide, 122-23, 137, 152,
212, 236, 255, 272-75
suit inns, 74, 83
Suzuki Shigetane, 119-20, 122, 287,
291
Suzuki Yaemon, 175-76, 178-81,
209

Takahashi Tarozaemon, 54-56
Tax Rice Cash Conversion
Company, 3, 187-92, 194, 198,
200, 202, 204, 205
tengu, 97-98, 139, 143
Tengu League, 138-43, 155-56,
171-72, 203, 285, 286, 287
Thompson, Edward P., 8, 19n, 24n
Three-way Fief Transfer Order:
anti-transfer protests, 77-98, 284,
286, 287; order, 77; rescission,
98-101
Tokugawa Nariaki, 67, 98-99
Tokyo nichinichi shinbun, 225, 234-
35
townspeople's faction, 274-75
Toyohara Village, 277n, 282
tributary polity, 5-6, 8, 288
Tsurugaoka: population, 33, 272;
renamed Tsuruoka, 268; sake
brewers, 109-110, 116; town
council, 275

Ueki Emori, 257-59

village group headmen, 32-33, 70-71, 143-44, 148-50, 166, 171-72, 192-94, 215-17, 237-39, 249, 263-64
Vlastos, Stephen, 143, 204

wappa, 2, 4
Waters, Neil L., 172
Wolf, Eric, 7

Yamamura, Kozo, 15-17, 22n, 24n, 43, 49

LIBRARY OF CONGRESS CATALOGING IN PUBLICATION DATA

Kelly, William W. (William Wright), 1946–
Deference and defiance in nineteenth-century Japan.

Bibliography: p.
Includes index.
1. Shōnai Region (Japan)—Politics and government.
2. Peasant uprisings—Japan—Shōnai Region.   I. Title.
DS894.39.Y349S546   1985   952'.18   85-42688
ISBN 0-691-09417-9

DATE DUE			
NOV 1, '86			